THE FIRST YEAR OF BEREAVEMENT

THE FIRST YEAR OF BEREAVEMENT

Ira O. Glick
Robert S. Weiss
C. Murray Parkes

A WILEY-INTERSCIENCE PUBLICATION

JOHN WILEY & SONS, New York • London • Sydney • Toronto

Library of Congress Cataloging in Publication Data:

Glick, Ira Oscar, 1927-
   The first year of bereavement.

   "A Wiley-Interscience publication."
   1. Bereavement—Psychological aspects. 2. Widows.
I. Weiss, Robert Stuart, 1925-   joint author
II. Parkes, Colin Murray, joint author. III. Title.

BF575.G7G63   155.9'37   74-12499
ISBN 0-471-30421-2

Printed in the United States of America

10 9 8 7 6 5 4 3 2 1

FOREWORD

This book, though its topic is death, is an enthralling human document that is likely to have personal meaning for every reader. The skill of its authors in incorporating quotations from recorded interviews fills their story with vivid life; and the story itself is an affirmation of the struggle of the human spirit and its eventual triumph over death.

The book is also one of the most important research reports to emerge from our Harvard Laboratory of Community Psychiatry. It records two main theoretical advances. First, it reveals our realization that Lindemann's early conceptualization of bereavement as a typical life crisis was an oversimplification. A central element of crisis theory, which Lindemann originally emphasized, and which my Harvard colleagues and I have corroborated over the years, is that the psychobiosocial forces for change during a crisis operate within a relatively short period of time; usually a few weeks limit the duration of the turning point. This has obvious consequences for organizing crisis intervention to promote a healthy outcome.

The book shows that there are indeed a succession of such

characteristic short crisis periods in the course of mourning, but what we have learned from this research is that the forces of bereavement and adjustment to widowhood usually operate over a much longer time period that is more appropriately labeled a "period of life transition" than a "life crisis." The focus of the present report is on the first year, but the book provides many indications that an even longer period is often significant. Many of our research subjects were still involved in an active psychosocial readjustment process during the second and third years of their bereavement.

In our earlier formulations we had thought that a widow "recovers" at the end of the four to six weeks of her bereavement crisis on condition that she manages to accomplish her "grief work" adequately. We believed that thereafter she would be psychologically competent to carry on with the tasks of ordinary living, subject only to the practical readjustments demanded by her new social roles. We now realize that most widows continue the psychological work of mourning for their dead husbands for the rest of their lives. During the turmoil and struggles of the first one to three years most widows gradually learn how to circumscribe and segregate this mourning within their mental economy and how to continue living despite its burden. After this time they are no longer actively mourning, but their loss remains a part of them and now and again they are caught up in a resurgence of feelings of grief. This happens with decreasing frequency as time goes on, but never ceases entirely.

The second main theoretical lesson has been an increased understanding of the "normality" and benign predictive significance of many of the strange individual reactions of widows that we had previously imagined to be unhealthy, for instance the continuation of illusions that the dead husband is still present in some form and should be "consulted" about current decisions. The book provides many examples of this thesis, and describes in more detail than any previous publication the variegated patterns of the mourning process among healthy people.

Some authorities have used a clinical model in conceptualizing mourning, as though it was essentially an acute illness with signs and symptoms of disability from which one might recover, or which might alternatively become a chronic disease. I have always maintained that, on the contrary, crisis, despite its turmoil and its unpleasant psychobiosocial side effects, should be thought of as an essentially healthy reaction of an ordinary person struggling to master a novel and burdensome situation. And yet, since I was applying the short time-frame of crisis to the mourning situation, I sometimes tended to evaluate continuing signs of strain or cognitive and emotional deviations of a widow a year or two after the death of her husband as either a manifestation of current pathology or a predictor of future illness. This book has led me to greater sophistication.

Eventually we may indeed validate some predictors of future illness in the behavior of bereaved individuals, but meanwhile the book urges caution in this matter. It persuades us to guard against thinking of individual widows and widowers as "cases" either of current pathology or of possible future sickness.

And yet, nothing in this book contradicts the findings of previous studies that widowhood does substantially increase the risk of mental illness and that this is related to lack of success in grappling with the burdens and challenges of the situation because of personal factors complicated by idiosyncratic stresses and lack of supports in the social milieu. I see no reason, therefore, to change my opinion that it is important for a community mental health program to ensure appropriate help for widows as a high-risk segment of the population. But nowadays I do not think that this help should take the form of guiding widows to accomplish specific "grief work" tasks according to a normative time table, as I used to advocate ten years ago. Rather, I believe that our efforts should focus on mobilizing emotional supports for a widow at the times when she feels in need of them and also on communicating to the widow the kind of information contained in this book, which can strengthen her by reassuring her of her own normality, and can provide her with a rough map of the ground she may herself have to cover in her struggles to readjust. It will also give her information about the wide range of methods used by other widows in mastering expectable burdens and challenges of the mourning process that may increase her understanding of her own options.

This book is the successful outcome of an interesting team effort spanning Boston, Chicago, and London. Ira O. Glick, Ph.D., is a Chicago sociologist with specialized skills in qualitative research. He is not a member of our research staff, but we invited him to collaborate with us on a part-time contractual basis for the circumscribed purpose of carrying out a qualitative analysis of the data that we had collected over a period of several years. C. Murray Parkes, M.D., a senior research psychiatrist from the Tavistock Institute in London, who has conducted a well-known series of studies of his own in the field of bereavement, came to Harvard for a year to take charge of our research project during the crucial period of our initial field investigation. He exercised a major influence on the planning and organization of our methods of data collection and analysis. He then returned to London and continued his participation by means of mail and occasional visits to Boston. He has been largely responsible for the quantitative aspects of our study and for integrating these with Dr. Glick's qualitative analysis. He also took major responsibility for the first and last chapters of the book. The "anchor man" of our reporting team has been Robert S. Weiss, Ph.D., the senior sociologist of our Laboratory of Community Psychiatry. It is he who welded together the contributions of the other authors, as well as his own; he took responsibility for the description patterns of recovery and the analysis of their relationship with anticipation, and for the description of widowers as a contrasting group. He has molded and enriched the document on the basis of his competence in both qualitative and quantitative research methodology, and also on the basis of his first-hand knowledge of our data, in the collection and analysis of which he played a major part. The fact that this team effort has resulted in a gripping and smoothly flowing cohesive narrative is mainly due to his efforts.

GERALD CAPLAN
Professor of Psychiatry
and Director of the Laboratory
of Community Psychiatry
Harvard Medical School

ACKNOWLEDGMENTS

A great many individuals have contributed to the Harvard Bereavement Study, of which this is one report. Dr. Gerald Caplan, Director of Harvard's Laboratory of Community Psychiatry, was Principal Investigator of the project, and was very much the leader of our research group. Marie Killilea and Joyce Brinton, members of the Laboratory administrative staff, were invaluable in that they made it possible for us to give our attention to substantive issues. Dr. David Maddison and Dr. Peggy Golde directed the study through its first phases. The third author of this report directed the study through its middle phase, and the second author through its last. Consultants to the study were Dr. Lenin Baler, Dr. Melvin Krant, and Dr. Phyllis Silverman. Research assistants were Miriam Arenberg, Barbara Brandt, Barbara Cronin, Rhea Delene, Caroline Lubell, Ron Oakland, Ellen Pollak, Gina Prenowitz, Carol Richmond, John Sargeant, Linda Silverman, and Brad Simcock. Interviewers were Mary-Lou Balbakey, Paul Conley, Mrs. Bernard Miller, Donna Morse, Charles Nichols, Gail Plotkin, Sylvia Schiffman, Kay Tolbert, and Gene Webb. Typists and transcriptionists were Sylvia Karoul, Betty Levine, Patricia Porter, Joyce Rosenthal, and Florence Zamcheck. Coders were Ellen Frankfort and Norma Rosenberg. Mrs. Ruth Abrams was a valued research associate in the analysis phase of the study. Project secretaries were Kathleen Callinan, Mary Coffey, and Carol DiNucci. Data handling was the responsibility of Mary Hyde, Dr. Kenneth Jones, and Mary McCrae. Suggestions for revisions of an earlier draft of the manuscript were made by Dr. Arlene Daniels, Mr. Peter Marris, and Dr. Lee Rainwater. Special thanks are due to Mrs. Marlene Hindley, who has been involved with the project as office manager, research associate, and finally as manuscript editor.

The project was funded by two grants from the National Institute of Mental Health, Grant No. 5 RO1 MH12042, "Mental Health Implications of Conjugal Bereavement," and Grant No. 2R12 MH09214, "Study of Community Mental Health Methods." Dr. Weiss's work was in part supported by a National Institute of Mental Health Research Scientist Award, No. 5 K02 MH45731.

In addition to these debts we acknowledge our very deep indebtedness to those widows and widowers who, in the hope of helping others, described their experiences to us.

IRA O. GLICK
ROBERT S. WEISS
C. MURRAY PARKES

Evanston, Illinois
Boston, Massachusetts
London, England
May 1974

CONTENTS

THE FIRST YEAR OF BEREAVEMENT

1

PREVIOUS WORK AND
PRESENT PROBLEMS

Sorrow and its vicissitudes have always been part of man's lot. Evocative descriptions of grief and perceptive insight into its nature appear in the literature of all peoples and times.[1] Yet until recent years few social scientists attempted to describe in a systematic way the experience of grieving and the processes by which individuals recover from grief.

Among the first to attempt to develop both an accurate description of bereavement and a theory that would offer some explanation of its phenomena was Thomas Eliot, an American sociologist. In a series of influential articles

[1] See, for materials from Western literature, Howard Becker, "The sorrow of bereavement," *Journal of Abnormal and Social Psychology*, Vol. 27, (1933), pp 391–410. See also A. F. Shand, *The Foundations of Character* (London: Macmillan, 1920).

published in the early 1930s, Eliot drew attention to some experiences in bereavement and emphasized the importance of bereavement as a crisis for individuals and families. He noted that among the immediate impacts of bereavement are a sense of abandonment, shock, and denial, colored by guilt and sometimes anger, and accompanied by intense and persistent longing for the one who has died. In addition he spoke of the disruption of accustomed patterns that bereavement produced.[2]

Eliot pioneered the empirical study of typical, uncomplicated reaction to bereavement in addition to distinguishing between successful and unsuccessful patterns of recovery. D. M. Fulconer, extending Eliot's work on typical reactions, conducted systematic interviews with seventy-two bereaved men and women. Fulconer described five stages of a recovery process, beginning with shock and ending with a stage of "repatterning" in which the individual had established a new and stable way of life.[3] An important contribution of both his work and Eliot's was the recognition that grieving was not a single emotional state that appeared at the time of loss and then disappeared abruptly when mourning had been accomplished, but rather a process with successive phases leading from emotional devastation to eventual readjustment.

In 1958, Peter Marris extended this work through a study of the consequences of bereavement in a representative sample of widows. He studied reactions to bereavement among a carefully drawn sample of seventy-four widows of

[2] See Thomas B. Eliot, "The bereaved family," *Annals of the American Academy of Political and Social Science*, Vol. 160 (1932), pp. 184–190. See also by the same author, "The adjusted behavior of bereaved families: A new field of research," *Social Forces*, Vol. 8 (June, 1930), pp 543–549, and "Bereavement as a problem for family research and technique," *The Family*, Vol. 11 (June, 1930), pp 114–115.

[3] David M. Fulconer, *The adjustive behavior of some recently bereaved spouses: A psycho-sociological study.* Unpublished doctoral dissertation, Northwestern University, 1942.

men aged forty or under whose deaths had been registered
in the boroughs of East London.[4] Although the majority of
Marris's respondents had been widows for an average of two
years, they had hardly recovered; they felt that their lives
were futile and empty. They had in large measure withdrawn from earlier interests and social ties, many had
become dependent upon their immediate families, and
many seemed apathetic in relation to their immediate lives.
Insomnia and loss of weight were frequent symptoms
among them; about a third thought their health had been
impaired.

More recently, Helena Z. Lopata investigated the later life
of older widows, many of whom had been widowed for
years.[5] She found great variation in the level of social
participation within her sample of 300 Chicago area widows, with corresponding variation in feelings of well-being.
Widows whose earlier life had provided them with little
preparation for autonomy, especially those who had had
little education, who had always lived near the edge of
poverty, and who now, as earlier, occupied relatively marginal positions in their community, seemed to have the
highest risk of isolation.

Despite these useful studies, Berardo's 1968 assessment
could still be defended: "The special problems that confront the widow both at the time of bereavement and beyond
have not undergone extensive sociological research."[6] When
we began this report, we too believed too little was known
regarding the way in which bereavement affects the individual's relations with family and friends and others, and the
way in which those relations in turn affect the emotional

[4] Peter Marris, *Widows and Their Families* (London: Routledge and Kegan
Paul, 1958).

[5] *Widowhood in an American City* (Cambridge, Mass.: Schenkman, 1973).

[6] Felix M. Berardo, "Widowhood status in the United States: Perspective on
a neglected aspect of the family's life-cycle," *The Family Coordinator*, Vol.
17 (1968), pp. 191–203.

state of the bereaved. One aim of this book is to provide a response to this need to understand bereavement as a social as well as an emotional event. Indeed, our view is that the social and emotional aspects are so intermeshed that neither can be understood apart from the other.

Exploration of the social aspects of bereavement seems to have a brief history. The emotional aspects of bereavement have, however, received more attention. Freud is often credited as having been the first to develop a systématic explanation for the psychodynamics of grief. Quite possibly his attention was drawn to the problem by the widespread grief in Western Europe that was one legacy of World War I. In 1915, responding to a paper by Abraham written four years earlier, he suggested that the mourner grieves because he can no longer deny the reality of death.[7] He revised this view in 1917 in "Mourning and Melancholia," a paper that has become the basis for the psychoanalytic theory of depression.[8] In it he discarded his earlier position that grief signals the breakdown of denial and instead asserted that grief is the means by which the energy that tied the individual to the object of his or her love is progressively withdrawn.

This energy was conceived by Freud as being bound to the memories and ideas that arose from interaction with the dead person. To become free of his tie to this person, the energy has to be detached by a process that Freud termed "hypercathexis," a process that requires the mourner to turn his back on the real world, and to invest free energy in the struggle to "decathect" the loved object. By focusing his mind on the lost person and bringing to consciousness each relevant memory, the mourner gradually sets free the bound up energy.

[7] Sigmund Freud, "Instincts and their vicissitudes" (1915). *Collected Papers* (New York: Basic Books, 1959), Vol. 4, pp 60–83.
[8] Sigmund Freud, "Mourning and melancholia" (1917). *Collected Papers* (New York: Basic Books, 1959), Vol. 4, pp. 152–170.

This process, which Freud called the "work of mourning" (or "grief work"), provides an explanation for the phenomenon we term "obsessional review," which is so prominent a feature of grief. Most newly bereaved people do spend a great deal of time going over in their mind the events leading up to the loss and focusing attention on their memories of the dead person.

Other aspects of Freud's theoretical model do not bear too literal an interpretation, however. What is the "mental energy" to which he refers? Does it really have the same qualities as physical energy? And if not, how far can the analogy to physical energy be taken? Since mental energy cannot be measured, these questions are unanswerable. A number of present-day writers, including some psychoanalysts, have developed alternative models that they find more satisfactory.

John Bowlby, an English psychoanalyst, has developed a theory of grief based on ideas from ethology, neurophysiology, information theory and psychoanalysis, as well as on observations of animal behavior and the behavior of human children and adults in situations of separation and loss.[9] He sees the human being as carrying within his brain a "working model of the world" derived from and constantly modified by his experience. Behavior is switched on and off by the external events that impinge upon him and to which his attention is directed by the complex mechanisms of perception.

In Bowlby's model an individual's previous experience and internal biochemical and neurophysiological changes determine his priorities in perception and action. Of very high priority are events involving the other individuals to whom he is attached and to whom he wishes to maintain

[9] John Bowlby, *Attachment and Loss.* Vol. 1, *Attachment,* 1969; Vol. II, *Separation, Anxiety and Anger,* 1973; Vol. III, *Loss,* Forthcoming. (London: Hogarth; New York: Basic Books).

proximity. Any form of separation from these individuals is likely to trigger behavior patterns that tend to restore proximity, and these are more strongly evoked if the separation is prolonged or either he or the other is perceived by him as being insecure or in danger. These mechanisms are of obvious importance in maintaining the integration of the living group in all social animals, including man. Only in the event of permanent separation do the mechanisms for maintaining proximity prove redundant. At such times the crying, searching, and inhibition of other activities, which normally would help to facilitate reunion, are clearly useless. But this does not prevent them from occurring, even though the human adult is well aware of their senselessness.

Parkes has pointed out that Bowlby's theory contradicts accepted psychoanalytic views of the function of grief.[10] These views argue that since grief appears to be a necessary consequence of loss it must have the function of detaching the individual from the one who has gone. Yet Bowlby's theory implies that far from promoting separation, grief has the biological function of promoting reunion. Only in the rare event of a permanent separation do the most obvious features of acute grief, pining and yearning, become gradually extinguished without reunion occurring.

In Parkes's view, grief is a process of realization, of making real inside the self an event that has already occurred in reality outside. Although a loved person may have died, the appropriate modification of the internal world takes time. The repeated awareness of discrepancies between the outside world and the internal representation of it accounts for much of the sense of frustration that is so often a feature of grief. But the repeated frustration of any behavior pattern will eventually lead to its extinction.[11] In

---

[10] C. Murray Parkes, *Bereavement: Studies of Grief in Adult Life* (London: Tavistock; New York: Basic Books, 1972).

[11] There are a few notable exceptions to this rule even in the animal kingdom. See, for instance, the account by Pollock (in the *International*

the end the intensity of pining and searching can be expected to grow less; other priorities will predominate once more.

The work of Bowlby and Parkes that has resulted in reconsideration of Freud's seminal statements has been paralleled by other empirical work that has for the most part accepted Freud's ideas, but has gone on to elaborate them and to provide additional detail. This line of inquiry was essentially initiated by Erich Lindemann and Stanley Cobb. On the basis of their therapeutic experience with bereaved survivors of Boston's Coconut Grove fire, they produced a set of extremely influential descriptions of the consequences of totally unexpected loss. The most important single statement to emerge from their work was Lindemann's 1944 paper, "The symptomatology and management of acute grief."[12] Subsequent studies have confirmed the correctness of Lindemann's observations of the acute reaction to bereavement. Indeed, his description of the pangs of grief has not been bettered:

> The picture shown by persons in acute grief is remarkably uniform. Common to all is the following syndrome: sensations of somatic distress occurring in waves lasting from twenty minutes to an hour at a time, a feeling of tightness in the throat, choking with shortness of breath, need for sighing, an empty feeling in the abdomen, lack of muscular power, and an intense subjective distress described as tension or mental pain.[13]

Journal of Psychoanalysis, Vol. 42 (1961), pp. 341–361) of the dog Hachi who continued to visit the railway station in Tokyo where he had previously met his master each day. This behavior is said to have continued for ten years, until Hachi's own death. A statue of the dog has since been erected and in 1953 Japan issued a stamp in his honor.

[12] *American Journal of Psychiatry,* Vol. 101, (1944), pp. 141–148.
[13] Lindemann, *ibid.,* p. 141.

Lindemann succeeded in drawing attention to the existence of acute grief as a definite syndrome with specific psychological and somatic symptomatology. He may have been less accurate, however, in his supposition that individuviduals might recover from grief rather rapidly. He believed that once grief work was accomplished, which might only be a matter of weeks, recovery proceeded rapidly. Our own work suggests strongly that the death of a spouse typically gives rise to a reaction whose duration must be measured in years rather than weeks. Even a year after a major bereavement grief is still prominent. It is more often during the second year of bereavement than the first that a widow can admit to thoughts of a hopeful future, and even three or four years after loss both widows and widowers may have recurrent moments of grief. Parkes's study of London widows and our study suggest that although the pangs of grief are most severe within the first two to five weeks of bereavement, grief may again be evoked many years later by the finding of a photograph or an article of clothing.[14]

Grief seems to encompass feelings and reactions that have their source in our nature as human beings rather than in our socialization into a particular society's patterns. In the past half-dozen years, studies conducted in many different settings have suggested strongly that grief reactions are similar the world over. Hobson's study of forty widows in a small English town; Harvey and Kistemaker's study of twenty-four widows of all ages in East Cleveland, Ohio; a study by Clayton, Desmarais, and Winokur of forty relatives of patients who died in a hospital in St. Louis, Missouri; and Yamamoto's study of fifty-five Japanese widows whose husbands had been killed in motor accidents are among such studies.[15]

[14] C. Murray Parkes, *op. cit.*

[15] C. J. Hobson, "Widows of Blackton," *New Society* (September 14, 1964), p. 13; and L. A. Harvey and M. Kistemaker, *The resolution of mourning through ego-adaptive mechanisms in women following separation by death*

One exception to the generalization that grief reactions are not especially affected by cultural settings should be noted. A sense of presence of the dead husband was reported often but not uniformly by American and English widows, but was reported by fully ninety percent of Japanese widows.[16] A possible explanation is that the dominant religions of Japan, Shintoism and Buddhism, both encourage the living to maintain a sense of relatedness to the dead, and even to discuss the events of the day with the dead at a family altar. Cultural emphases can therefore produce somewhat different expressions of grief, even though the experience of grief is nearly universal.

The pathological potential of grief has long been recognized. Medieval writers considered grief-induced depressive withdrawal, which they termed "melancholy," one of the most common and serious of afflictions. Some of the therapies prescribed by them and by their successors are remarkable, and suggest by their forcefulness how much power they assumed melancholy to have. Benjamin Rush, an influential American physician of the nineteenth century and a signatory of the Declaration of Independence, recommended bleeding and purges along with opium "in liberal

---

of their husbands. Thesis for M.S.W., Smith College School of Social Work, (1965); Paula Clayton, L. Desmarais, and G. Winokur, "A study of normal bereavement," *American Journal of Psychiatry,* Vol. 125 (1968), p. 168–178; J. Yamamoto, K. Ohonogi, T. Iwasaki, and S. Yoshimura, "Mourning in Japan," *American Journal of Psychiatry,* Vol. 126 (1969), p. 74.

[16] We might note, in relation to just this issue, that Rees, on the basis of work with a large sample of Welsh widows and widowers, reported that about half his sample experienced the illusion of hearing the voice or catching sight of a dead spouse or of being strongly impressed by the spouse's presence in the room. The frequency of such phenomena was highest during the first ten years of widowhood, but even after ten years was still quite high. The phenomena seemed more likely to occur among those who had been happily married for a long time and who missed their spouse greatly. Many of them considered the experience pleasant, indeed comforting. See W. D. Rees, "The hallucinations of widowhood," *British Medical Journal,* Vol. 4 (1971), pp 37–41.

doses."[17] Less heroic, but equally bizarre to the modern mind, was his recommendation for fending off melancholy. He said that those present at the death of someone dear to them "should be carried from the room in which their relations have died, nor should they ever see their bodies afterwards." Rush was a great believer in the efficacy of tears for relieving grief and considered how they might be obtained while fending off the grief itself: "From the relief which the discharge of tears affords in grief, pains should be taken to procure it. The means of this purpose are obtruding on the mind a sorrow of a less grade than that by which it is depressed." The fact that "sorrows seldom come alone" was, for Dr. Rush, an example of the goodness of Heaven, since the lesser sorrow provided means for the relief of the greater.

In the present century, medical regimes for the treatment of grief for a time simply disappeared, as it was no longer seen as an illness syndrome. Grief no longer appeared on death certificates as a cause of death nor, for that matter, was it listed in medical textbooks. More recently there has been a resurgence of interest in grief as a form of stress, but this new development is still in its beginnings.

The decline of medical interest in bereavement accompanied a more general decline in the importance attributed to mourning in most Western cultures. At one time a bereaved individual assumed a special dress, entered into seclusion, and expected and received special treatment from those he encountered. Now mourning is treated as a private event; after a brief period set aside for grief, the bereaved are expected to appear no different from anyone else. Mourning clothes now seem odd, a tactless anachronism.

Yet signs of changes in social attitudes as well as in medical attitudes are at hand. To some extent motivated by

[17] Benjamin Rush, *Medical Inquiries and Observations upon the Diseases of the Mind* (Philadelphia: Kimber and Richardson, 1812), pp. 319–321.

the work of Lindemann and Cobb, a number of programs have been developed for helping the bereaved. These are in addition to the therapies available from individual physicians, which in general consist of reassurance augmented by tranquilizers or sedatives. Widows' groups offering community and understanding have been organized and administered by individuals, many of whom have themselves been bereaved. And there are occasional professionally sponsored programs of advice, consultation, and support, such as the Widow-to-Widow Program developed by Phyllis Silverman.[18]

One issue that remains undecided, but that is of major importance in the development of services, is whether some bereaved persons are at special risk of lasting emotional disturbance. In a second volume now being prepared, we are attempting to identify the various determinants of what might be described as good and bad outcomes of the recovery process after bereavement. But one factor in particular seems of such critical importance in relation to later recovery that we deal with it in this volume as well. It is the factor of what may be considered preparation for bereavement, the difference between, for example, nursing the spouse through a long illness whose terminal course is apparent, and losing the spouse suddenly and without forewarning. Our work shows that, in the young widows and widowers whom we studied, the presence or absence of forewarning of eventual bereavement was of enormous importance in determining the course of recovery, though we are still uncertain why this should be so.

The importance of anticipation for the course of recovery has been recognized for some time. One way of thinking about the possible role of anticipation was implied in the

[18] Phyllis R. Silverman, "The Widow-to-Widow program," *Mental Hygiene*, Vol. 53, No. 3 (July, 1969), pp. 333–337. See also P. Silverman, D. MacKenzie, M. Pettipas, and E. Wilson, *Helping Each Other in Widowhood* (New York: Health Sciences, 1974).

concept of "anticipatory grief" developed by Lindemann.[19] As Lindemann used the term, it referred to a capacity to experience grief and come to terms with loss before the loss actually occurred. The individual experiencing anticipatory grief would experience in anticipation the emotions that would otherwise have followed the loss. When the loss actually occurred his grief would be much diminished. This concept, it might be noted, rests heavily on the interpretation of grief as a loosening of emotional bonds, an interpretation closely related to Freud's theoretical analysis.

There is some reason to question whether anticipation of grief has the effects Lindemann proposed for it. A careful empirical study of widows, most of whom were older than ours, found that those who showed evidence of depression and grief before bereavement were no less grief stricken afterward than those who showed no such evidence.[20]

Nevertheless, anticipation of a spouse's death does matter greatly. As we show in our final chapters, the impact on survivors of a long-forewarned death is quite different from the impact of a totally unexpected death. The way in which they differ is *not* that anticipation has permitted the eventual survivor to begin to reorganize himself or herself both cognitively and emotionally so that the loss, when it comes, is already partially grieved for. If this were the case, anticipated grief and unanticipated grief would follow the same course, though anticipated grief would begin it earlier. This is not what happens. The grief that follows unanticipated bereavement is different in both form and duration from the grief that has been anticipated.

It appears that those whose loss is not anticipated have less likelihood of regaining full capacity for functioning and for happiness. There is as one expression of this, a tendency

---

[19] Erich Lindemann, *op. cit.*

[20] Paula J. Clayton, James A. Halikas, William L. Maurice, and Eli Robbins, "Anticipatory grief and widowhood," *British Journal of Psychiatry*, Vol. 122 (1973), pp 47–51.

for women especially but to an extent for men as well, to be wary of remarriage if their first spouse died suddenly and unexpectedly. We say more about this in Chapters Twelve and Thirteen.

For none among the bereaved does recovery mean forgetting. Even after they have established new lives and regained their energy and capacity for happiness, the loss and their reaction to it will not only have been a major determinant of the people they have become, but will emerge, again and again, in their thoughts and feelings.

We hope in this book to make clear just what does happen in the first year of bereavement and, in a more condensed way, in the years that follow. We are concerned with the sociological phenomena of bereavement: with the changing roles and statuses of young widows and to a lesser degree widowers; with the social forms and ceremonies that mark these changes; with the changing response to them of others. We are also concerned with more psychological phenomena, the ways in which the bereaved come to terms with their loss and then go on.

The specific questions to which we attempt to respond in this report are the following:

1. What are the experiences through which young widows, and widowers, move from the time of their loss to the time of its resolution? What are the meanings to them of these experiences? What are their relations to others during these experiences? What expectations do they have of others and what expectations do they believe others have of them? What are the roles and statuses that they and others seem to believe to be appropriate for them?

2. What are the emotional and psychological phenomena associated with bereavement? What phenomena can be considered to be within the range of the usual or expectable (and in at least this sense, the normal)? How do widows and widowers come to terms with their loss emotionally?

3. What seems to help, or to hinder, recovery? And, indeed, what forms might recovery take? What are the characteristics of "failure to recover"? Are there early symptoms of difficulty that might alert observers to the likelihood that a particular individual may in part or in whole fail to recover?

Recognizing the dilemmas these questions imply, we intend this book for a mixed readership. We hope it will be useful to members of the helping professions in contributing to their understanding of bereavement, and thus allowing them to be more effective in their work with the bereaved. We also hope that it will be useful to widows and widowers. By describing for them the nature of the social and emotional situation in which they find themselves, it may at least relieve them of some measure of perplexity.

Our final chapter, "Dealing with Loss," is addressed primarily to professionals, but we hope that, like the rest of the book, it will be useful to the bereaved as well.

2

**THE METHODS USED
IN THIS STUDY**

The aim of this study was to learn how bereavement affected the emotional and social lives of those who had lost a spouse, and also to learn about the course of their recovery and the social or psychological factors that facilitated or impeded that recovery.

Previous work had demonstrated that although bereavement is always a severe emotional blow, it is especially traumatic among younger people. It seemed to us that it might be important to learn about their special problems associated with bereavement. In addition, we felt that younger widows and widowers would display the phenomena of bereavement uncomplicated by the other losses and ills to which advanced age is liable. We therefore decided to limit our sample to individuals no older than forty-five.

We were aware that there had as yet been little longitudinal study of bereavement—that is, study that considered the experience of a single person over time. But we felt that only through longitudinal study could we identify different processes of recovery and distinguish those that had more satisfactory outcomes from those that seemed to lead to inferior outcomes. We also hoped to be able to identify early indicators of the direction an individual's recovery would take. We therefore decided that we would interview our respondents three different times over the course of the first year of their bereavement.

Our first interview would be as near to the time of the loss as could be managed; we anticipated that this would ordinarily be about three weeks. We wanted our next interview to be held after the immediate reaction to loss had subsided, when the problems of establishing a new way of life might first be presenting themselves, and thought this might be about eight weeks after the loss. Finally, we wanted to talk with our respondents at the end of the first year of their bereavement. But we were concerned that if we scheduled an interview for exactly one year after the death we would encounter feelings and memories stirred by the anniversary. We therefore scheduled our third interview for thirteen months after the individual's loss.

Appended to our schedule of topics to be included in the third interview was a list of questions dealing with the respondent's current health. We also selected a sample of individuals from the community matched to our respondents in age, occupation, and region of residence who had not been bereaved and asked this control group to respond to the same health questionnaire. The results of this comparison will be explored at length in other reports from this study, but will be referred to here as well when they are relevant.

The longitudinal study design proved invaluable in that it permitted us to deepen our knowledge of each respondent beyond what might have been possible on the basis of a single interview or even several interviews in a brief period of time. Because of the longitudinal design, we came to understand our respondents not only as individuals to whom a particular experience had happened but also as individuals who struggled to deal with that experience. We learned not only about the nature of the initial disruption of their lives but also about their efforts to regain some measure of stability.

Some previous studies had directed their attention to the experience of individuals who had appeared at a clinic or had in some other way identified themselves as patients. We wanted to be sure that our study was not limited in this way. This meant that we would have to present ourselves to individuals who had not already established a relationship with an institution, and hope that they would accept us and our study.

We were intensely aware of the assault that fate had visited on the people we hoped to recruit into our study, and we were determined not to become a further burden for them. We therefore decided that we would invite potential respondents to join our study, but would forego the usual pressures used by survey studies to assure themselves of an adequate response rate. In particular, we would let potential respondents know we were going to call on them before we actually did, and we would not attempt to convince the initially reluctant that they should nevertheless participate.

Beginning in 1965 and continuing through the following year we arranged with the Office of Vital Statistics in Boston to inform us when there was a death of an individual from natural causes or from accident—not suicide or homicide—whose spouse was aged forty-five or younger. On being informed of such a death we sent the widow or widower a letter describing our study and saying that we would soon call. We then telephoned, or in a few cases of homes that were without phones, visited in person. We described in this contact the aims of our study and the interviewing schedule we hoped to follow. We then asked the widow or widower to participate in the study. If the potential respondent did not want to participate for any reason, we let the matter drop.

Table One describes the filling of our sample. A total of 231 names of widows and 118 names of widowers were received from the Office of Vital Statistics. Almost one widow in five could not be contacted because she had moved or because she was not at home at the time of our telephone calls. Almost one widower in three could not be contacted for these reasons. Of those contacted, forty-four percent of the widows and forty percent of the widowers refused to participate. We did not press them.

Not all those who agreed to participate proved eligible. and suitable. A number had been separated from the spouse at the time of the spouse's death. A few of the deaths had involved suicide or homicide, without this appearing on the death certificate. A few spoke so little English that inter-viewing was difficult. Several had moved to a far suburb, and we could not arrange transportation for the interviewer. Two turned out to be patients in a mental institution at the time of the first interview and were dropped for this reason, although a widow who was hospitalized after the first interview was retained in the sample. Twenty-seven widows and thirteen widowers were dropped from the sample for one of these reasons.

Some respondents who had agreed to earlier interviews refused to be interviewed a second or third time. A variety of reasons were offered, but a major reason seemed to be their unwillingness to review painful memories. Widows and widowers seemed equally likely to have this reaction. Three widows moved away from the Boston area during the first year of their bereavement. Adding all these sources of sample attrition, fifty-eight widows and twenty-seven widowers were dropped from the sample or left the sample after the first interview.

Forty-nine widows and nineteen widowers completed the sequence of three interviews. This represented twenty-six percent of widows contacted and twenty-one percent of those whose names had initially been received. Among widowers it represented twenty-three percent of those contacted and sixteen percent of those whose names had been received.

TABLE ONE. PARTICIPATION AND NONPARTICIPATION IN THE STUDY

	Widows	Widowers
Total names received	231	118
Unable to contact because had moved or for other reason	40	35
Actually contacted	191	83
Refused to participate	83	33
Interviewed, first interview	108	50
	(56% of those contacted, 47% of those whose names were received)	(60% of those contacted, 42% of those whose names were received)
Found ineligible or unsuitable (see text)	27	13
Refused later interview	28	14
Moved away	3	0
Total leaving sample	58	27
Completed all interviews	49	19
	(26% of those contacted, 21% of those whose names were received)	(23% of those contacted, 16% of those whose names were received)

One way of assessing the potential bias due to self-selection is to compare those who participated in the study with those who did not, both in relation to demographic characteristics and in relation to the experience they had in the first year of their bereavement.

Demographic information regarding some characteristics of refusers appeared on the death certificates available to us. In addition, we determined husband's occupation (or own occupation, for men) and ethnicity for a sample of refusers.

We found only a few differences between participants and refusers. We did find a difference among the widows in the ethnicity of respondents. We do not know why this should have happened, but there seemed to have been significantly fewer refusals among Black widows than among other widows. As a result, twenty-four percent of widows who participated in the study were Black, compared with only ten percent of widows who refused to participate. There was no similar disproportion in racial composition among accepting and refusing widowers.

We suspect that our sample of widows is weighted toward the lower end of the income continuum. When the occupational distribution of those in the sample is compared with the occupational distribution for the Boston area population, we find the sample to be somewhat fuller in blue collar occupations. Those among the sample of refusers for whom occupational data was available were also disproportionately within blue collar ranks. It may be that early death is disproportionately a blue collar experience.

There does seem to have been a difference between those who participated in the study and those who refused to participate in the frequency with which the death of the spouse was caused by cancer. Participants more frequently had had spouses who had died of cancer. Since death from cancer tends to be long foreshadowed, our sample may be more heavily weighted toward widows and widowers who had some preparation for their eventual bereavement.

Because our sample was drawn from the Boston area, it displayed in general the ethnic, racial, and religious composition of this particular community. We have noted that about twenty-four percent of widows were Black, a somewhat larger proportion than we would find in a more representative community sample. But an even larger proportion of the sample of widows, thirty-one percent, were Irish American, almost all of them Catholic. Another twelve percent of the sample were Italian Catholics. The Catholic population as a whole—including some Black Catholics—amounted to fifty-eight percent of the total sample. This is undoubtedly a much larger proportion than one would have found in most other metropolitan areas. Among widowers, the proportions of both Black and Catholic respondents were somewhat smaller.

To assess what might have been the social or psychological differences between those who cooperated and those who declined, about two years after we had first called them we again telephoned a sample of those widows who had declined. We said in the call that we hoped they would tell us, first, why they had initially declined participation, and second, what had happened to them in the years since we had first contacted them. Few of them could remember very clearly what had led them to decline. Some said they had wanted to recover from their grief and feared the study would force them to dwell on it; some said they had had all they could manage without the study. But when they described their experiences since their bereavement it became clear that these had not been dissimilar from the experiences of our study population. This observation, together with our assessment that there were not major demographic divergences between those who participated and those who refused, makes us feel that our respondents constituted a fairly representative sample of younger widows and widowers.

In 1969, four years after we interviewed our first respondent, funds became available for follow-up interviewing. Although we had not previously planned to interview respondents after the thirteenth month, it seemed likely to be valuable to learn how their lives had continued in the years that had since passed. Because of funding requirements, the follow-up interviews had to take place within the same fairly brief period. Since the respondents had been recruited over a two-year period, this meant that follow-up interviews were held anywhere from four years to two years after the death of the spouse. We were successful in gaining follow-up interviews with forty-three of the forty-nine widows and with seventeen of the nineteen widowers.

Our interviewers throughout the study were experienced social workers selected for maturity and tact. The interviews were kept as informal and open-ended as possible, although the interviewer had a list of questions for discussion and was expected to make sure that all of these questions were answered at some point in the interview. All respondents were asked to give details of the circumstances of the spouse's sickness and death, of their reaction and the reactions of others, and of how they had managed the problems that ensued. They were also asked to answer a short list of questions about feelings that are commonly reported by bereaved persons. The interview was primarily concerned with the respondent's experience in dealing with the impact of bereavement and in reestablishing an acceptable pattern of life.

All interviews were tape-recorded and transcribed with careful attention to detail. A set of issues was developed—for example, presence of anger or of guilt—in respect to which each of the interviews was coded. The coders not only read the transcriptions of the interviews but also listened to the tape recordings. Because so much of the information required judgment and inference, all transcripts were coded twice, and only those items where reliable appraisal proved possible were retained in the final analysis.

We plan to prepare several reports of the material in our interviews. Some of our reports will be quantitative and will deal with, among other issues, early indications of the quality of the widow's later recovery. The present report is more qualitative, utilizing primarily description and quotation. Its aim is to describe and as far as possible explain the experience of the first year of bereavement.

Except in Chapter Thirteen and infrequent brief comments elsewhere, we concentrate our attention on the experience of widows. We may here note that the immediate emotional response to bereavement seems very much the same for widowers as for widows, but thereafter the expressions of mourning and the directions taken by their lives differ in important respects. Although the psychological and emotional reactions to loss appear to be quite similar, their sense of the continuing obligations of their marriage, the demands on them of other roles, and their sense of the proper way to go about dealing with grief, all seem different enough to make it difficult to discuss the experiences of widows and widowers together.

The process by which this report was developed should be noted. We began by selecting from our sample of forty-nine widows a subsample of fifteen who seemed to represent a range of income levels, of extent of forewarning of the husband's impending death, and of apparent quality of recovery. We developed a quite detailed description of the phases of the first year's experiences for this subsample. We next made explicit the structure of assertions of this description. Finally we used this structure to organize statistical findings based on the entire sample. Most of the following chapters draw both on the qualitative descriptions and the quantitative percentages. For the chapters on types of outcome, however, we worked with the entire sample of forty-nine widows. The comparison of widows and widowers is also based on the entire sample of both groups.

In summary, our aim in this report is to describe and, as

far as we can, explain the experiences of the first year of bereavement. Our approach is qualitative, emphasizing the unfolding story. But where it has been appropriate, we have used quantitative assessments to structure our account, and we have throughout corroborated our account by reference to the quantitative findings.

3

THE IMPACT OF THE DEATH

Twenty-one percent of the widows lost their husband suddenly and without warning through heart stoppages or through accidents. Twenty-three percent had some intimation that their husband was unwell, but had not expected him to die. In the remaining cases, the husband's death followed illnesses of obvious severity that lasted from several weeks to several years.

As we note in the first chapter, preparation for the husband's death seemed to be of great importance for the eventual course of recovery, but not because of the occurrence of what Lindemann termed "anticipatory grief." Virtually all the widows and widowers who had known of the impending deaths of their spouses believed that although they had begun to grieve prior to the actual death, this did not reduce their subsequent grieving. Some of those whose spouses had died after a long debilitating illness were relieved that the end had come at last, but they were no less desolated by their loss.

Nevertheless, there was a positive correlation between longer advance warning and eventual satisfactory adjustment to widowhood. The value of advance warning seemed to be that it allowed emotional preparation for the loss. Loss without preparation seemed almost to overwhelm the adaptive capacities of the individual. Grief might not be augmented, but capacity to cope seemed diminished.

Preparation for loss did not ordinarily lead to realistic planning for the management of life after the spouse's demise. Thirty-six percent of our sample of widows had been told explicitly that their husband was dying, but fewer than half of them made any plans at all for what they would do after the death. There seemed to be somewhat more planning among widowers with preparation, but our sample is too small to permit more than surmise. Most widows, although they consciously believed that it would be good for them to have plans, could not bring themselves to make them. They may have feared that planning would somehow hasten the spouse's death or indicate that they wanted it; or they may have been unable to deal with the pain they felt when they considered their own impending widowhood. Or they may simply have been unaccustomed, after years of marriage, to planning for themselves.

When there was a long period of illness most wives, perhaps despite themselves, accepted the inevitability of loss. Many found that at some point in the terminal phase the husband's condition had become intolerable for them as well as for the husband. They then began to wish, even to pray, that death would release the husband from suffering and themselves from continuing witness of that suffering. Once death occurred most felt relief mixed with the shock of loss. Wives who had had no preparation for loss tended to have a more severe shock reaction; they might for some time be unable to grasp fully the reality of events. But grief was as deep among those who anticipated the death of their husband as among those who did not.

As we have noted, forewarning of loss affected in a major way the nature of later recovery. Widows and widowers who did not have forewarning were more likely to display symptoms of still unresolved grief at the end of the first year of their bereavement. In the follow-up interview two to four years after the death of their spouse, a number of widows and widowers in this group still displayed diffuse anxiety.

To suggest both how the death of the husband might be responded to, and the difference made by forewarning to the immediate experience of loss, we present excerpts from the reports of two widows, one whose husband's fatal cancer had long been recognized, and one whose husband died in an automobile accident.

WHERE DEATH IS ANTICIPATED. Mrs. G, thirty-four years old, Irish Catholic, with three children, had known for three years that her husband was dying. For some time before his condition was diagnosed her husband had complained of ill health, but his complaints had been vague and she had discounted them. Then it suddenly became clear that he was indeed ill, and that medical attention was necessary. At first the medical personnel were reassuring.

> Three years ago, exactly, he complained of pains in his chest a lot. But he was an overactive man—he worked very hard, played golf every day after work that he could, every weekend, his whole life was golf—and we kept telling him that he was doing too much. This one night he woke up in the middle of the night and complained of a terrible pain in his chest. I called the doctor. The doctor told me that he was having a heart attack, to get him to the hospital immediately. I called the neighbor to stay with the children. Being the type

of person that doesn't call for help, I got him into the car myself, which I never should have done. I should have called the police or called someone to help me. He passed out on me when I got to the square. But I did finally get him over to the hospital and they took tests of him and took X-rays and led me to believe that it was a slight heart condition.

Despite their reassurance, Mrs. G inferred from the behavior of the doctors that they suspected something more than a slight heart condition. They were evasive when she sought information, but finally when she insisted and voiced the possibility herself she was told by the doctors that they believed her husband had cancer.

They had taken cardiograms for a week and he had taken all kinds of tests and X-rays, and in the meantime I noticed that it was getting to be a daily thing to take quite a bit of blood from him, that they were doing extensive tests on his blood and they had oxygen on him all the time. For two weeks I called or talked to those doctors and they would tell me nothing and finally I went to one of them and I said, "I want to know exactly what is wrong and you have to tell me." And after I said, "Do you suspect cancer?" he said, "Yes, we do." But I was still under the impression that it was lung cancer because his brother had died of it. He said, "We'll have a talk with the doctors and we'll have you present."

I was six months pregnant at the time. They called me in, but they didn't know I was pregnant because I didn't show that much and I never said that I was. In fact I had forgotten about it myself. I went in and I talked to them and they said they suspected leukemia, at which I was shocked. I had no idea or even any suspicion of this. I took it very calmly, but I think it's not that I took it calmly, I think I was really more shocked than anything. And I walked out of there and they asked me if I was alright and I said, "Yes."

Mrs. G's husband, as is almost customary in such situations, was not informed of his diagnosis. Many doctors prefer that a dying patient be unaware of his condition.[1] There may be advantages to permitting patients to deny the seriousness of their condition but whatever its values the state of what Glaser and Strauss call "closed awareness," in which the patient is supposed not to know, robs the wife of the figure to whom she would most naturally look for support. The wife is under obligation to dissemble with her husband and she must deal with her own anxiety with a relative, with a friend, or alone.

> I asked the doctor if they were going to tell him and they said no, that they were not going to tell him. I went up to his room and acted like nothing had happened. This doctor who was from Ireland came into the room to make sure that I was alright and of course he saw that I was in a maternity dress. I had my coat on before. Right away he got very nervous and asked me who my doctor was, and I told him. And he must have called him, because when I got home that evening the doctor called me and said that he didn't want me to be by myself.

> So my girl friend came to stay with me for a few days. But I was almost in a state of shock, really, I would say. I never cried, I never let go at all—which I later realized was not a good thing—but I kept it all in and went to the hospital every day and saw him. He came home and, well, it wasn't until a month later that I really let myself go and fell apart and really let it out— to my mother, though, and his brothers, not to him.

Mrs. G was perhaps unusual among our widows in being able to contain for as long as a month the knowledge that her husband was dying. Yet her attempt to avoid "letting go"

[1] See Barney Glaser and Anselm Strauss, *Awareness of Dying* (Chicago: Aldine, 1965).

was quite typical of the strategy followed by most of our respondents. Mrs. G found support in the solicitude of her own doctor and the loyalty of her friend. With their help and the help of her family she began coming to terms with the impending loss of her husband. But most important for her, her husband broke through the condition of closed awareness. After that Mrs. G was no longer quite so alone.[2]

> One night Jack said to me, "Kitty, I have something to talk to you about," and I said, "What? Are you feeling alright?" And he said, "Yeah, I'm feeling fine. But I think I'm much more seriously ill than the doctors have said." And I said, "Why?" "Because I read an article in the paper today," he said. "I think I have leukemia." So I said, "Oh, Jack," I said, "You don't know this," and he says, "Have the doctors talked to you and told you this?" I said, "No, they told me you were ill." And I didn't know whether to agree with him or tell him and I just said to him, "Well, why don't we wait until you go for your checkup, and we'll discuss it with your doctor."

> When we did go for his checkup the doctor—it was a blood specialist—told Jack to go into the examining room and while he was there I said to him, "He knows." He said, "You didn't tell him?" And I said, "No, he read it in the newspaper. He put himself right into this picture, because of all the tests and everything." And the doctor said, "Well, why don't we wait to see what he says to me."

> When he got through examining him, Jack walked back into the office and he said, "I know I have leukemia. I don't want you to fool me. I want to know exactly what is wrong, what I have coming in front of me, and how long I have." The doctor just looked at him. He was

[2] Only twenty-eight percent of those widows who had forewarning of the husband's death said that they had frankly and realistically discussed with their spouse the prospect of his death. Fifty-five percent say they consciously avoided discussion of the death.

floored. And he sat us down and then he said, "Yes, Jack, you do."

Jack wanted to know how bad it was. The doctor said, "At this point it could be within six months or a year. It could progressively get worse, but with the drugs they have come out with, it can be kept down. But you will have to come and see me every single week. You will have to be under constant medication." The doctor said it was very good because tests he wanted to take, things that he wanted to discuss with Jack, he could do it freely, because he knew about his condition and I knew.

When Mr. G was entering the terminal phase of his illness, the doctor again began to withhold information. But until then he was accessible and candid, and this seems to have been helpful.

He was very good with us. Any questions we had, he was very willing to discuss and talk about. Until the last, when Jack got very bad. Then he would put me off.

Mrs. G began to rearrange her life long before her husband's death. To an extent this helped prepare her for subsequent life as a widow. Her husband's decreased functional capacity required that she assume more responsibility in the house, with the children, even with the car. She became of necessity less dependent. Meanwhile her husband tried to maintain his usual routine, going in to his office every day, maintaining control over his small business.

For a year and a half he worked, but the last two months, he had all he could do to get up and go to work. But he pushed himself to work, which I was against. He felt as long as he could get up on his two feet he was going to continue working. He even played golf, and the fellows used to say to him, "Jack, would

you please just play nine holes?" But he was a very
determined man. I don't know whether he was out to
try to prove something, that even though he was dying
he was still going to continue to live his own life and
do what he had always done.

As the disease progressed and the husband withdrew from
active participation both outside and inside the home, Mrs.
G gradually increased the time she gave to nursing him and
keeping him company.[3] Like other wives in this situation,
she devoted less and less time and energy to other interests
and other relationships. Her husband became her constant
preoccupation.

Usually at some point the husband could no longer be
cared for at home and was forced to enter the hospital. But
even though his care then became the responsibility of the
hospital staff, his wife was likely to continue in constant
attendance. Mr. G went rather quickly from maintaining his
activities, though perhaps with some difficulty, to requiring
the specialized care of the hospital. There was only a brief
period during which he could be nursed at home.

> Progressively he got so very weak that he just could not
> work, he could not do anything, it was an effort for him
> just to walk up and down the stairs. He just got worse
> every single day, progressively worse. I mean it was
> noticeable to anybody that would see him from day to
> day.
>
> He finally went into the Veterans Hospital. I had lost
> my Blue Cross, because once they have paid within so
> much time or so many months, you are dropped from
> them if you have an incurable disease. I couldn't afford
> to keep it up on my own, because I was on a group, so I
> gave it up and I told the doctor that I would just have to
> have him go over to the Veterans. They were marvelous
> to him over there. Very, very good to him. He was given

---

[3] Fifty-two percent of the forewarned widows said they played some part in
the nursing care of their spouse prior to death.

a private room because when he finally did go in he had got to the point where the pills would not help the pain. He had to go on morphine shots.

The course of a terminal illness is likely to leave a man ever weaker physically, and ever more regressed socially and psychologically. An ill person can well become angry and depressed at this. And these reactions, too, the wife was required to share:[4]

> About three months before he died he went into a semicoma. He did not know where he was or what was going on around him. And when he came out of the coma then he went into a terrible mental depression. They had a psychiatrist come and talk to him who also talked with me. The way he explained it to me, Jack had prepared himself for death. He knew he was dying, he had accepted it, he said he had no fear of it. He had fear for me and the children, but as far as death was concerned, he wanted to get it over with. He had suffered too much and he was the type of man that could not accept being an invalid and being cared for and being waited on by me, like a child. This was degrading to him. I think most men feel this way, any man that has been a very self-determined man, that it's degrading to have to be taken care of like that. So when he came out of it, he did not want to come out of it. He said he would just have preferred that he died.

Mrs. G brought her husband home, sent the children to live with relatives, and devoted herself to her husband's care.

> I had him home here for a week and at this point I neither slept day or night. The children were sent to

[4] Thirty-four percent of widows said that they were upset by the pain suffered by their spouse prior to his death. Forty percent were upset by the deterioration in his physical appearance.

relatives and he didn't want me to bring the children home. I think it was because he always was a very possessive man.

Mr. G was soon forced back into the hospital. Mrs. G continued to be devoted to him.

When he went back into the hospital I did bring the children home because I missed them terribly. I said to him, "I've got to bring the children home, Jack, I will be in here as much as I can." So I would send them to school, I would drop the baby off to my girl friend's or among one of my sisters or sisters-in-law, go into the hospital and stay the morning and come home and be home for them when they came home from school and give them their supper and then get a baby-sitter and go back in at night and stay until ten or eleven. And this was the way I arranged it.

Finally, the husband died. Those widows who were with their husband at the moment of death seem to have imprinted on their minds the particular scene, the particular words that were said. [5] For a time after the death they obsessionally reviewed all of the details.

The last time he went in I had gone to the doctor and I said to him, "How bad is he?" He said, "He is very bad, the leukemia cells have gone into everywhere in his body." He said, "He will either go in two weeks or a month." His legs had swollen up and when we saw this, of course, knowing as much about the disease as we did, each symptom that he got we knew what it was.

The doctor had said to me, "You think you are prepared for this, but you are not." I said, "Well, it's not like it's going to be a terrible shock to me when it happens. I know that it's coming." He said, "Yes, but no one is really prepared." And I found that out. The doctor had

[5] Thirty percent of widows reported that they had been present at the death of their spouse.

said, "Make any arrangements that you have to." And I said, "I don't have to." Because Jack had gone out and bought his own lot a year and a half ago at the cemetery. He had made all the arrangements, what he wanted and what he didn't want. People were shocked by this, that a man could go and do this, but that's the type of man that he was. He said, "I am making arrangements so that when it happens everybody won't be up in the air and not know what they're going to do, what they're not going to do. It will be all arranged and taken care of." The lot was paid for and everything. He was really thinking of me, that he didn't want me to be put through that. It was true to his personality. He was going to have things the way he wanted it. This is the type he was.

When it finally came, I had left him an hour before. He was conscious while I was there and we talked and he said, "Gee, it's not going to be so long." And I said, "No, Jack, I don't think so." He was in an awful lot of pain and I had gone out to the nurse and said to her, "Please, he's in terrible pain, could you give him a shot?" And she said, "I've just given him pills two hours before." "Well, he's very bad," I said, and she told me to see if I can talk to him to see if he can wait a half an hour. So I went in and we were talking and discussing things. He was very weak. I said to him, "How about my shaving you?" "Oh, I don't feel like getting a shave," he said. Well, I shaved him, because it would take up the time. And I washed him. His legs and hands had become very black.

And then she came in and she gave him the shot and I said to her, "Would you help me pull him up on the pillow?" She went on one side and I on the other and we went to pull him up and he gurgled and I looked at her. And she said, "What's the matter?" I said, "Nothing." So he went off to sleep for a little while and I went out and I said to her, "He's not going to come through the night." She said, "Oh, you've seen him this bad for a week." I said, "No, he's not going to come through the night. He's going to go."

I was standing outside the door and he called me. So I went back in. And he said, "The injection isn't working." I said, "Oh, Jack, have a little patience. It will in a few minutes." He said, "I don't think I'm going to get through the next few minutes. I think I'm going." I said, "Oh, don't say that. Don't be silly." He said, "No, I just feel that I am." So I said to the nurse, "He's going to go tonight. I don't want to go home. Would you call my aunt? Because the children were at my aunt's. And she said, "No, I want you to go home." She must have known that he was dying and didn't want me to be there. Of course, they thought he would take a hemorrhage, and the doctor had told all of them that if he did, that he did not want me in the room. And he had told me that if he had started to take one I was to get out of there immediately. They did not want me to have this memory.

She would not let me stay and I said, "Well, let me stay until he falls asleep." So I held his hand and we'd talk every once in a while. Finally he just went out, completely, to sleep. And he never regained consciousness from then on. He just went to sleep and died in his sleep, but he never hemorrhaged or anything. I was there. He died within the next hour. He just went to sleep.

I didn't realize he was dead. I went home and picked up the children and I didn't realize he was dead. I thought he was asleep, because I had said to her, "Let me stay until he goes to sleep." And then when they called, the doctor said he had died.

THE UNANTICIPATED DEATH. Mrs. E, a Black woman, with four children, was just thirty when her husband, also thirty, was killed instantly in an automobile collision. She began the interview with us by saying that she did not believe that it had been the collision that had killed her husband. She could not believe that something so catastrophic could have been an entirely avoidable accident. She felt he must have had a heart attack, after which the collision followed.

> I really believe he had a heart attack. He used to complain at night about this severe pain in his chest and he would wake me up and talk to me. He said "Oh, God, I have to turn over because of the pain hurting me so bad in my chest." But they didn't rule it that way on the death certificate. They said skull fracture and some other two big words there, and one of them was pertaining to the neck. But I still don't believe it. Because he was a good driver, he drove for a living.

Mrs. E then went on to talk about how the accident might have been avoided had her husband driven a different car. Accompanying her insistence that her husband's death had been the inescapable result of a heart attack was a quite contrary feeling that it all could have been changed had he done something different, had she been more insistent.

> He got this light car, it was a sports car, but he was used to something heavy because he drove this big truck every day. And when he got it, one night he picked me up and I told him, I said, "Well, you got to be careful." He was taking off so fast. I said, "This car is so much lighter."

> I told him, "Get a station wagon, don't get that sports car. We have four children and we need a wagon." So when I came home one night he met me and I said to him, "Why did you get this car?" And he said, "Well, I didn't have enough money to pay down on a station wagon, so this was the only one I could get, so this is what I got."

Mrs. E, like other widows and especially those whose husbands had died suddenly, dwelled obsessively on what had happened and continually searched for its cause. Her incompatible convictions expressed themselves in turns. At times she felt that the death was her husband's fault, a consequence of his thoughtlessness in buying an impractical car; at other times she would return to the view that his death had been caused by a heart attack and so was no one's fault.

> I prayed to him, I begged him not to get that car. I said, "Take that car back. You don't need a car like that because that's strictly a sports car." It wasn't for nobody with a family, noways, because they have bucket seats. I asked him, "Now where are we going to put the children?" He said, "We'll put all four of them in the back." The children never rode in it. We just had it four weeks.

Mrs. E reviewed again and again how she had learned of her husband's death. Some widows whose husband had died by the roadside learned of the death from the police. Mrs. E was told by friends.

> It happened on Sunday, about 11:30. Some of his friends were going down the same street and they recognized the car right in front of the service station. So they got out and they inquired at the service sation. They told them that the driver was killed. Then they came over here to my house. They pulled up in front and they blew the horn. So naturally, I said, "I wonder why they're stopping when they don't see his car." Because on Sunday they'd come by and if they didn't see the car they didn't stop. And at that time my heart got so big and so heavy I just wanted to cry right then. I said, "Oh, God, something's happened." So I sent my oldest one down to open the door.
>
> And this guy came in and I said, "Well, wait just a minute. I got to sit down." I could just see it all over his face. He was asking my husband's license plate and all that stuff and I told him. I said, "God, he just had the

car for four weeks. All I know is the number." "Well, is
475 the last three numbers?" I said, "Yes." He said,
"Well, that's your husband's car."

Often, in cases of accidental death, there is a period
during which the widow is unsure that it was really her
husband who died, when she hopes that there may have
been a mistake in identification, or a too quick diagnosis of
death. It was difficult for these women to accept the reality
of the death even on viewing their husband's body.

They knew my husband was dead because they had
told them at the service station, but they didn't want to
get me upset. So they took me down to the hospital. I
went to the accident floor and I asked about it, "A case
about a half-hour ago, an accident on Wellington
Street." She told me, "We admitted just the passenger.
The driver, the other man, is unidentified over in the
morgue." So all the way to the morgue I just prayed,
"Lord, don't let him be driving." Because sometimes
he didn't drive, he let the other guys drive the car.

We went in and told them what we were looking for
and that we wanted to identify him, but he was already
identified. They had his name down, just like it was on
his pocket. The man finally came up and took us down.
You know, you have to go down, walk down the steps.
And I knew he was dead. And if you know that, if you
know somebody's dead, you just can't walk right in
there, this pantry like, and look right in there on him,
"Now you walk in there and you look and see that it's
him. I'm going to stand right here." Because· I just
could see him. I knew he was laying in there, but I still
didn't have enough courage to walk in at first. I
couldn't be first. And he didn't walk in, he just walked
to the door and he turned around, he bowed his head,
and then I had to get up enough strength and courage
to walk in there and look at him.

I walked in and I felt his skin. It was just as warm as
mine. He was laying there just like he'd be in bed some

nights, with his eyes half opened. And I closed them and I rubbed and called him for twenty minutes. And the man told me, "Lady, your husband didn't even go to the accident room, your husband came right here, because he was dead when he left the scene." And I stood there and I called him because he was so warm.

You know, you don't picture a dead person as being warm. You picture a dead person as being very cold. The window was open and it was bitter cold that Sunday and I said, "Please close the window off my husband. He's not dead." He said, "Lady, your husband's dead. He was dead when he got here."[6]

The death of any young husband seems to his widow to be nearly insurmountable, but an unexpected death and especially an accidental death seems doubly so. The widow may be unable to believe she can ever end her grieving.

I'll never get over this. Never. I'll always remember that Sunday I had to walk in and look at him. I never will forget that for all my life. I never will forget him for the rest of my life. But just to walk down and look at him laying there, the only person that can say, "Well, I know what you are going through," is a person that went through it. I mean if it had been in the hospital and he had just died from sickness, then you'd say, "Well, at least he's out of his misery, he's not suffering." But accidental death, that is something else.

When death comes entirely without warning, the pain of grief is compounded by shock. Mrs. E reported that she cried uncontrollably. Other widows whose husbands died unexpectedly reported a period of numbness in which there was no feeling at all. These are not unusual reactions among all new widows, but among unforewarned widows there

[6] Sixty-three percent of respondents who had little or no warning of the death said that their initial reaction was one of disbelief. Twenty-four percent of those who had had warning also reacted with disbelief, despite the warning.

was greater intensity to these reactions:

> When I got home from the morgue, I was just out for
> the rest of the day. I just couldn't help myself. I
> thought I would have a nervous breakdown, and my
> heart was going so fast. The man at the morgue said,
> "Well, if you don't stop crying, you're going to have a
> nervous breakdown." But all I could do was cry. That's
> all I could do. And I told him, "If I don't cry, God, my
> heart will burst." I had to cry, because he wasn't going
> to be back no more.

Whether the husband's death was expected or not, its
occurrence presents the widow, despite her grief, with
responsibilities. Children and kin must be told. Arrangements must be made for funeral and burial. Most widows
find at this time that family and friends come to help, and
generally some close family member acts to support them.
Mrs. E was somewhat unusual in having to manage alone.

> When I first found out he was dead I thought I would
> never get him buried and get myself started again. The
> only thing I did was ask that God would give me
> strength. Because I said, "How can I do it? I don't
> know about making arrangements for a funeral." I
> didn't even know the first step, because I never had this
> in my family. I never had death in my family, no more
> than my grandparents, and they weren't living with us.
> So it was hard. How do you go about doing this? That's
> what you say to yourself. And what are you going to
> do? Everything was on me. I had to do everything.

Many new widows, but perhaps especially those whose
husbands died unexpectedly, begin to fear that they will not
be able to manage the burdens of loss and isolation. They
are surprised and frightened by feelings that seem strange
and foreign, and in some cases become concerned that they
are headed for nervous breakdown. Their trust that the
world they live in is relatively predictable and benign has

been attacked. And, very often, they must cope with their own tendency to permit themselves the illusion that their husband is just on his way home, is perhaps just now coming to the door.

> I lay here at night and I hear the door close outside and I'm listening for that key in the bottom door. I got his keys in my pocket, but I still lay here and listen for him. And that's been like that since he died three weeks ago.

> You know, it's so lonesome here at night. I mean after the children go to sleep and everything. The children go to bed early. My boy, he sits up with me, and the others go to sleep. He doesn't have to go to school until later. He's good company. If I didn't have the children, I'd be a nut. I'd be in the nuthouse if I was here in this house alone because, God, I thought I'd have a nervous breakdown.

> I couldn't describe my feelings those first days after he died. I really couldn't. It was a feeling I never had before. That's for sure. I mean I went through something I never have been through, because I never had grief and sorrow to go through with.

> I couldn't describe it if I had to. I really couldn't, because I was in another world and I was expecting things that wouldn't ever happen. I was expecting him to come home. I got his keys and everything and I went over and looked and identified him, but still I said, "Well, he'll be home." I know he's there, but right now I don't believe it. I still don't. I got it in my mind he'll come back home. And it's a mystery for a grown-up to say that, but I really have.

4

EARLY EMOTIONAL AND PHYSICAL
REACTIONS TO BEREAVEMENT

M ost widows (sixty-four percent of our sample) reacted to the death of their husband with disbelief, shock, or both. It could not be so, or they could not feel it—they were cold, without emotion. Shock and disbelief were especially prominent where there had been no forewarning. Ninety-two percent of the widows cried; some collapsed in tears. Eighty-eight percent became sad and despairing. Sometimes shock and disbelief alternated with anguished sobbing. Psychophysical symptoms began for some; these included sleeplessness (reported by forty percent) and loss of appetite (reported by thirty-six percent). Some became unable to organize their thoughts and energies and, responding to this, began to fear breakdown and collapse. Forty-four percent reported some loss of self-control.

These reactions persisted or recurred, though ordinarily

with reduced strength, throughout the first year. But in the early weeks of bereavement, shock, physical distress, bewilderment, and deep despair dominated the picture. At the same time, and with steadily increasing effectiveness as bereavement progressed, widows attempted to regain their balance. They tried to be realistic, to cope with their difficulties as they presented themselves. Indeed, if there was a single principle governing the behavior of our respondents, it was to carry on. They made strenuous efforts to inhibit the expression of their grief when with strangers. Even in solitude they tried to maintain composure. Forty-six percent spoke of the need to control feelings for the sake of others.

Some widows attempted a regimen of grief in which they would give the morning to crying and would thereafter be done with it, or give a week to sorrowing and thereafter return to their responsibilities. This was impossible, of course; they could neither cry on demand nor set a date for the cessation of sorrow. But when it proved impossible, some blamed themselves for indulging their grief.

For the most part, by self-imposed restrictions and with the active support of others, through the distractions of people and activities and with the help of medications, our respondents managed the initial bereavement period in ways that they themselves thought of as successful. They gave way to grief only at more or less appropriate times, to an appropriate extent, with appropriate others. Not quite half said they felt free to express their feelings with at least one other person. Most felt they did best to restrain their grief until they were alone. They managed the various rituals and ceremonials of memorializing and burying with at least some competence, and they were able to deal with the relatives and friends who called on them. Often they were distressed that the pain of loss lingered and recurred regardless of their attempts at self-discipline, but eventually they usually decided that on balance, given everything, they had done fairly well.

There were exceptions. One widow's grief simply would not abate, and her intense religious beliefs proved of little help. Another who seemed at first relatively unaffected gradually slipped into more and more confusion. The norm, however, appeared to be intense distress in this initial period, accompanied at times by fears of being unable to manage. Nevertheless the widows demonstrated an ability to deal adequately with the tasks that required their attention: arranging for the funeral and burial, helping the children to reestablish a routine, maintaining a functioning home. As they recognized their own reliability, widows reassured themselves that they would in time regain some equilibrium.

SHOCK AND DISBELIEF. The initial reaction of the majority of wives to news of their husband's death was, as we have said, a form of shock. They felt cold, numb, dazed, empty, confused. At the edge of consciousness, for many, was a fear of being overwhelmed, of being submerged, drowned, by grief. Yet at the same time the death might seem unreal and incomprehensible; it could not be grasped, could not be felt. Frequently they said that when they were told that their husband was no longer alive they were surprised to notice that they were devoid of any feeling. Later they usually felt that numbness at that moment had been a blessing, preferable to the pain that they were not sure they were then ready to bear. The numbness constituted a brief moratorium from feeling, a time when they might know as a kind of external fact that their husband had died, but would not yet have to deal with the knowledge emotionally.

Shock was reported as regularly by women whose husbands died after an extended illness as by those whose husbands died suddenly, although in the former case the shock was more subdued and tended to stem less from the fact of the death than from the time at which it came. No amount of preparation could really be adequate. "The doctor from the hospital called and said, 'Your husband has succumbed,' and as much as I thought I was going to be prepared for this, I said, 'Oh, my God.'"

The inability of these women to prepare themselves fully for the reality of death even though they knew their husband was on a fatal course may have been in part an expression of loyalty to the husband in his fight for continued life. It may be that only if the husband himself acknowledged his terminal course could the wife also acknowledge it. In the few cases where the husband did help his wife plan for the period after his death, the wives reported comparatively less shock and disbelief.

But there were some cases in which the husband's death had long been predicted and should have been expected, in which the wife had been present when the husband stopped breathing and knew that the death had been confirmed by an attending doctor, and yet wanted to deny the finality of the event, to believe the husband had only dropped off to sleep, would awaken, was still alive. In fact, thirty-six percent of the forewarned respondents reported reactions of this sort. Mrs. D, whose husband died after a long illness, was among them. She described her reaction to his death in this way:

> He was just like he was when he was sleeping, you know. He was still warm, although he was very pale. I didn't want to believe it, yet I saw it right there. So it was as though I were torn between what I wanted to believe and what was really there.

When the death had been accidental and sudden, the widow might find it almost beyond her powers to believe that the death had actually occurred. She might not at first be able to understand what she was being told, to grasp the import of the statement by the doctor or police officer, "He's dead." Or she might understand but expect that somehow the report would prove wrong, that there was some mistake. On seeing her husband's body, she might even expect that by some miracle his life would return. Mrs. K, whose husband died suddenly of a cerebral hemorrhage, described such a reaction:

> I never expected this to happen, but for years he had very high blood pressure and it just caught up with him, I guess. It happened while he was sleeping. He was in an awfully heavy snore and after a while it wasn't like the snoring he usually did. So I tried to wake him and I couldn't. It was ended within an hour after it started.
>
> I just couldn't believe it, even when the doctors came. I said, "Can't you give him something to start him breathing again?" I mean, you just don't believe it until the undertaker comes, I guess. I kept thinking I saw a little pulse or something in his neck. So I thought, well, he just needs stimulating, somebody rubbing his heart, or to give him something to start him going again. But they said no.
>
> After they all had left I touched his cheek and it was cold and that did it.

The initial grief reaction of shock and disbelief is most acute in the days immediately following the death, and through the succeeding first few days. It appears to give way when the widow responds to the request for her permission for a postmortem examination,[1] in her participation in planning for the funeral and burial, through the insistent

[1] Sixty-three percent of our sample reported that an autopsy had been carried out. Another ten percent said that one had been requested but that they had refused permission. It would appear that responding to a request for an autopsy is becoming a normal part of the postbereavement ritual when the death occurs in a hospital.

sympathy of friends and kin, and as there is recurrent recognition of the husband's absence from her usual surroundings and events.

EXPRESSIONS OF THE EMOTIONS OF GRIEF.   As shock and disbelief were reduced, the widows' underlying feelings of almost all-encompassing sorrow emerged, to be expressed in sadness and in weeping and crying. During the first week or so of bereavement the pain of loss when not actually manifest seemed to be lying in wait, ready to take the widow by surprise. Brief intervals of momentary forgetfulness might occur, only to be shattered by the realization that the death had indeed occurred.

Only eight percent did not cry at all during the first week after the death. Nineteen percent described themselves as having cried for extended periods. The remaining seventy-three percent cried only intermittently, in brief outbursts. For most widows confrontation with the fact of the death during the funeral service, in conversation with family and friends, or on encountering an individual or an object associated with the husband would almost certainly elicit quiet sobbing or a welling of tears.

Grief continued to be strong among all respondents through the time of the husband's burial, but after that its form and intensity varied a great deal. With some it increased and became more visible; with others it decreased or became more covert. By the three-week point about half our sample reported themselves to be crying less.

At times the widows' crying and sadness seemed almost to be reflex expressions of their dazed condition and traumatized feelings, without particular content. But at other times, and this seemed more and more the case as the immediate shock abated, there was deep grief for the loss of a beloved figure, on whom had depended the structuring of many sectors of the widow's life. Widows cried both for their husbands and for themselves. They grieved for their husbands for the years that had been taken from them, and they grieved for their own desolation. Distress seemed to be intensified if the widow felt herself in any way blameworthy because of difficulties in her relationship with her spouse while he was alive, or because of failure in her attention to him while he was dying. This was illustrated by the case of a widow who had been away from her husband's bedside when he died, and who thereafter blamed herself for what she felt had been a desertion, and in the cases of several widows who blamed themselves for not having gotten their husbands to medical treatment earlier. In these cases self-blame was an additional source of pain. In a quite different and extreme situation, a widow who had been unfaithful to her husband during his final hospitalization later appeared unable to release herself from her own condemnation. Guilt feelings for sins of omission or commission in the marriage were infrequent—only fourteen percent expressed some sense of guilt or self-reproach regarding their past relationships with their spouse—but thirty-six percent found some basis for self-reproach in connection with the death itself.

Anger seemed to be expressed more frequently than guilt within our sample. Thirty-eight percent blamed others— doctors, above all—for having failed or misused their husband. A very few widows felt that they had been badly treated themselves. Twenty percent of our sample expressed feelings of anger toward the husband for not having cared for himself better or for having contributed in some other way to his own death. Anger toward the husband was especially marked among widows of alcoholics, for whom their husband's death seemed to be a final outrage. Two widows of alcoholic husbands, however, while expressing bitterness over their husband's self-destruction, also remarked that the death had brought them relief.

Another element in the emotional constellation of new widows was their anxiety as they contemplated carrying on alone in a future they saw as uncertain for both themselves and their children. They knew that the children, especially the very young ones, could not grasp the implications of their father's departure. Sometimes they grieved for their children's fatherless future and were anxious because of its financial and moral perils. Fifty-eight percent of the sample said they were anxious about their children, and seventy percent were anxious about their own financial or occupational or domestic futures.

Underlying the sometimes florid emotional expressions of grief, although seldom referred to explicitly, was deep and pervasive sadness. Respondents assumed that those who knew them would understand this. They usually felt that it was not wrong of them to cry when with kin or friends who knew of their grief and to an extent shared it. And although they also wanted to avoid inflicting their grief on others, most widows reported at least one public situation in which, to their embarrassment and regret, they had broken down.

At first widows might be led to cry by meeting those who had been close to their husband and themselves, "people you know your husband loved the most and that you had the most fun with." But as bereavement continued, crying became a more solitary activity; in the presence of others feelings of grief were inhibited, delayed, or disguised.

In the very beginning many widows wanted to cry because they believed that crying would lessen the internal pressure of their grief. Some nevertheless found that they could not cry as freely as they thought they should, and thirteen percent said they were quite unable to cry despite feeling choked up. Some of these widows gave credit to their self-control, but were puzzled that they had so much of it.

This may be one expression of a generally held belief in our society that painful feelings are best dealt with by being fully expressed, at which point they are done with. This model assumes that sorrow can be treated as an entity that exists in a certain quantity, and that expressing sorrow uses it up or expels it. Therefore, it should be possible for the individual to "get it all out," to fully externalize or discharge it. It is consistent with this model to believe that crying should continue until sorrow is fully expressed but that once this is done further crying is self-indulgent. Thus some of our widows experienced disappointment and self-blame when their grief lingered despite their attempts to get it all out.

Some widows maintained their composure even in the first weeks because they were afraid that open confession of sadness or depression or bitterness would be the beginning of a loss of control from which might stem still further loss. At this time widows were just beginning to recognize that they were on their own, and that if they did break down there might be no one to care for their children—or themselves. In addition they did not want to alienate their friends and kin, whose support and potential help were now especially important.

Gradually most widows came to what might be character-ized as a manageable strategy for the expression of their grief. Maintaining control was of great importance for them, but so was the relief they expected from tears. Therefore, they seemed to believe, the prudent approach to expression of feelings would be to remain composed when in the presence of others, thus demonstrating their strength, and then in the safety and privacy of their own home to grieve as openly as they could, being careful not to go too far. Some who followed this strategy later regretted that they hadn't permitted themselves more release. Mrs. K said:

> It's like you're in shock ... Through the whole thing I didn't cry. If I had I would have been better off, I think, because the next day, that night—when I was awake I could control myself—but as soon as I started dozing off something was taking over me, I don't know what, what it was, but I went through a loose spell. I don't know what you'd call it, but the next day my whole

shoulder, everything was tight for days ... You're
almost ready to pass out. Whereas if I had been crying,
even like this [she was crying during the interview]
during the wake and funeral maybe some of it would
have come out ... I just forced myself, I kept going and
going, I just didn't think too much about anything. You
can't think too deep or it will hit you, you know.

Other widows believed that even though their crying
would at first have been accepted by others, it was better,
more dignified, more worthy of respect, to comport themselves with stoical composure. Jacqueline Kennedy's display of self-control was taken by some of them as a model of
how to behave. Before he died, Mrs. M's husband suggested
that his wife think of Mrs. Kennedy and the dignity with
which she had carried her grief. His wife attempted to
behave with equal dignity when her turn came.

Last year he said to me, "If anything ever happens to
me I don't want you to go to pieces. I want you to act
like Jacqueline Kennedy—you know, very brave and
courageous. You've got to have class," he said. "I just
don't want you screaming and hollering."

So I just prayed to God to give me the courage to do
that, and He did. I didn't even cry at the funeral, and it
was an impressive funeral. But I did what he asked
me to do. I behaved as he wanted me to.

I was worried how I was going to react at the funeral
home: "Gee, I hope I don't—I hope I'm alright." Then
when it was the day of the funeral: "Gee, I hope I'm
alright." I didn't know how I would react. But I acted
very good. I just cried quiet, I prayed, I said my final
prayers, and I touched his arm, that's all. I just kept
thinking about him telling me not to cry. Now I don't
break down very often—once in a while when I'm
alone I will—but during the Mass I didn't shed one
tear. And at the cemetery I didn't shed one tear.

Widows were aware of the contagious effects of crying and felt some responsibility not to make it more difficult for others to retain their control. Moreover, they felt that the open expression of their grief, even though accepted by others, might make it more difficult for the others to interact with them. They were concerned that the loss of their composure would make interaction stiff and uncomfortable, and constrain the others to act as sympathetic onlookers.

Widows were discouraged from emotional display by physicians, relatives, and friends. From the moment of death (and often before) and through the period of the wake, funeral, and burial ceremonies, they were cautioned, instructed, cajoled to control themselves, not to give way to their grief, to think of their children or to think of all they had to live for. Generally they found such injunctions unhelpful. Indeed it was those kin and friends who permitted and encouraged the expression of grief who were likely to be seen as helpful.[2] Nevertheless as time went on they might be threatened openly or by implication with the loss of the respect of those relatives and friends on whom they had come to depend, if they could not maintain their composure.

Widows perhaps exaggerated the inability of others to tolerate their grief. Yet they repeatedly reported receiving praise for maintaining composure and, at most, understanding and indulgence if they broke down.

Some of these themes are apparent in Mrs. L's report, in which emotional control was equated with "doing well." Describing the funeral, Mrs. L said:

> They told me I did very well. I know I broke down, but I didn't scream and holler like some people. I don't believe in that. I know I broke down and cried, but

[2] People who permitted and encouraged the expression of grief were seen as helpful by sixty-seven percent of the widows; only twenty-eight percent of the widows thought it helped them to be told to exercise control.

they got me out of there quickly. I tried to compose myself as best I could, and they just took me and we came home. And then for the preburial Mass we all did very well through it, the whole family, including myself. Everybody held up very well.

Oh, I certainly did cry, and I still do. I still have my moments—I could cry right now—but I can compose myself, you know, a little bit. I talk about it, and I get that choked up feeling, but then I can try to hold it in for a while.

So for others, if not for herself, the new widow after a brief period restricted the expression of her sorrow.

DISORGANIZATION. The death of her husband, more than any other loss, would seem likely to disorganize a woman's life profoundly. Not only does it bring about fundamental disruption of her living arrangements and social environment, but it also removes the key relationship in her emotional life and at the same time attacks one of her bases for security. It introduces into her life new difficulties and leaves her to deal with them alone except for the help she may for a time receive from friends and kin.

This experience of personal disorganization might be expected to lead to feelings of anxiety and despair, depression and anxiety. And indeed we find much of this in the widows' reports. We find, too, descriptions of changes in personality or behavior that can be traced to the upheaval in their emotional life. A woman whose relationships with her parents or with her in-laws had always been pleasant might find them suddenly disrupted by bitterness and hostility. In several cases widows who previously had been loving mothers, though fully intent on giving their children the affection they knew they now needed more than ever, found themselves impatient and irritated and unable to respond to their children's needs.

Although our respondents went to considerable length to maintain their self-control, to fend off their feelings of vulnerability, to prevent themselves from acting on anxieties and irritations that seemed very different from anything they had previously felt, they were aware of changes in themselves, of angry feelings they knew to be unjustified, of new susceptibility to despair, and to bewildering thoughts of self-destruction. The result was that even when the widow was in fact able to control her behavior, she might experience a frightening feeling that "something is happening to me," perhaps that "I might do something I'll regret."

Flirtations with self-destruction were not unusual. Three weeks after their husband's death twenty percent of our sample said they would welcome death if it were not for their children, and another six percent said they would simply welcome death, without qualification. None of the women in our sample in fact attempted suicide or appeared seriously to consider it, but many out of despair and with a desire to undo their loss, to regain the husband, thought in abstract and fleeting ways of this possibility.

Yet opposed motivations were present at the same time, not least important of which was the belief that they must go on living for their families, and especially for their children. A substantial number of respondents said that it was only such considerations that sustained them during the first days, and that without them, "I don't know what I would have done." Three weeks after her husband's death, Mrs. F told us:

> I think I'd really go out of my mind if it wasn't for my daughter. The other night I was ready to take some sleeping pills in my hand. And I thought, "Well, gee, what would happen to her? Well," I said, "Forget it." So I put them back in the drawer again.

Widows believed that others were afraid they might be contemplating suicide. Perhaps they exaggerated, or put into others' minds thoughts that were in their own. But there was some evidence that relatives did worry about this possibility. Widows were repeatedly warned against permitting themselves to become depressed, and were hardly left alone during the first days and weeks of bereavement.

The expression by others of the fear that the widows might somehow fall prey to their depression tended to reinforce the widows' own distrust of their physical and psychological frailty. It heightened their fear of the possibility that they would break down.[3]

During the first weeks of bereavement, many lacked confidence that they would be able to "make it through." Their concern was phrased in various ways: a fear of "breakdown", of "losing my mind," of "ending up in a mental institution." Thirty-eight percent admitted to some fear that they might have nervous breakdowns, fears that were apt to be especially prominent during the first few days after the husband's death, and then to decline somewhat when the social phase of mourning was at its high point, when other people were around and there was much to do. The fears tended to reappear, sometimes in more severe ways, when the widows were again left alone and began settling into their new lives. Three weeks after her husband's death, Mrs. F reported:

> Some days I'm worried about having a nervous breakdown. Sometimes I get more nervous than others, and I just feel like I'm ready to scream, especially if I'm alone. Like sometimes at night I'm sitting here and I just feel like I'm ready to scream. I'll put the music on to listen to that, or I'll sing to the records, just something to do, so that you're not talking to yourself. I think it helps. It helps me. I don't know if it would anybody else, but I'll just put the records on and I'll sing along with the records. Some people think I'm soft, but it really helps me.

[3] This process has been documented in another setting by Arthur L. Kobler and Ezra Stotland in *The End of Hope* (New York: Free Press, 1964).

As time passed, and as the widows achieved some new mode of living and thus regained confidence in themselves, the fears gradually subsided. Even quite far along in bereavement, however, a bad period might again provoke fear of emotional breakdown.

The drastic and abrupt changes in the widow's world led in most cases to experiences of bewilderment or a sense that their lives were no longer entirely real—sixty-four percent reported that they had at some point felt that "it's not real." Widows were sometimes unable to recall events of that period, including matters that had required their attention and that had been important to their welfare. Sixty percent of our sample reported that they could not concentrate well, nor think with their usual clarity. Some widows realized that they were not able to perform routine tasks that had previously been part of their everyday pattern of life, or to make decisions of almost any sort. It was not that they had lost their capacity to function. Even at those moments when they thought of themselves as disoriented, they might be impressed by how well they were doing, and months later they might congratulate themselves on how much they had accomplished and how well they had performed during the crisis period. But while in the midst of the crisis both the widow's perception of herself and the picture of her held by others and communicated to her through verbalized and unverbalized messages was of someone whose competence had been reduced.

Outside of a clearly protected setting, such as that afforded by the interviews, widows tended to keep their feelings of diminished capacity and, even more strongly, their fears of emotional breakdown very much to themselves. Protective of their dignity and desirous of retaining the respect of others, they did not share such frightening fears with even the closest of their kin and friends. Perhaps they were right not to tell others about these anxieties. It is by no means certain that they would have received reassurance that breakdown was not imminent, that their anxieties were not incompatible with normal response to traumatic loss. They might, indeed, have confirmed the fears of those around them that they were doing badly, after which they would have been treated with even more caution and concern.

In some cases fear of breakdown appeared to have a regressive impact on widows, forcing them into passive and somewhat childlike roles, perhaps abetted by family and friends who might recommend that they take it easy, that they not exert themselves. Fear of collapse might overcome the desire to retain independence; they might increasingly ask others for company and for help, at the same time asking less of themselves and restricting their social activities. Anxiety regarding their ability to manage on their own led a few widows to retreat for a time to the safety of their parents' homes. Loss of confidence in their own judgment led some to lean heavily on the advice of a brother or brother-in-law.

Most widows followed a different course, making deliberate attempts to counteract both their feelings of incipient breakdown and their impulses to let others take over. They tried instead to keep themselves busy, to fend off the frightening fantasies and fears, and in general to reassure themselves that they were indeed capable of managing something, be it only the painting of a room. They tried in this way to "get control" of themselves and to give themselves the confidence to attend to the ordinary demands of their lives.

They were often helped by drugs that gave promise of preventing runaway anxiety, including tranquilizers, sleep-

[4] Twenty-eight percent of the sample said that their alcohol consumption had increased and twenty-seven percent that they had taken tranquilizers. Compared to the matched nonbereaved sample, these changes were statistically significant. Compared to the sample of widowers, widows tended more frequently to have taken tranquilizers, less frequently to have increased their consumption of alcohol.

ing pills, and alcohol.[4] But to an extent widows felt the same conflict about medications that they felt about dependency on others. They feared a permanent change in their character, a permanent inability to function independently. While many of them accepted the need for tranquilizers and sedatives during this early period of bereavement, almost all of them were afraid of becoming permanently dependent on pills. Some who were given a prescription by a physician used the drug only infrequently, when they felt that they absolutely could not manage without it. Others were reluctant to go to a doctor to begin with, lest the drug they would be given prove too satisfying.

Resistance to the temptation of dependency showed up in other ways too. A few respondents refused the offer of a relative to stay with them, and a number refused the offer of parents to house them and their children. Despite their fears of collapse—perhaps in part because of them—widows tended to avoid supports that might interfere with their achievement of self-sufficiency.

Many respondents reported a desire for the help and support of others together with a fear of dependency. The resolution of these conflicting tendencies differed from case to case. It is our impression that most widows, despite uneasiness and extensive discomfort, succeeded in maintaining their integration through the initial phase of bereavement. A few had serious trouble later on, as we note in Chapter Twelve. It appears to us that the real danger for a widow is not so much immediate collapse under the impact of the trauma of loss, but rather an inability thereafter to summon her capacities to reorganize her life in a way she finds satisfactory. The failure to begin to reorganize satisfactorily may not display itself until several weeks or months have passed.

PSYCHOPHYSICAL REACTIONS.   Our respondents reported a

varied set of physical symptoms after the death: changes in sleeping and eating habits, in energy levels, and in tension states. Aches and pains often developed in various parts of their bodies, accompanied at times by a sense of fatigue or of oncoming illness. It was common for such symptoms to begin within a few hours after the husband's death, together with the initial reactions of shock and grief, and to persist through the first weeks and months of the bereavement period. Like other difficulties described in this chapter, they often intensified and diversified after the funeral and burial, when mourning no longer had prescribed forms to follow and fewer friends and relatives were around.

Sleep disturbances tended to be the most troublesome psychophysical symptoms, and along with reduction of interest in eating were the most common symptoms early in the bereavement. They were reported by thirty-one percent of our sample when interviewed three weeks after their bereavement. New widows were apt to define sleep as very important for them. Many of the women felt tired to the point of exhaustion by the time their husband died, and badly needed rest. Most also looked to sleep as an escape, if only a transitory one, from their grief. In addition most hoped that rest might provide them with the energy they would need to manage the new kinds of decisions and activities with which they were constantly confronted.

Yet many of the widows reported difficulty in falling asleep, and a tendency to wake again during the night. Attempting to avoid this experience, they became reluctant to go to bed. They stayed up late with others or, when there was no one around to talk with, they did chores in the hope that they would become tired, or simply to delay the point at which they would have no alternative to their empty bed. Once in bed they were beset by the fear of a lonely and sleepless night, and by the fear that if they did find sleep it would be interrupted by nightmares. A number of respondents reported that their sleep patterns had become so disturbed three or four weeks after the death of their spouse that they had sought medical help, and were using sedatives or tranquilizers.

Two reports suggest the quality of sleep problems in this early stage. The first was made by Mrs. N:

> The night before the funeral, I just couldn't sleep. I tried. Actually my sister came home with us after the wake and she made a hot toddy to see if that would help me sleep. Nothing. It just was, I don't know, it was just—everything I seemed to touch reminded me of Tom.

The second was made by Mrs. K:

> I feel I'm awfully tired lately, but yet I can't go in and lay down. I couldn't go to sleep—I just can't, I tried a couple of times—even with the pill I had. I'm tired enough to sleep but I don't.

Difficulties in eating and consequent weight loss were less troubling although equally common psychophysical symptoms. A year after bereavement fifty percent of respondents referred to changes in appetite. Twenty-six percent had experienced ups and downs—for the most part downs—in their weight. Most widows accepted appetite loss as a natural reaction to stress and believed that as they recovered their balance they would again be able to eat. In time some found the weight loss to be not altogether displeasing—our one-year interviews suggest that they rather liked the improvement in their figures. And there was not at any point fear that anorexia might become entrenched, as there was in relation to insomnia.

Lethargy, loss of energy, and decreased strength and stamina were another group of symptoms reported by widows during early mourning. Sometimes complicating the picture were feelings of restlessness and irritability, often held in check by a controlled, subdued manner, but contributing to difficulties in concentration.[5] These symptoms, if seen in severe form in a psychiatric setting, would be termed "agitated depression," but they seemed as characteristic of early mourning as simple sadness. Such feelings aroused a good deal of anxiety in widows who had not experienced them before, and could not realize that they were common and transitory expressions of grief.

Other physical symptoms that were reported by several women as having occurred during the first three weeks of bereavement included headaches (by twenty-four percent), dizziness (by fifteen percent), menstrual irregularities (by nine percent), and muscular aches and pains (by fifteen percent). In some instances these were ailments previously experienced by the women, perhaps, as in the case of headaches, when they were angry or upset or in conflict. In some instances the symptoms were entirely new to the women, and as such contributed to their anxiety regarding what was happening to them. In a few cases women experienced symptoms similar to those of the illnesses their husbands had died from. Although these turned out to be transient, they were intensely worrisome while they were present, and the women sought medical attention to reassure themselves that they were not embarked on the same terminal course their husbands had followed.

None of the women permitted their ailments to interfere with their participation in the wake and funeral, or to limit their accessibility to those who called on them. Widows were as unwilling to give in to physical symptoms as they were to give in to their underlying feelings of distress. However, many of their ailments continued to appear, often only briefly, during the first year after the husband's death.

---

[5] Forty-one percent of the sample agreed, after a year, with the self-description, "Sometimes I can't get myself to do things." Fifty-five percent agreed with "I'm so irritable." Sixty percent agreed with "I can't concentrate."

MANAGING. During the early period of bereavement, although a good many widows called on physicians to help them control their physical symptoms,[6] few sought out professional counselors (including priests or ministers) to help them with their emotional turmoil. Perhaps they did not seek help for their emotional difficulties because they believed that their grief was without remedy, and that all that they could do was maintain their self-control. Their physical symptoms were however considered manageable with proper medication. At times widows seemed to seek physical treatment for essentially emotional distress. Mrs. K, for example, said:

> I think the hardest part was right after the funeral was over, because you're kind of let down. Before then you just kept going, you just go through each day. But finally it was over, and then I kind of fell apart a little bit. That's when I started knowing I needed some pills. I needed help in some way. I told the doctor how I felt and he got some pills into me right away.

A similar pattern of reliance on physicians persisted for months after the death. Indeed, physicians appeared to be the primary professional source of support for widows. But even though widows received advice and sympathy from physicians they did not think of them as counselors. Rather, physicians were professionals who could prescribe drugs that might reduce aches and pains and promote ability to sleep and to accept adequate nourishment.

For the most part our respondents did not rely on professionals at all, but instead relied on their own determination to maintain control and to meet their responsibilities. Later, in recounting the experience of the first days of bereavement, respondents sometimes said they could not

[6] Thirty-six percent consulted a doctor in the first three weeks of bereavement and forty percent between the first three weeks and the first eight weeks.

imagine where they had gotten the strength to carry on. Mrs. L, whose husband had died suddenly of a heart attack while at work, described how she managed to keep going with just a bit of help from her family doctor.

> I can't believe it. I just don't even remember what I said to the policeman who came here with my brother-in-law. I just couldn't believe it. All I was concerned about was how I was going to tell the children.
>
> I don't know where you get the courage at a time like this. Somebody is watching over you all the time. I told them, and I tried not to break down as I told them. Of course my family and everybody was here in half an hour, I don't remember who, how or when, and then my own family doctor came, who is also a personal friend, and they gave me some pills and tried to clam me down.
>
> I mean I remember going through everything. I tried to keep my wits, and in fact I tried to give everybody else the courage. Like I said, "I'm alright, as long as the children are alright."

Most of the widows in our study believed at the time, and in retrospect, that they had maintained rigorous self-control through the first period of their bereavement and that all in all this had been a good thing. A small number of highly controlled widows later felt that they had given too much energy to fending off their feelings. Most, however, like Mrs. J in the report below, felt that they had been right to maintain their self-control:

> I was able to do everything I had to do—watch over the children and everything—without getting emotionally upset. I was busy, and I had no time to think about myself until everything was over, and he was buried, and the children were in school. Then I had time for myself to think back, and afterwards I thought it was

very hard. While I was doing things nothing bothered me—I won't say nothing bothered me, but I knew things had to be done and I knew I couldn't be emotional. I had to keep a stiff upper lip for the children's sake and do everything like I always did, and I did it.

5

THE AVAILABILITY AND USE
OF HELP

The first phase of grieving occurred in a context of relationships with fellow mourners—kin and friends and co-workers of the widow or her husband, people brought together by the death of a man who had been related to them in many different ways. These fellow mourners established a kind of community, ordinarily solicitous of the widow and understanding of her grief, which provided her with services and support through the first weeks.

In the previous chapter we described the emotional state of the new widow. In her initial shock and bewilderment, her subsequent sensation of emptiness, and her need to cope with the continuing physical as well as emotional symptoms of grief, the widow had little energy for coping with routine household and work tasks. Such energy as she had was likely to be preoccupied by the demands of the rituals of mourning and interment, and beyond these by the need to deal with the misery of her immediate situation and the bleakness of her future prospects.

Widows usually did not intentionally avoid others, but they did become less active in seeking others out, and less able to be fully responsive to those who called on them. Yet despite appearing at times indifferent to those who offered condolences and help, they were generally grateful to them for their reassurance and for their concrete help. Some widows, because they could not adequately express these feelings, achieved a withdrawal they did not really want. This withdrawal was then facilitated, as we note below, by the expectations of others that the widows might desire to withdraw for a time from social life.

People whom respondents said had helped them fell into three groups. First were those associated with the events preceding their husbands' death. Friends or kin who had looked after the children while the women had visited their husbands in the hospitals, who had prepared an occasional meal for the children or put them up overnight, or who had helped the women with shopping and cleaning had made it possible for them to devote themselves to their husband's care. Still others had made themselves available when the women needed to talk about their distress and had provided them with support beyond that which they could gain from their husbands. Some women were also helped at this time by physicians, nurses, and other hospital personnel who kept them informed regarding their husband's condition and suggested, directly or indirectly, how they might best conduct themselves with their husband.

After the death a new cast of helpers ordinarily appeared, overlapping the earlier cast only slightly. These "postdeath helpers" included a wider set of family members, friends, and neighbors than those who had earlier supported the women and their households. Co-workers of the husbands (and of the women, if they had been employed) might now appear.

Simultaneously another group of helpers would have been enlisted, the professionals in the management of death. Funeral directors and clergymen were most prominent here. Physicians might be consulted for help with the more physical consequences of bereavement—tension and anxiety and sleeplessness. Insurance agents would be called and asked to help the widow apply for benefits.

Widows said that in the first weeks of their bereavement they were treated well by others. Their distress was recognized and accepted. They were offered counsel and support from many directions. And it was not only the assistance others provided, but their very presence that proved valuable. The widows agreed that people had turned out to be much nicer, more solititous and more sensitive, than they had imagined they would be.

The supportive community of mourners existed only briefly. Many widows expected that they would be able to count on others longer, that the community of supporters would continue to exist through the later stages of their bereavement. But after the interment and the postcemetery gathering at the widows' homes, most of those who had rallied round returned to their own concerns, though some of those closest to the widows continued for some time to worry about their welfare.

The sudden emergence and nearly as sudden fading of a supportive community should not be surprising. The family, friends and co-workers who made up the community had come together only partly to provide comfort and help to the widow. In addition they had come to pay their last respects to the man who had died and to express their grief. With the end of the ceremonies their relationship with the dead man was formally ended, and now it became apparent that their relationship with the widow was not of a sort that would justify altering the routine of their lives to care for her. Near kin and especially devoted friends might remain in touch and solicitous, but others could do no more than offer the widow assurance of their continued desire to help should the widow ask for help.

HELP RECEIVED AS WIFE TO A DYING HUSBAND. Let us return to the situation preceding the husband's death. Respondents whose husbands had suffered an extended illness were likely to have organized daily routines around their roles as wives of hospitalized men. They stopped performing less necessary household chores, and as far as possible they shifted responsibilities for child care to older children, to relatives, or to neighbors. Instead of giving time to home tasks that did not absolutely require attention, they spent their afternoons with their husband in the hospital and, when their husband had a crisis, their evenings and sometimes their nights. They also dropped their routine responsibilities when their husband was ill at home and dependent on them for nursing. This last was by no means an unusual experience: fifty-five percent of our total sample played some role in their husband's nursing and about half of these women played a major role.

Some families, especially low-income families who still identified themselves as members of an Italian or Irish community (although they might share none of their parents' or grandparents' sense of nostalgia for the old country), had chosen to settle near the wife's mother or sisters. When their husband became ill it was relatively easy for the wives to call on nearby kin to help out with the running of the households. These same women were likely also to have old friends living nearby who, like them, had chosen to be geographically immobile, and who could drop in to help. In other families, including those of many of the more middle-class respondents where there had been greater residential separation, helping seemed more difficult to arrange. Nevertheless all were able to find someone among kin or friends who would baby-sit, care for the house, shop, chauffeur them if they didn't drive, and on occasion provide advice and support. Before and just after the death almost all our respondents felt they could legitimately ask others for help. Those they called on seemed to respond immediately to their requests, if they had not already volunteered.

The widows usually had not planned, during their husband's illness, what they would do after he died, but they had not been able to prevent themselves from recognizing that they would soon be alone. Even if they sought to fend off this realization, a relative's allusion to the impending bereavement would break through their denial. Medical personnel also might contribute directly or indirectly to forcing recognition that the husband was on a terminal course. A woman could observe the medical treatment her husband was receiving and compare it with the treatment of the other patients. She could infer the staff's prognosis easily enough. Many widows did not have to rely on inference; they were candidly informed by physicians. But others found the medical staff unwilling to discuss their husband's prognosis with them.

Most widows whose husbands had died in a hospital after a long illness were convinced that the best of care had been given, and were grateful to the doctors and nurses who had provided that care. In contrast, a number of widows were angry with medical personnel who had seen their husband earlier in their illness, and who had made what the wives believed to have been mistaken diagnoses or who had prescribed ineffective treatment. Anger toward medical personnel who were in attendance at the time of death was somewhat more common when the husband had been stricken by a sudden illness; then widows sometimes suspected that he might have been saved had medical attention been available more quickly.

The physicians and nurses who had cared for the dying men during their last days had sometimes treated the wives as untrained colleagues to whom they could delegate simple and tedious tasks. But more often extended contact between the women and hospital personnel had led to recognition of shared concerns, and sometimes the hospital personnel had come to express solicitude for the women. When the men died these relationships ended; only occasionally did a nurse or physician get in touch with a widow to find out how she was. But it was enough for widows who had been fortunate enough to gain the sympathetic attention of the hospital staff that those overburdened professionals had gone out of their way to help them as well as their husband.

In the few cases in which medical personnel did express continued concern for widows after the husbands had died, the widows invariably were deeply grateful. Only in one case did a husband's physician call after the husband's death to ask how the widow was managing, but in several cases nurses phoned. These gestures not only communicated continued solicitude; they also assured the widow that the treatment given the husband had been something more than mechanical medicine.

The following report by Mrs. O may suggest the way in which hospital personnel might constitute a supportive community for the wife who knows that her husband's illness is terminal.

> As far as the doctor was concerned, and the nurses, they were just fantastic. Even the ward helper, the floor scrubbers even. I mean I was just like a member of the family in there. At 3:30 every afternoon I went down to the kitchen and made a pot of tea and we [she and her husband] both had a cup of tea. And I just had my dinner in there if I stayed. They just served me off the tray. Any time I went down to talk to the doctors, they were more than helpful to me, and any time that Bill

asked for anything they gave it to him immediately. So that is the one thing I know, that he had the best of care, the very best.

Even when he was at home, I'd call the doctor—I was always calling them there—and they were always so patient. As soon as his temperature would start up I'd—not panic, but, you know—get in touch with the doctor, and they were all so patient, even to calling them at home. At different points I thought I was just being a plain nuisance, but they were very, very patient and very, very good.

Another respondent, Mrs. M, remembered the intensity of personal involvement of her husband's doctor:

The doctors at the hospital were terrific. There was a little woman doctor, she was terrific. She worked on Tom while his heart had stopped, to get him to breathe again. She was more upset, I think, than I was, because I half expected it. I mean, I was the one who sat there with Tom when he couldn't lay on the couch, he couldn't lay on a bed because it was too flat—he used to sleep in his chair at night because he could breathe when he sat up. And she felt terrible. She turned to me, she grabbed my hand, and she said, "He was too young to die."

Most widows felt it was an obligation, an implication of their fundamental commitment to their husband, to be with him at the time of his death. Yet only thirty percent of widows were in the same room as the husband when he died. The remainder, because they had been temporarily away from the hospital, or because death had occurred unexpectedly, tended to be remorseful at what they regarded as a personal failure. Widows of men whose deaths had been unanticipated felt distressed, almost guilty, that their husbands had died among unfamiliar faces in unfamiliar settings.

The person who notified the widow of her husband's

death, in those cases where the widow was not herself present, was remembered thereafter with complete clarity. Often this was a person they did not know. To the extent that our data permit generalization, it would seem that most widows regretted bitterly being told about the husband's death by a stranger. Very likely they would most have wanted to be told by the physician who had been responsible for their husband's care, in part because they had by that time developed a relationship with him. More important, perhaps, this would have assured them that the physician had been with the husband at the end and that the husband had not died unattended or attended only by strangers.

It seemed to have been especially harrowing to widows to be notified of their husband's death by the police. The impersonality of an announcement made by a policeman at the door, even if he was accompanied by a neighbor, seemed to exacerbate the trauma of being told that one's husband had died.

HELP RECEIVED AS A WIDOW.   After learning of the death of her husband, it was the widow's responsibility to insure that kin and close friends were told. Notification was not her job alone, but ordinarily it was up to her to begin the process, perhaps by calling her brother or her husband's brother and by asking him to call others. It was also her responsibility to decide who must be called and in what order. Generally blood ties were acknowledged, irrespective of the warmth of the previous relationship. Death, like birth and marriage, was first of all a family affair. The husband's and wife's parents, siblings, and grown children were likely to be telephoned immediately. If they could not be reached by telephone, they would be sent a telegram. Occasionally a widow felt that the news would come as a severe shock, and she should deliver it in person rather than by phone. Children were usually told by the widow herself, often in a setting from which others had been excluded. In a few cases another relative told the children.

Only the closest of friends were notified by telephone. Indeed, to call friends was to treat them as kin. If the friends were genuinely close, this would be an acknowledgment of the relationship, but if the friends were more distant, this might have been an imposition, an implicit request that they assume the obligations appropriate to kinship. Not surprisingly, widows sometimes found it hard to know whether to call friends or not.

Mrs. D was somewhat more active in the calling of people than many other widows, most of whom preferred to delegate some part of the task. The order in which Mrs. D called others, and her concern regarding who should be told in person, illustrate typical procedures followed by respondents. Also typical was Mrs. D's uncertainty regarding how to notify friends.

He died on Tuesday night. The wake was Thursday and Friday and the funeral was Saturday morning. I called my brother in California myself. My mother called me to see how John [the husband] was doing. I had planned to go down and tell her personally because I felt it wasn't something to do over the phone. She called, so I told her then anyway.

I called the priest to ask him if he'd come and say Mass, and also I called this other friend of ours who is a priest, one of John's buddies who has been ordained, and he was the deacon. I called my uncle, too. I called both my brothers, and I asked my brother to go down and tell my grandmother because I didn't have time and I didn't want to tell her over the phone. He wasn't able to, so I called one of my uncles and he went over there and told her.

I called two of my girl friends and a few of our close friends that I knew would want to know, but at a time

like that you don't know who to call, whether you're
imposing, whether they already know, or what. I just
didn't know whether they knew or whether to call them
and they'd feel they had to come or something. It was
kind of a predicament. I didn't know what to do.
Fortunately all his people somehow or other found out.

Many of those notified of the death, including some only
remotely connected with the family, called on the new
widow with offers of help and support. Some of the offers
seemed primarily to be devices for expressing solicitude for
the widow, but others were intended to be accepted as
stated. Widows might be offered assistance with housekeeping and child care; many had received such assistance right
along, and this would constitute only a continuation. But
there might also be offered to the new widow a new kind of
help, based on the recognition that she was herself in need
of care. A sister or a female friend might now offer to stay
with her so that she need not be alone, or her mother might
suggest that for a few days the new widow come to stay with
her.

The help that kin provided seemed especially valuable at
this time. Seventy percent of our widows said that their
family had been of more help than friends. Within the
family it was the female kin who proved most helpful:
thirty-eight percent reported they got most help from a
sister, twenty-four percent from the mother, ten percent
from an aunt, and only ten percent from a male relative.

Mrs. D described in the following way how the women
among her kinfolk helped:

> My cousin has been very helpful and several other
> cousins called and offered to take the children and
> offered to baby-sit for any of the rest of the family that
> needed baby-sitters and things like that. Everybody
> was very, very helpful. One of John's aunts made
> supper for everybody. She must have been cooking all
> morning because she had lobster and spaghetti with

lobster sauce, all homemade pizzas, all kinds of things like that. She must have cooked all morning because she had been there in the afternoon and she couldn't have done it in the time she had left. On Thursday I went to my mother's and Friday I went to John's mother's.

In general, the women close to the widow—her mother, sisters and sisters-in-law, aunts and cousins, but also her neighbors and her girl friends—took responsibility for ensuring that food was bought and prepared, that visitors were welcomed and made comfortable, that household chores were done, and that the children were cared for. Even though, at least for the first few days of her bereavement and often for the first few weeks, the new widow was likely to be absolved of responsibility for these home-management chores, she might perform some nevertheless. From habit or to distract themselves, several women washed their floors to prepare their homes for visitors, for example. But most of the bereaved and most of those who came to help believed that widows should be relieved of their usual tasks. Other women were there to replace them, so that they might be freed for grieving and for management of their new tasks.

Almost all widows reported that someone stayed with them immediately after their husband's death. In some cases this was in response to their request, but more often family or friends were themselves insistent that widows not remain alone. It appears that ideally the person chosen to remain with a widow would be an unmarried female without competing responsibilities: a sister, widowed mother, cousin, aunt, or close friend.

The woman who stayed with the widow usually took responsibility for keeping the house in good order and for holding the children to their routine. She served as a companion to the widow and also as a protector, screening the demands made for the widow's time or attention by solicitous friends or unknowing strangers. But most important in the view of our respondents, the woman who stayed with a widow made sure that the widow cared for herself: that she ate, slept, and groomed herself, and that she did not entirely withdraw into desolation.

How long the companion stayed appears to have depended on many factors. If the widow seemed to those close to her to be fragile, or if the husband's death had been devastating, as might have been the case if it was unanticipated, and if she would otherwise have been alone except for small children, then it might be felt that she should have someone with her for as long as possible. But a widow who appeared competent and strong, whose husband's death had been long anticipated, and who had older children who could share some of the responsibility for care of the home, might be stayed with only for a day or two or three. Much depended, too, on the widow's own attitude, on how insistent she was on getting back on her own.

Almost always widows remained in their own home. An exception was sometimes made for the first night after the husband's death; a widow whose children had been staying during her husband's last days or weeks at her mother's or sister's home might now stay with the mother or sister herself. But widows generally did not want to be away from their own home; there was comfort in its familiarity. In addition they wanted to reestablish their children's routines and end the disruption of their children's lives which had been a secondary consequence of their husband's illness. Many widows also seemed to fear that if they once permitted themselves to depend on their kin they would not regain their independence for some time.

An additional motivation of widows for keeping their home going was that the homes became planning and organizing centers during the first days of bereavement. The widow was the central figure in the postdeath activity. She decided the nature of the ceremonies of mourning, and her emotional state was itself a focus of concern for most of those in the community of mourners. The husband's parents, brothers, and sisters might be commiserated with and offered consolation, but their needs and wishes were understood as less imperative than those of the widow. (Sometimes, however, there was conflict on this issue.) As for the young children, although there was recognition that they had suffered fearful loss, people seemed not to be sure how fully they recognized their loss, and were therefore uneasy with them. This further established the central role of the widow, since it was her responsibility to deal with her children's grief.

In addition to persons who could help them in their homes, widows in the early period of their bereavement were likely also to need others who might provide them with support, advice, and, in some instances, comfort and resolve. Help in the home was generally provided by women; help with functioning and planning was often provided by men. Most of our respondents reported relying for support and advice on a man who was almost designated by their family or their husband's family or who had volunteered himself, perhaps after they had made some initial request of him. Almost always, where it was possible, this role seemed to be filled by the husband's brother.[1] Second choice for this supportive role was the widow's own brother and a distant third was a sister's husband. But only if the husband had no brother or if the brother was unavailable because of geographic distance or unsuitable because of age or personality or familial estrangement, would the widow call on her own brother or a sister's

---

[1] During the first three to six weeks thirty-six percent of widows regarded a brother-in-law as the most helpful member of their husband's family. This was virtually all widows whose husband had a brother who was suitable as a helper. Fourteen percent of widows said that most helpful within the husband's family had been a sister-in-law, fourteen percent said a mother-in-law, and four percent named others. Thirty-two percent said that no member of their husband's family had been helpful.

husband. Rarely, it seemed, would a widow call on her own
father or her husband's father.

For that third of the sample who had an appropriate
husband's brother, he would be among the very first to be
summoned after the husband's death. Generally he assumed
a good deal of responsibility in arranging for the funeral and
in dealing with the other tasks that emerged in the aftermath
of the death. He was often described as having been
extremely solicitous, and the widow sometimes hoped that
she might continue to rely on him for advice regarding her
home and finances and for help with the children. In time
the widow might well be disappointed in her brother-in-law
when the attention of the latter returned to his own family
and affairs, but in the period immediately following her
husband's death the brother-in-law was likely to be an
entirely reliable figure. Mrs. J reported:

> Well, they told me I'd have to inform my undertaker if I
> had one, that whoever I have as an undertaker I should
> go to him and find out what to do. So I went down to
> my brother-in-law's, his brother, and his father was
> there, and we called up the funeral home. My brother-
> in-law came with me. I had never done this before and
> he had done it for his mother, so it would be much
> easier for him. And if there was anything I would
> forget to ask the undertaker, he would tell me.

A similar report was made by Mrs. H:

> His brother went with me. I went with his brother and
> a couple of his friends, because we didn't know
> anything about making arrangements. His brother
> more or less took over everything. He's the next oldest,
> and he paid half the funeral expenses and he said what
> I get from the Veterans and Social Security will pay the
> other half. And he bought all the flowers and he gave
> fifty dollars toward the rent. He was very good.

Still another report indicated the continuing support the

husband's brother could offer during the first phase of bereavement. This report was made by Mrs. I:

> My husband's brother has been a great help to me. In fact he's always here. My husband was his only brother and it's been very, very hard for him, too. He was with me that night [of the death] and he came home with me and sat with me for a while, and the next morning he came and we both made the arrangements together. We had to come back here to the apartment and get clothes [in which the husband would be buried]. He called where my husband worked. Neither of us had ever done anything like this before. We didn't know where to start. We just plunged right in. You're numb, you just don't know. My brother-in-law was at my side constantly, and he was like the Rock of Gibraltar.

Although the repeated descriptions of the assumptions of responsibility by the brother-in-law made it evident that we were here witnessing a reliable implication of our kinship system, widows themselves seemed to have little awareness of the socially patterned nature of their calling on the brother-in-law for help. Rather each who did this seemed to feel that her brother-in-law was someone she respected and that for some reason peculiar to their relationship it was natural and proper to call on him.[2]

The pattern of reliance on the brother-in-law may well, at the time of our study, have been part of our national imagery because of the reliance of the two Kennedy widows on their brothers-in-law after each tragic loss. But our respondents did not have the Kennedys in mind when they decided that the husband's brother more than any other male within their kin network should share with them the responsibility for the interment of the dead husband.

Widows sometimes explained their choice of the brother-in-law by saying that among the husband's relatives it was

---

[2] The men who died did not have grown sons. In an older age group with mature sons we might find a different pattern.

his brother who was most directly and deeply affected by his death. One widow, for example, said that she thought her brother-in-law had been grieved by her husband's death almost as much as she. Another said that her brother-in-law had been hospitalized with a heart ailment just after her husband had died from a coronary, and thought of this as displaying the closeness of the brother-in-law's identification. Still another said that her brother-in-law had so idealized her dead husband that he now intended to model his own life after his, and this demonstrated his commitment to his memory.

A number of widows felt that their brothers-in-law to some extent continued the life or character of their husbands. The latter feeling might be especially strong if the brothers had looked alike or had similar mannerisms. Some widows had thought of the husband and his brother as "part of one another," in a fashion not unlike the way in which they understood their own relationship to the husband. Because of this they could easily believe that the brother-in-law shared their sense of loss. Some widows admitted that the presence of the brother-in-law led them momentarily to question why the brother-in-law had lived and their husband had died. But ordinarily this was only a fleeting thought, quickly rejected in recognition of shared grief.

At the same time that immediate family and close friends rallied to the widow's support, support of another kind was offered from more distant relatives and friends. This other kind of support came in the form of cards and gifts accompanied by expressions of sympathy and testimonials to the worth of the dead husband. A number of widows received messages of condolence from people they hardly knew. Sometimes these more distant connections offered the sort of help noted earlier—food for a family meal, transportation, or services as a baby-sitter—but generally widows declined these with thanks; they were already being helped sufficiently. Flowers and sometimes money, in a few cases fairly large sums collected by the husband's co-workers, were tangible ways of expressing sympathy and concern. Many widows were almost overwhelmed by what appeared to be an outpouring of affection for their husbands and themselves. But some widows had more mixed feelings, and questioned whether expressions of sympathy were responsive to their genuine needs. Mrs. A was one of those who viewed the gifts with some ambivalence:

> I felt everyone was very loving and helpful. They helped me financially, which really hasn't been needed in my case. People have given money and I sometimes wish that some people instead of donating so much— well, I don't know if they knew that I didn't need the financial help—if they did know, instead of giving so many flowers, I'd rather had them give to the deceased person's church or any organization that he is really interested in or active with.

During this first week of bereavement an atmosphere of warmth and concern surrounded the widow, whatever the appropriateness of its expression. Ordinarily people had come through for her, had been warmer to her, and had done more for her than she could have anticipated. A few widows reported bickering or other unpleasantness between family members, perhaps over some detail of the ceremonies, but most widows felt that during this time the usual family hostilities and interpersonal difficulties had been held in abeyance, and potential disagreements deliberately smoothed over, out of deference to their distress. "Society" seemed to them at its best at this moment; people acted well to one another and to them.

THE HUSBAND'S ROLE IN PREPARING THE WIDOW-TO-BE. Infrequently the better educated widows—and only rarely others—had been helped by their husbands to deal with the coming change in their situations and identities. (Only eighteen percent of widows had discussed with the husband in realistic terms the prospect of his dying.) It seemed to require a particular sort of marriage relationship for this to be possible, one in which there had been a history of frankness in expression of feeling and of mutuality in planning. It appeared, too, that communication between husband and wife about the husband's coming death had to be initiated by the husband. Even then the discussion was painful for the wife. Yet in those few cases where there had been realistic discussion, the wife later seemed to find it easier to manage.

Except for those few couples, husbands and wives did not deal openly and realistically with the knowledge of the husband's impending death. A number of couples, however, talked about what might happen should the husband die without ever confronting the fact that the husband's death was nearly certain. In some of these couples the husband might voice his hopes for his family and how he wanted them to live should he chance to die, without actually raising the possibility that his present illness might be terminal. The husband might comment on the location of wills and insurance policies, make suggestions regarding the schooling of the children, even make clear his wishes regarding the kind of funeral he would want and whether he hoped his wife would eventually remarry, all without referring to his illness and without asking for response from his wife. In other couples there seems to have been somewhat more interchange, though still without acknowledgment that the husband's death was imminent.

There were yet other ways in which husbands implicitly communicated their wishes to their wives. If there was a woman whose management of widowhood seemed to him worthy of emulation, the husband might express his admiration of her and suggest, in an offhand fashion, that he hoped his wife would pattern herself on that woman should he die.

Indirect as this approach was, it might nevertheless define for the wife how she should attempt to manage her grief. We earlier noted how the husband of one of our respondents had commended Mrs. Kennedy as a model of how a widow should behave, with the result that his wife tried hard to keep control of herself during the husband's illness and after his death.

Among those husbands who talked with their wives about what they wanted to happen after their death without acknowledging that they knew they were soon to die it was not uncommon for the message to be disguised as banter, reducing its emotional impact without sacrificing its clarity. Mrs. I reported that her husband had handled his coming death in this way:

> He spoke about it to prepare me. I'd feel bad when he'd talk about it and I'd tell him to stop and then he'd smile and say, "Well, I was joking," or something like that. But he talked about it and about the kind of funeral and where he wanted to be buried. And he used to joke with me about our having a very happy marriage—we were only married five years, but it was very happy—and he used to joke with me about my getting married again, and say he'd write me a letter of recommendation. This would make me feel just terrible, just awful. And then he'd joke and laugh.

OTHER INFLUENCES. Jacqueline Kennedy, as we have noted, was taken by a few widows as an admirable model of widowhood. But some new widows had available other models, closer to their own lives: their mother or an aunt or grandmother. A few of our respondents said that they had deliberately attempted to pattern themselves on such a model. Mrs. I said:

> I think you do kind of follow somebody else's example. My aunt's husband died three years ago and my

husband and I were very close to both of them. He was
an older man, and of course it's very different when
someone is older. But it's even more sad when someone
is young, because you think of the potential they had in
the life ahead of them. I can remember that she was
composed, although she was numb. I can remember
that at the time she was very brave and very courageous. I think you don't want to have people see you
crying. You don't want people to pity you. At least this
is the way I feel.

Along with the overt or covert directives of the husband,
and the woman's own remembered models of how a widow
should behave, the expectations of those who rallied to her
side after her husband's death helped widows decide how
they would comport themselves the first days of their
bereavement. The descriptions by our respondents of what
happened at this time suggested that their own inclinations
to withdraw from normal activities were strongly encouraged by the people around them. Often the widow's kin and
friends suggested that it was proper to delegate to them
much more of the housekeeping and other tasks than was, in
fact, absolutely necessary. Aside from periods of very short
duration in which the new widows were truly incapacitated
by grief, they all felt able to be active and, as we have noted,
often wanted to be active to distract their thoughts and
feelings. Other people sometimes insisted on relieving
widows of tasks the widows would have preferred to be
permitted to perform themselves. The expectations of the
people who surrounded the new widows, that their lives had
been devastated and that they therefore wanted to retreat
from everyday events, played a major role in encouraging
many widows to accept temporary retirement from activity,
whatever their own feelings about the matter.

All those who provided the widow with help or expressed
sympathy for her communicated their view of her as no
longer being a wife. In this way early bereavement became a
learning period for the new widow. By the behavior of

others toward her she learned what she as a widow might be expected to do and to feel, which behaviors and feelings would be accepted and which would not, what sort of person others thought her to be. She might herself accept these definitions or resist them, but in either event she became aware that she was understood as now having a different status from the one she had occupied as a wife.

Some widows accepted their change in status without great protest. Others found the notion of widowhood repellent. For some it was a kind of stereotype that felt entirely foreign and yet into which they were expected to step. For others it was a demand that they relinquish their status as wives, and for a time at least they would insist that they were wives still, although their husband had died.

6

THE CEREMONIES
OF LEAVE-TAKING

The social management of the husband's death is both structured by and expressed through a series of ceremonies: a wake or viewing, ordinarily in the funeral home, where the body is visible and the family receives callers; a funeral service, either in a church or in the funeral home; and a burial or committal service at the grave. There might at a later date be a memorial service. More Protestants than Catholics held the funeral service in a chapel of a church. The Jewish rites differed from the Protestant and Catholic in omission of the wake and provision of a memorial week during which the family received callers. In addition to religious differences in rites there seemed also to be differences related to the socioeconomic standing of respondents and to their ethnic backgrounds, but these differences appeared relatively minor.

Like other time-honored ceremonies, the ceremonies of leave-taking respond to profound human needs. They provide an orderly and proper way of dealing with and disposing of the body, in which there is recognition both that the body is now lifeless and that only days before it was a living, loved person. They also provide settings in which the community of kin, friends, and co-workers can take leave of the deceased, and can express, indeed can celebrate, the role he played in their lives and the meanings he had for them. In these settings, too, others can support the former wife in the transition to her new status of widow.

For most respondents the ceremonies went well. The proper forms were observed, and the proper people attended. In some cases, people who would hardly have been expected to have cared came as well. Afterward there was often quiet approval that communicated to widows that the ceremonies had been successful. Knowing that they had been able to see to it that the departure of their husband had been properly accomplished helped many widows begin their first year of bereavement somewhat stronger and more assured than would otherwise have been the case. They were reassured that despite the shock and upset they were suffering, they could manage and indeed were managing effectively. They were reassured that they had met their responsibility.

Contributing to the widow's trust in herself (at a time when this might be shaken) was the understanding implicit in each ceremony that it was the widow who was in charge and that the success of the ceremony was a credit to her. Many widows did not at first accept this. They had gradually to be led to recognize that they were defined by others as the responsible figures by the systematic consultation of their wishes and the deference their preferences received.

Hospital personnel, police, undertakers, and clergymen all contributed to this definition of the widow as the responsible figure. Often its first expression was the sometimes subtle, sometimes clumsy, request by hospital personnel for a postmortem, which the new widow had authority to permit or refuse. The new widow would also be asked to decide who should be notified and how. Family and friends, if not the hospital personnel, might next press for her decision on the undertaker. Although the husband's family, in particular, might seek to influence that decision in ways the widow might find unacceptable, they too would recognize that hers was the final authority. With some exceptions, and occasional ambivalence, everyone in the widow's community, even the husband's family, accepted the widow as the new family head. From the moment of the husband's death to the time of his burial they recognized that the husband's body was hers to dispose of, and that she had final authority to plan the ceremonies of leave-taking.

None of our respondents attended to these matters entirely by themselves. Because of their grief they felt incapable of managing alone. But in addition it would seem inappropriate to attempt to arrange for the ceremonials of death without consultation with others; there would be something secretive, furtive, in this. Nor had many of these young widows much prior experience with death. Often they did not know the name of the undertaker used by their family or community.

To deal with these issues the widows consulted the family members: the husband's brother, preferably; or the husband's parents or sisters if there was no appropriate brother. If these were not available, then members of their own family were consulted. They wanted to know what undertaker, ceremonies, and cemetery would be felt proper by both their own family and their husband's family. Occasionally there was conflict here and the beginnings of intrigue when the practices of the two families differed, but generally the conflict was resolved quickly and apparently amicably. New widows seemed to listen to all suggestions and to accept those they could—there was neither time nor desire nor emotional strength for dispute. Later, disagreements regarding the management of the ceremonies that had been smoothed over in the interest of family peace might become a basis for continuing resentment or antagonism. But there seemed at this time to be little overt conflict.

Mrs. O in her report suggested the way a new widow might accept responsibility as the new family head even while remaining dependent on others for support and guidance. Her description begins with events following a physician's statement that her husband had just died.

> My brother-in-law asked me at the hospital who I was going to get for an undertaker, and I said I hadn't even given it a thought. My father-in-law came and he explained how, [my husband] being a veteran, the privileges they have. Well, we agreed to get this particular undertaker, and then we called him and he came up and he arranged for the funeral, in detail, just all about it.

The undertaker now chosen, Mrs. O was led by him to her next decision, choosing a casket. She consulted with her family here to be sure she would choose the most appropriate.

> He told us about the different steps and so forth. He showed us all the different caskets, the choice we had. We wanted to stay within the limit of how much we had to spend for the casket and everything. In selecting it I asked everybody, were they pleased with it? Everybody agreed that wood would look better for a man. Everybody agreed that it was a nice one. You know, I wanted it to be a nice one and yet I wasn't going for that elaborate kind of thing. I want things simple and yet, you know, within the budget.

Still further decisions now presented themselves—the plot, the proper clothes—but with the help of the funeral director they were surmounted.

He being a veteran, they took care of the burial ground. I didn't have no kind of plot or anything, but the undertaker told me that he being a veteran they would take care of it. Then I went shopping for a black dress.

There was a viewing of the body at the funeral home, and finally the ceremonies of funeral and burial. "A lot of people came," and Mrs. O felt sustained by this display of caring. Then there were the announcement cards, in which task again Mrs. O took responsibility, although guided by the funeral director and helped by kin.

There were a lot of people came to the funeral. It made me feel—I felt much better. A lot of them were from where I work—they all came. I appreciate it very much because it meant a lot to me. And they came over and I talked with them.

Of course I was going in circles because it was something that I wasn't familiar with, I didn't know what to do. I sent out cards and things which I didn't know about, but his cousin was telling me how you go about it because she lost her father and mother and husband, so she was familiar with all these things. She did it, at least she sent cards. I just gave her the addresses. They were cards announcing his death. You send them to your friends and relatives. The funeral director gave them to me.

Despite their grief and the disorientation and feeling of unreality which often accompanied it, widows were caught up, in the days immediately following their husband's death, by what some felt to be endless decisions and activities and encounters. They came together with their own and their husband's nearest kin to console and to consult. They told their children and tried to comfort them. They responded to the sympathy of friends and neighbors. Against this background of continuing social interchange they had to plan, organize and participate in the social ceremonies of the wake, funeral, and burial.

These ceremonies were of great emotional importance for all respondents; there was nothing of empty ritual in widows' participation. Indeed it is difficult to capture all the meanings the ceremonies might have had for a widow. They were first of all complex things to do in relation to the death, so that the death did not leave the widow empty of response; then they provided recognized, structured settings in which the widow could share with others her love and regard for the husband; and then they were themselves final offerings to the husband or at least to his memory, final expressions to him of who he had been and what he had meant. The ceremonies also offered kin and friends an opportunity to express to the widow their continued affection and regard for her. And the ritual elements of the various ceremonies seemed to be seen by some widows as making more nearly comprehensible an event otherwise beyond their grasp.

The widows wanted above all that the ceremonies be fitting and proper. They were not especially concerned with keeping costs down, although many were limited in what they could spend. Nor did they allow their decisions regarding the ceremonies to be affected by what had been the nature of their marital relationship. Even in those instances where the marriage had been marked by tension or estrangement, widows wanted the ceremonies to be the proper ones. Widows felt that in arranging the ceremonies they continued to express the love, devotion, duty, and attachment they had felt for their husband through their marriage. And those widows who felt their marriages had been only too deficient in these respects saw in the ceremonies of leave-taking a last chance to repair the lack.

If the husband had indicated the kind of funeral and burial he wanted, either in the course of idle conversation early in the marriage, or later on recognition of the severity of his illness, the widow generally followed his wishes closely, whatever her own wishes or those of others. Although in the course of their marriage she might have brought her own desires to bear on major family decisions, here the widow felt obligated to carry out without modification her husband's wishes. A few widows did somewhat more than they felt had been wanted: they had a more elaborate funeral, or a more elaborate burial rite. But most widows would not go against a husband's clearly expressed wishes even to this extent.

The next most important determinant of the forms of the ceremonies was tradition. The tradition, to be sure, might be made known to them by the funeral director, and so his ideas of what was proper would have influence. But family and very close friends also would be consulted.

Forewarned widows had felt that it was important that their husband die in familiar surroundings in the presence of loved others. Now they wanted the handling of the body to be entrusted to undertakers who were in some way related to them. A funeral director associated with their husband's community—with his ethnic group and even better, with his family—seemed especially appropriate.

For similar reasons widows sought clergymen who were linked with their husband, one who officiated at a church the husband had attended or where the children went to Sunday school, who was a boyhood friend, or who had read the funeral service at the death of a relative, for example. They wanted the husband buried in a cemetery where there were others of his family or of their own family. At the same time they wanted him buried near enough to their home so that they and the children would be able to visit the grave. The widows wanted, so far as they could, to avoid releasing the husband's body or his memory of the ceremonies surrounding his death to an impersonal outer world.

THE FUNERAL DIRECTOR. Much of the literature on funeral directors, undertakers, and morticians[1] is critical of

[1]"Undertaker" is the term most often used by the public, although the terms "funeral director" or "mortician" are much preferred by the trade. "Undertaker" is the oldest term and has had the most time to assimilate to

them, emphasizing their exploitation of grief for profit and their sometimes unscrupulous business behavior, which can include sales of unnecessary services and products. They also have been caricatured in the mass media as combining with an overeagerness for business a comic lugubriousness. Yet none of our respondents spoke of funeral directors in these terms; nearly all were grateful to the funeral directors with whom they dealt for the helpfulness and kindness they had displayed. There is surely in our society ambivalence toward undertakers, perhaps founded on repugnance toward those who find their livelihood in preparation of the dead, which displays itself in derisive anger toward them when they are not needed and great dependence on them when they are.

Almost all our respondents believed that the funeral directors with whom they dealt had provided support and advice that went beyond anything that could have been expected of them had they been mere businessmen. Instead these men seemed to them to have acted as conscientious professionals providing a service in a time of need. Widows felt that their charges were entirely justified, given their services.

The funeral director often advised the widow how much she should spend by interpreting to her the nature of proper ceremonials for someone in her husband's social niche. Critics of the American funeral have suggested that this gives the funeral director a socially undesirable opportunity

---

itself the negative images described in the text. Trade associations now actively discourage use of the term, saying that it referred to carpenters and cabinet makers of bygone days who contracted for a variety of funeral services as adjuncts to their real specialty of making and selling coffins. "Funeral director," the term now preferred by the trade, suggests the management of ceremony, which is in fact a major responsibility in the modern funeral. "Mortician" is at present used to describe anyone who is professionally employed in the management of death, essentially either a funeral director or an embalmer. Ordinarily funeral directors are also embalmers and managers of funeral homes in which wakes may take place.

to promote costly items and practices. Nor, as they point out, is he restrained by competition. No one in our sample shopped around for a cheaper mortician.

We have no criteria by which to evaluate the true cash value of the funeral director's services. We can only present to the reader the positive evaluations made by the widows whom we interviewed. Perhaps if the widows had not generally had insurance or other death-related funds, including gifts, with which to meet undertakers' bills, there might have been more criticism. Widowers were more restrained in their gratitude toward undertakers, and some of them *were* critical of their charges.

Most of our widows had little if any previous contact with a funeral director before their husband's death and consequently did not know what to expect of them. Invariably the funeral directors proved sympathetic and easy to talk to. The experience of Mrs. C, whose husband was killed in an automobile accident, was typical, although atypically she encountered a woman at the funeral home. Mrs. C said:

> I didn't even know the first step because I never had this in my family . . . but the lady at the funeral home was so nice. She instructed me in every step. She told me the other day when I was there, she said, "Anything you have trouble with and don't understand, just call me and I'll try to give you instruction."

Those widows in our group who had to arrange their husband's funeral with limited financial resources, far from being critical, were especially positive in their descriptions of the way they had been dealt with. There were, to be sure, three widows for whom paying for a sizable funeral bill later constituted a major problem. These were widows whose husband's insurance had not covered the funeral expenses and who later had to budget payments to the funeral director out of meager incomes. At the time of the death, however, later problems regarding payments seemed a minor matter.

A report by Mrs. N suggests how an undertaker can behave so as to relieve some of the worries of even a relatively impoverished widow. Note in her report how the undertaker effectively shared with Mrs. N responsibility for managing the burial. Mrs. N was accompanied in her call on the undertaker by a girl friend. Neither she nor her husband had living parents, and their siblings were far away.

> You don't have a cent in your pocket and your loved one dies, what do you do first? I wanted him buried close so the kids would be able to go to his grave once in a while, to take a little plant out. It isn't going to hurt them.

> So we went to the S—— Funeral Service. This man greeted us at the door, took us into his office, and sat us down. I explained to him that I came in to ask a few questions. He said, "If I can answer them, I'll answer them. And then we'll see about burying somebody." He said, "I know that's what you're here for." So I explained my circumstances to him, and that Ted was a veteran. He took it all down, very nicely, and he said, "Don't you worry about a thing. You sign this slip of paper giving me permission to first of all pick up the body," which I did. Then he took us out and showed us the casket. Then we went back to the office and wrote up the death notice for the papers, and in the meantime he also gave me an estimated bill for the amount of what it would cost me to bury Teddy.

> A man I had never met before, who was so kind at a time when you need a friend, was that man. And all his workers up there, they were terrific to me. The next morning he asked me to bring up Ted's suit of clothes and his shirt and a tie for him, which I did. And then he made other arrangements—I never, never knew you could have friends until I went through this trouble. . . .

> Teddy had a lovely funeral. It went off as well as could be expected.[2]

[2]At the time of interviewing many widows were entitled to a $250 Social Security death benefit and those whose husbands had served in the Armed

This woman, more isolated than many others in our sample, had special need for the "friendship" she received from the funeral director. Others, with greater access to kin and friends, did not feel so strongly that the funeral director had become personally involved, although their assessments of the funeral director were often equally favorable.

Some part of the gratitude felt toward the funeral directors may have derived from their role as intermediaries between the widows and death. But for the most part the widows' gratitude was a response to what they felt to be their professionalism. The professionalism of funeral directors was displayed, widows felt, by their ability to be unruffled yet solicitous as they led the widows through grief-burdened decisions regarding the rituals of the wake, funeral and burial, and by their mastery of the many details regarding when and where each ceremony should be held, how the rooms should be furnished, what notifications should be made, where the family should sit or stand, how individuals should distribute themselves among the cars in the procession to the cemetery, and so forth. They suggested how everything should be managed, but did so without usurping the widows' final authority.

So successful were funeral directors in establishing a professional stance that widows did not conceive of them as salesmen or even as businessmen, and made no reference to any attempt by them to sell a particular casket or a particular service. As they reflected on it later in our interviews, the buying and selling aspect of their contact with the undertaker had been entirely incidental. The undertaker, in the course of helping them plan the various ceremonies, had informed them of what might be proper for purchase. They

Forces during a conflict were entitled to an additional $250 Veterans Benefit for funeral expenses. The exact sum a widow received from these sources might be somewhat different from these figures, depending on circumstances, but a widow whose husband had been a veteran and who also was covered by Social Security could have an inexpensive funeral paid for even though she thought herself without funds.

did not feel, then or later, that he had taken advantage of their helplessness or their confusion.

There were many secondary ways in which funeral directors seem to have helped. Some widows found in the undertaker's solicitous and deferential consultation an affirmation of their importance and worth which helped them to continue to function effectively. Others reported that an undertaker had intervened in their favor in family controversies regarding the form or place of burial. And still others were grateful for the undertaker's reassurance that the ceremonies they had decided on were the proper ones.

THE WAKE AND THE VIEWING. About seventy percent of our widows chose to have formal wakes and all but three viewed their husband's body after they had been "restored" by the mortician. Many of the widows had major reservations about the value of the viewing, although most felt that the wakes, if not helpful to them, were at least not harmful. Of those who had wakes, forty-eight percent found them helpful and only fourteen percent thought that their effects on them were primarily negative.

It was important to most widows to have their husband's body restored so that they might appear as they had when alive and well. Some widows were fearful, when they approached the viewing, that they would see in the casket a grotesque or misshapen corpse. Others, not permitting themselves imagery so precise, were fearful of some vague sense of death. These widows were momentarily relieved when their fears were not realized and they saw only a body, the body of their husband. Yet this was itself repellent. As one widow said, "Just to look at him after they fixed him up, I knew it wasn't him any more. It was just a body—there was no life in it."

The morticians' attempts to produce the illusion of sleeping life usually failed. Some widows tried to recognize the morticians' efforts and complimented them on the beautiful job they had done. But on viewing the corpse most widows experienced a different sort of dismay from the sort they might have steeled themselves against. Instead of horror they were confronted by lifelessness. Mrs. I said:

> The biggest shock was when we got to the funeral parlor and looked at my husband in the casket. I had expected him to look as he did right after he died. It was a big shock to us. It just wasn't my husband there as far as I was concerned, it just didn't look like him at all. When a person is dead they just don't look the same as they did alive, the animation. And my husband was always smiling and his eyes were always twinkling and he had bright red hair and he was a very colorful person, very much full of life and vitality. And there he was, you just don't look the same. Of course I realize that it was just his body, not his soul, that his soul wasn't there. I knew that, but he just looked so different.

Most widows tended to find repugnant the whole business of viewing the corpse. Fifty-two percent said that the effect on them had been on the whole negative. About twice as many (thirty percent) regretted having seen the corpse as were glad they had seen it (fourteen percent). Even when the widows felt that their undertakers had achieved marvels of restoration they disliked confrontation with the fact that their husband's body could now be molded like any other inanimate substance.

Mrs. J, whose husband's last illness had caused his body to become misshapen, suggested the mixed feelings produced by even a relatively successful restoration. Fearful anticipation was followed by relief, as these fears were not realized, and then followed by a sense of strangeness, of alienation from the corpse, expressed through viewing the restoration as a job—"I think they did a very good job."

Considering they only had two hours to work on him I
think they did very good ... Of course he didn't look
exactly like him because he had swollen five times his
size before he died. The part that was most swollen was
in through his mouth and through the chin, and there
he didn't draw it all down. From his nose up it looked
just like him, but his mouth didn't, and the swelling
through the throat—he had a very tiny mouth and it
was quite swollen—it was impossible to bring down.
Of course, his face was discolored and needed a lot of
makeup. But I think they did a very good job on him. I
mean, I can't complain.

Many widows reported that there were moments on
seeing the dead body in the open casket, or just on
confronting the floral arrangements that unmistakably
communicated death, when the pain of their loss suddenly
became almost unbearable. Before the funeral service they
had often allowed themselves to be distracted from grief by
confusion and busyness. Now they could neither deny nor
avert their attention from their loss. One widow, not
atypical, said: "I didn't believe he was dead until I saw him
in the casket."

Despite the evident lifelessness of his body, some widows
placed a last kiss on the husband's cheek or lips. The effect
on these widows was further to demonstrate the fact of
death: the husband's body was cold.

A more satisfactory gesture was found by widows who
deposited mementos of their marriage in the coffin, perhaps
a picture of themselves, perhaps a ring or pin. The small
object then went with the husband, a bit of themselves
accompanying him forever.

All these gestures had in common as one of their elements
a refusal to accept the finality of the death. The gestures
were directed to something of the husband that still existed.
Yet the stubborn fact of the husband's death constantly
intruded. Mrs. B's account displays this conflict between
wish and reality:

When I saw him in the funeral house, that was pretty hard on me. Just to look at him after they fixed him up —I knew it wasn't him any more. It's just a body, because there's no life in it . . . I had a picture of me that he took and he always carried it with him and I put it in the casket . . . and a tie I gave him for his birthday and things like that, that he loved most, I wanted to be sure that they were on him right. But when I first looked at him in the casket, his expression was still there and it looked so real, but his face, they just put so much powder on him—from a distance it looked like him but not from close. It was not so much the makeup, I guess they had to do it, but it was so different from the day I saw him in the hospital. I mean, it's not him any more. But then I looked at his hands—the skin on his hands— and I was holding his hands for, I guess it must have been for a while, and it felt so warm that all of a sudden I thought he might come alive again. Then I looked at his face and I was so disappointed.

THE FUNERAL AND BURIAL SERVICES. It was the widow's prerogative to select the clergyman who would officiate at the funeral and burial services. If the widow and her husband had been churchgoers, the clergyman was almost always automatically the priest or minister of the church she and her husband had attended. Only if they had not been churchgoers did the widow have to stop and consider. Then she might confer with the husband's relatives to decide if there was a priest or minister who had known the husband, or who for other reasons might be appropriate. Irrespective of the religious commitment of the widow or her husband, all of the funerals and burials were held within a religious context, and a religious service was a matter of course.

The widows were less generous in their praise of the clergy than they were of the funeral directors, but their attitudes were on the whole positive. Most clergy seemed to appear only in the limited, though essential, role of religious representative; few attempted to give solace or counsel in a

personal way. Only eleven widows actually talked with a
clergyman; four of these reported that the talk had been
helpful, one that it had definitely not been helpful, the
remainder that it had been neither one nor the other. Except
for the case of one upper-middle-class Irish Catholic widow, whose priest had long been a close friend of the family,
and for the cases of widows who had belonged to small
congregations (a Christian Scientist and a Seventh Day
Adventist) in which leaders and members knew each other
well, the clergy seemed to enter widows' lives only as their
ceremonial role required. A sample with a larger number of
rural or Protestant widows, or greater representation from
the upper middle class, might have displayed more frequent
personal relationships with the clergy.

In truth few widows seemed to want closer contact with
clergy than they had. They had little enough energy for
anyone outside their intimate family and friends, and they
might have felt especially reluctant to play hostess for a
courtesy call from a priest or minister they previously had
met only on Sunday mornings. The professionals on whom
widows called at this time, other than funeral directors,
were physicians, not for words of advice or comfort, but
rather for medication that might help them to get through
the days and nights. Few of our widows thought of the
clergy as having anything comparable to offer.

In their sermons the clergy often attempted to minimize
the loss of the husband by suggesting that on the one hand
he had lived a full and productive life and on the other that
his spirit or his works would live on. These intertwined
themes of ending and continuation appeared in many of the
sermons to which widows responded most positively.
Except in this respect widows seemed to treat religious
rhetoric and doctrine as worthy of respect, but essentially
irrelevant to personal behavior. Nevertheless they seemed to
accept fully the religious tenet that only the husband's body
had died, while his soul or spirit continued. At the time of

the ceremonies few widows disputed even in private this definition of death; it seemed to them not only comforting, but right.

Few widows actually remembered much of what was done or said during the funeral service and the burial service. Their grief, together with their determination to behave properly, led them to focus their attention on themselves. They were aware that others had come, and were grateful for their attendance. Most were later pleased that they had had appropriate ceremonies and that they had comported themselves properly.[3] But their feelings during the ceremonies had been anguished, and they had only blurred memories afterward of what had transpired. Mrs. B, for example, said:

> We had it [the funeral] at the school chapel, which is a small one. I was just sitting there. I couldn't quite believe it and I didn't hear a word the minister said. I don't know, I guess the word is numb—and really sad. The service, I was told, was very short. A half-hour altogether. I don't remember it. I know there were a lot of people there, but I don't remember. I didn't really like to go. But I knew I had to. I was pretty nervous. I felt that I wished I was not so young, so I could join him sooner. I was very, very sad at the service.

All of the widows had their husbands' body buried rather than cremated. For many widows the cemetery rites, during which the last vestiges of the husband entered the ground, were the most difficult of all. Among those who found the burial hard to bear was Mrs. F.

> Father Thomas came up and said the rosary at the funeral parlor. He was buried from St. Anne's Church.

[3]Forty-seven percent of those thirty-six widows who expressed an opinion thought the funeral service had been helpful to them; twenty-eight percent thought it had been unhelpful. The remaining twenty-five percent were neutral in their evaluation.

I don't remember what went on at the church. We said
the rosary. I was all right through the rosary. It was
afterwards that I broke down. I don't know, I was
alright at the church. My daughter started crying, I
remember. She wanted to go to the bathroom and there
was no place in the church until after the service and of
course she threw up. All I could think of was trying to
console her until after the Mass. I felt alright until I got
to the cemetery. I think that's the worst part of it, going
to the cemetery. A couple of times there I almost passed
out. My brother was behind me and he asked if I
wanted to go to the car and I said, "I don't know. No."
The hardest part of it was at the cemetery, at the
graveyard, because it was so final.

Yet it would be a mistake to suggest that full acceptance of
the husband's loss occurred with his burial, just as it would
be a mistake to suggest that shock and denial immediately
on learning of the husband's death had prevented all
emotional recognition of his loss. Acceptance of the husband's loss seemed rather to proceed by fits and starts, now
succumbing to denial, now reemerging in response to
insistent reality. Feelings of continued connection
expressed themselves even in selection of a cemetery plot
close to home so that the widow and children would be able
to visit frequently. Some widows bought a plot that adjoined
an empty plot where they might themselves be buried one
day.

THE NEW WIDOW AND THE COMMUNITY OF MOURN-
ERS. The ceremonies that followed the husband's death
were, of course, social ceremonies providing settings for
interactions between the widows and others in their com-
munities. They made it possible for the widows to join with
others in defining the nature of the men they were together
mourning, to offer one another their sympathy and support,
and to reaffirm their continued ties.

Almost always there was opportunity for the widow and her immediate kin to meet in an informal way with friends and with more distant kin. Usually this was at the wake although some widows also met with others immediately after the funeral service. Widows valued the expressions of sympathy offered to them and through them to their husband at the wake and elsewhere. They also valued the mere presence of others. They interpreted their attendance at the ceremonies as a testimony to their regard for the husband, and an expression of their concern for the widows themselves.

Virtually every widow was aware of who had attended the various ceremonials, though many had only a blurred recollection of the ceremonials themselves. If someone prominent had attended, his presence would certainly be noted at the time and referred to later. If someone had traveled a long distance to attend, that too would be noted. In general the widow learned from the assemblage the standing her husband had had in the community, and the standing she now had. She learned from whom she could expect recognition, from whom deference, and from whom help.

Mrs. I, like most widows, had her husband "waked" in the funeral home. The first evening, because there was no announcement, only family attended. But the next evening, after an announcement had appeared in the local paper, "there were hundreds and hundreds of people." Having many people come to the funeral was interpreted by Mrs. I as "a great tribute"; it was the attendance itself, rather than anything special that was said, that was the tribute.

> The first night it was mainly family at the wake because we didn't put in the visiting hours in the paper. I would have liked to have had my husband waked at home, but that was impossible here in the apartment. And his mother, I don't think, could have taken it. Her house is

small and I think it would have been too much for her.
So we picked a very nice funeral home that was really
more of a home than it was a funeral home. The first
night there was just the family. But the second afternoon and night there were hundreds and hundreds of
people. I don't remember what I said to people, or who
was there and who wasn't. But I remember we were
there two hours after the visiting hours were over and I
thought, you know, we'd never get home. He had a
great tribute paid to him. This means quite a bit to me.

He had a very large funeral and of course when you're
young you have not only your own friends, but your
family and your family's friends, and he had thought a
great deal of many of the people who came. It was very
dignified and very simple. It was the way he lived, in a
very dignified and simple manner. This meant a lot to
me, that so many people would pay him such a great
tribute. It was a tremendous funeral procession and the
church was packed. I think he would have been kind of
proud to have known this.

Many widows reported that in these ceremonies "Everyone was wonderful to me." This was a time when only good
feelings, only constructive and supportive approaches, were
permitted expression. There were among the reports of our
widows exceptional episodes in which an in-law became
suddenly and unexpectedly hostile, and indeed there was
ample opportunity for animosity to develop over differences
between the widow and her in-laws regarding details of the
ceremonies. But these animosities were held in abeyance, if
not forgotten, in deference to the solemnity of the occasions
and the intensity of shared grief.

Engagement with distant kin and friendly acquaintances
was not restricted to the open ceremonies. Widows whose
husbands had been socially active often were caught up in
receiving and acknowledging gifts, calls, and sympathy
cards. Mrs. D, for example, made the following report.

I bought 200 stamps and I think I have six left, and I wasn't even sending notes to people who sent only sympathy cards or to people who came that I was grateful to see. At that point I just felt I had written so many I couldn't write any more. And I wrote them all in the first week or two because I felt if they were kind enough to share with us, that was the least I could do.

Mrs. M's husband had also known many people and she too found reciprocity demanding. She said:

I received hundreds of cards from people and I responded to the ones who sent me Mass cards, who came to the funeral or sent him flowers, and that's not counting the people that came to see him. I was going to go through that list, but when I went through the list of people that gave me cards and it came to over five hundred, well, then I just couldn't do it. To most I just sent out the acknowledgment card, but it will be between thirty and fifty personal notes I will be sending out. Like, for instance, my aunt and her family, they gave me a large sum, and his uncle gave me a large sum. And of course a couple of priests sent me nice notes and one sent me a beautiful painting. I haven't answered him yet, but I do intend to thank him for that. And the nuns have been very good to me and I'll have to thank them personally. I feel as though I shouldn't just write a note. And the city manager, he was very good, so I have to write him a personal note, which I haven't done yet. ... And even my undertaker, I was thinking of getting a basket of fruit. He really went out of his way. I think you should do little things like that to show your appreciation.

In time many widows lost the sense of being an integral part of a community which the ceremonies fostered. But one of the consequences of the ceremonies of leave-taking for many widows was that for the brief period immediately following the death they did not feel entirely alone.

7

GRIEVING

W ith the completion of the ceremonials of leave-taking a new phase of bereavement began. The distractions of arranging for the ceremonials could no longer serve as defenses against grief. The people who had earlier rallied around now returned to their own occupations. The ceremonies behind her, the widow was forced to recognize the need to establish a new routine and to plan her future life. More than before, the widow was likely to feel quite on her own. Although most widows now cried less than they had before, their sadness was apt to be more pervasive. Some reported that symptoms such as sleeplessness became worse. Several became deeply depressed.

This phase of the bereavement, in which widows were first confronted with the daily reality of their loss, seemed to last from several weeks to several months. Many of our respondents, when interviewed about two months after the death, seemed already to have passed through the worst of it. They were no longer beset by unrelenting despair, although pangs of grief would recur whenever their loss was brought to mind. In this phase of bereavement, however, widows were almost constantly aware of their loss, as a background to their thoughts if not the focus of them.

INDICATORS OF GRIEF. As though provided by society as signs to warn others of their grief and so prevent the embarrassments of inappropriate interaction, certain patterns of dress and decorum seemed to be prescribed for widows during this period of early mourning. Widows thought they were expected to wear somber clothing, avoid bright-colored accessories, and either forego makeup or limit it to the plainest and simplest available. In addition most felt they were expected to withdraw socially. Quite apart from the anticipated expectations of others, widows felt that somber clothing and some degree of seclusion expressed how they felt.

In practice few widows wore only black or gave up makeup entirely, but virtually all modified both their dress and their appearance enough to feel they had donned mourning. And for a time almost all widows did sequester themselves. One attended a social evening at a friend's house about two weeks after her husband's death, and two, perhaps thinking the experience might give them relief from their feelings, went out with friends at about the same point. They were, however, exceptions.

While almost all widows accepted the prescribed patterns of mourning at first, they soon modified them or dropped them entirely. Some questioned the validity of mourning dress at all; they felt it to be not only out of place in the modern world, but a repellent attempt to trade on grief, to wring sympathy from casual observers. Even at the beginning of mourning many chose to dress in a dark costume whose difference from normal dress was so slight that the uninformed would not recognize its significance.

Some widows had been told by their husband not to wear mourning. Typically these widows continued to use cosmetics, but could not bring themselves to wear bright-colored clothing. Mrs. M said her own feelings would have been violated if she had dressed gaily, despite her husband's wish. In addition she was certain that her doing so would be misinterpreted by others. Outside her home she wore a black dress of attractive design—sober, but hardly widow's weeds. At home she wore a light-colored dress. She said of her various compromises:

> My husband didn't want me to wear mourning clothes. He didn't want me to, but I've been wearing them. I mean, around the house I'll wear this, but I've been wearing black to work. But he didn't want me to, and maybe in another week or so I'll get away from it with a grayish or some other color ... I used to like to wear bright colors, and most of my things are Kelly green, reds. I felt so low that even though he told me, "If anything happens I don't want you to wear black," I just couldn't do it. If I went to wear a bright color, I couldn't. Of course now everybody is wearing black stockings anyways—you don't know who is in mourning and who isn't—so I had the stockings. I do wear the black, but I wear earrings and jewelry with it, and I wear lipstick.

Many widows ended their seclusion and returned to normal dress earlier than they thought would be approved by the more conservative of their friends and neighbors. In defense of their decision to cut short their period of formal mourning some argued that grief was essentially a private experience, and to wear mourning costume burdened others. They said that there was no disloyalty to their husband's

memory in returning to ordinary clothes and a less seques-
tered social life because their grief, though they did not
parade it, was genuine enough.

Feelings of ambivalence regarding formal mourning were
especially marked in the case of a widow whose husband
had been involved with another woman. This case is
instructive in displaying the force of anticipations of the
reactions of others and the conflicting force of the widow's
own feelings of what is genuine expression. The husband's
infidelity had been known to all the widow's kin and friends
and to many acquaintances. The widow thought it hypocrit-
ical to wear black—and ridiculous, given that everyone
knew about her husband. But at the same time her husband
had died and she felt impelled to recognize that fact in her
appearance.

> I was wearing black and everything but I said, "Well,
> after what's been going on—and everybody knows—
> why should I go around in black?" Under the circum-
> stances everybody in town knew, so why should I more
> or less go around like in a shroud, carrying on, which I
> can't. But I don't know. I wear it once in a while. I put
> on brown stockings.

As this report suggests, widows felt that no matter what,
immediately after their loss they could not present their
ordinary appearance to the world. But at the same time they
did not want to become ostentatious mourners. So even in
the beginning they adopted a style that while somber was
not unambiguously that of mourning, and rather soon they
moved away even from this.

In a similar way widows at first insisted on some measure
of withdrawal from their ordinary social life because this
felt right to them, but rather soon thereafter began to reenter
social life. For a time they stayed close to their own homes
and saw only family and close friends, avoiding entertain-
ments or parties or the like. But gradually they essayed a

movie, a lunch, or an evening with a sister or with friends, began considering joining organized social activities, and in this way reconstructing a social life.

Some widows justified their return to social life in terms of their need for distraction. Mrs. L, three weeks after her husband's death, said that she had decided not to sequester herself because it would be bad for her children and, incidentally, for herself.

> I'm not going to have any special period of mourning. If the children and I want to go someplace, well, we're going to go. I'm going to make a life for them. In fact, we had planned to take them to see "The Sound of Music" on their vacation, and I took them. Last week my sister and I took them to see "The Sound of Music" as my husband and I had planned. My husband's idea of life was, "Life goes on." When he lost his mother, and then my father died shortly after that, he kept saying, "Life has to go on. You can't stop living when a person dies." So I've tried to remember that and tried to keep going.

Only in one important respect did most widows not return to a normal social life: they completely avoided men who might be interested in them as dates. Some widows did not want to be alone even with their insurance agent or with men who had been close friends of their husbands. The possibility of a man becoming interested in them threatened their commitment to be loyal to their husband's memory. And, given their new vulnerability, they might have felt afraid of a man's interest in them.

To sum up, widows felt that a decent length of time should elapse before they resumed their normal appearance and schedule of activities. But they began moving toward this normal state rather soon after the burial. They gave up first one and then another observance of mourning: those who worked went back to work fairly soon; almost all gave up wearing black in a few weeks if not sooner; most soon thereafter returned to their usual clothing, spent an evening with friends as well as family, and became willing to celebrate a special event, especially with immediate family.

Widows felt observance of mourning should be a matter for individual conscience, and not a social requirement. Because of this they believed that the type and extent of mourning should be left to their own discretion. They assumed that any widow would express her grief by some change in dress and behavior, and that any widow would also be sensitive to "what others think," but they believed that just what changes a widow would make in her life and how long she would continue them was best left to her.

There were problems for widows in this permissive view of the matter. Without an established pattern to adhere to, how could a widow be sure that she had shown adequate respect to her husband's memory yet had not prolonged mourning beyond the time appropriate to her own feelings and needs? If she cut short her formal mourning would this not suggest callousness? If she prolonged her mourning might it not constitute a failure to try to emerge from her grief, to the cost of all those around her as well as herself? In several cases the uncertainty prompted widows to ask our interviewers for their opinion in relation to ending formal mourning.

There also appeared to be a good deal of defensiveness in widows' explanations of the reasons for their decision to return to normal clothing and nearly normal social activities soon after their husband's death. Their assertions that their husband had not wanted them to grieve, or had wanted them to end their grieving after a brief period, that protracted mourning had undesirable effects on their own mood and on the well-being of their children, and that in any event their grief was simply private, unsharable, and almost inexpressible, were all volunteered honestly and may well have been true. Yet they seemed also to be intended to fend off an accusation that they appeared to be grieving too little.

Some widows, when they considered an early ending of their observation of formal mourning, sought reassurance from their husband's kin that in doing so they were not failing in their duties to their husband. Their husband's kin, they seemed to feel, could be trusted to judge what would be proper observance of their obligations. Mrs. D, three weeks after her husband's death, said:

> I took the kids to see "Mary Poppins." Maybe some people might have thought I was terrible, but I felt it was something they had been looking forward to seeing. I didn't know whether I'd make it myself or not, the way I was feeling. My father got tickets for my brother and his wife and the kids. But we all went. When I mentioned it to my mother-in-law, she says, "Gee, that's good." At least I know she didn't feel as though I was disrespectful or anything.

This use of his kin to represent the husband's interests occurred a number of times in relation to movement away from formal mourning. It also would occur later in the cases of a few widows who would consider engagement or remarriage even though they were uncertain that adequate time had elapsed since the death. Ordinarily, it seemed, in-laws expressed approval and so implicitly gave permission, but we encountered a few instances among respondents in this study where they did not, and tension and resentment ensued.

By the time of our second interview, about eight weeks after the death, almost all the widows had for the most part ended their formal mourning. They might still be reluctant to attend a party and for many months to come would find repellent the idea of interest in an eligible man, but with these exceptions they now treated their grief as a private affair, perhaps alluded to only when with the closest of kin and friends, but no longer a justification for appearing in public to be different from others.

OBSESSIONAL REVIEW AND THE SEARCH FOR MEANING. During this period of intense mourning the widows returned in their minds again and again to the events of their husband's death, compulsively reviewing the course of the illness or accident. They did this both in reverie and in conversations with others. Again and again they asked themselves why it had happened. They seemed to have little control over "dwelling" so on their experience.

Obsessional review—going over and over the same scenes —seemed to be an integral part of the mourning process. It was distressing to the widows that they were so absorbed by the review and could not simply recognize their loss and be done with it. But they seemed unable to stop. Why might this have been the case?

Obsessional review was sometimes useful in that it helped the widow integrate the reality of the death emotionally as well as cognitively. Each review, as it reconstructed the sequence of events leading to the husband's death, identified a number of contingency points at which another path might have been taken—the initial indication of the fatal illness, or the initial decision to embark on the activity that ended in a fatal accident—and the widow was able to explore what might have been alternatives. "If I'd only insisted that he see a doctor then," she might fantasize, or "If I'd kept him from buying that car." But as she developed the alternative paths from each contingency point she recognized that these alternatives were not taken, that only one path was followed, and it was one that led to the next contingency, where again only one path was followed, and so on to the death. Each time she reviewed the sequence she might find another possible branching path, another possibility for having turned away from the fatal course. But each time she would have to accept that the alternative paths were not followed, that the path toward death had been chosen, that the death had occurred.

Many widows described to us their fantasies of alternative outcomes. Generally they described these in a series of "If, then," propositions: if he had done this, then that might have happened and the death might have been averted. "Had he taken better care of his health," "Had he not gone out that morning," "Had he not been working so hard," "Had he listened to my advice," "Had he followed the doctor's orders," "Had he given up drinking"—these were the materials of obsessional review.

It seemed to make little difference whether a widow held a fatalistic view of death, believed in predestination, or held that life and death were in the hands of God. Whatever her beliefs, the review process, the exploration of alternative outcomes, and the fleeting fantasies of undoing the fatal outcome were pursued.

To an extent there was a class difference in the content of the obsessional review. Widows of solid middle-class backgrounds often had planned and worked closely with their husbands. Now they took comfort in those realizations of plans the husband had lived to see, and found bitterly ironic the plans and wishes that remained unfulfilled. Widows of lower socioeconomic backgrounds instead were likely to review their husband's contributions to their families in their several roles as provider, father, and companion, and to comfort themselves with his goodness of intent if not of performance.

Nearly half (forty-seven percent) of our respondents gave some indication of self-reproach when interviewed eight weeks or so after the death. In their obsessional review they had almost predictably come upon acts of omission or commission that might have contributed to the death. Repeatedly they said something like, "Maybe I could have prevented the death in some way." About a fifth agreed with the statement, "I feel somehow it was my fault," a surprisingly large proportion to express so great a sense of responsibility. An additional ten percent expressed some guilt at having failed to have been a better partner to their husband when he was alive. Four said they felt guilty for having been unfaithful in thought or deed. The remorse of

the woman who had been sexually unfaithful while her
husband was in the hospital seemed almost boundless.
Another four felt guilty for not having cried more or for not
having grieved more deeply. Three felt guilty, eight weeks
after their husband's death, for having let him slip from
their thoughts now and then. Three felt guilty for having
permitted themselves to think about remarriage.

Given the tendency to engage in obsessional review, these
ruminations are hardly surprising. But perhaps it is surprising that half of the widows, rather than expressing self-
criticism or self-reproach, listed the ways in which they had
tried to save their husbands as a way of demonstrating that
they had done all they could. They emphasized their
devotion and their own suffering, described how they had
attended their husband faithfully through his last days or
how they had struggled without avail to get him to take
better care of himself or to be more careful. We felt that
many of these widows who displayed self-approbation
rather than guilt protested excessively, and that their attitude was a defensive response to the same deep uncertainty
that was expressed more directly by other widows.

Despite the residual guilt in at least that part of the sample
who expressed it directly, and perhaps as well in a portion of
the remaining who disclaimed it, there seemed reason to
believe that many widows found that the wake, funeral, and
burial provided opportunities for partial expiation. These
ceremonies, easily understood as providing a last opportunity to contribute to the husband's memory if not to the
husband himself, made possible ritual expressions of devotion and self-abnegation. They sometimes became settings
for acts of reparation by the widow, and in smaller measure
by the husband's immediate family and others in his
community who might have had similar feelings of guilt.

Their behavior during the ceremonies would later support
the widows' definitions of themselves as having done all
they could, at least after the husband's death. Our data do

not provide information regarding what would be the consequence if these mechanisms for the dispersion of guilt were to be blocked, but we would suspect that guilt might then be an even more lingering, even more disturbing element in the widow's attempt to recover from her bereavement, lessening the chances for a forward looking, constructive resolution.

A somewhat curious element in the obsessional review of several widows was an insistence that they or their husband had had premonitions of the coming death. This might be understood as an attempt by the widows to deny the thought that the death might have been the fault of a human agency, themselves or another. Mrs. M said:

> He said to me that he would never reach fifty. He was forty-five and he said, "I'll never reach fifty. When things are going to come easy for me, I'm going to go." He always liked politics, and he became a city official a year ago—this would have been his second year—and he just told me that when things got his way, which they were getting, "I won't live to see it."

Mrs. E, whose husband died in an automobile accident said:

> He told me, "That's one thing you never have to worry about, me getting sick, because when I die I'll go right out. I won't be sick. You won't have me to wait on." That was a year ago. So what can you do? He worked for this wholesale grocer place, and before he died he stopped by the house and he asked me, "Do you need any flour?" And I said, "No, we got plenty of flour. Don't bring me flour home." He said, "Well, I got a broken bag on the truck there. If you need some, you better get it, because it's going to be a long time before you can get some more." That's exactly the words he told me on Wednesday, before he got killed. I said, "Well, I don't need no flour. Forget it. When I need it, you can get it. If not, I'll buy it." He said, "Well, it'll be a long time."

Premonitions, as we have just noted, may have provided reassurance to the widow that she was guiltless by suggesting that the husband's death was fated. In addition it seems possible that in the cases of sudden death the memory of premonitions may have helped place the death in a sequence of events, and so have made it less arbitrary. It is as if the widow by finding possible forewarnings could construct a history of signs and omens like that provided by a fatal illness, though one requiring a rather mystical view of reality. But sometimes these memories of premonition were interpreted in the obsessional reviews as contingency points at which something might have been done, some action taken to set matters on a new course and ward off the coming death, and so became bases for self-reproach.

Widows occasionally were concerned with the reasons for the death—not now the causes, but rather the purpose of the death, its significance in the larger moral order. These questions seemed especially perplexing and urgent to our sample because their husbands had died at a time when their deaths should properly have been far in the future. This search for meaning was different from the obsessional review of the events leading to the death, but may well have had the same emotional roots. It too seemed to be an attempt to make sense of the death.

Having had forewarning of the death did not seem to make much difference to the widows' likelihood of engaging in a search for meaning, nor did being able to account for it in medical or scientific terms entirely offset the need for some such search. Nor could the search be put off by simple religious homilies—that it was God's Will, for example. Even the more religious widows, who had no difficulty in believing that their husband's death represented the Will of God and who felt in addition that they should be able to accept it without question—that it would be arrogant to attempt to understand God's motives—found themselves searching for further explanation.

Some widows could not accept that men as young as their husbands might die. Some widows objected that others older than their husbands, including their husband's parents or their own parents, continued to enjoy life. Some objected on moral grounds. Their husbands had been good men; why did they die when evil men lived on and prospered? Often the widows said bitterly that their husbands had had such high hopes, had worked so hard, that it was unfair that through no fault of their own nothing would now come of any of it. Other widows described how many problems and how much unhappiness the husband and the family had survived, only to be rewarded with this cruel ending. As if to underline the injustice, a number of respondents stressed how their lives had only recently become easier, how their husband had just begun earning more money, how their marital relationship had just improved, or how the children were doing better in school, when death came along to make it all futile. And, finally, fifty-eight percent asked in similar words simply, "Why did this happen to him?" Mrs. E said:

> I wish somebody could just sit down and explain to me why a young man had to die. A lot of people have died, but I still want to know why it had to happen to him. With the children, you say, "God does things." But I still can't understand why he had to die. I know it's God's way, because he wouldn't have died if God hadn't intended it for him, he'd have went through all that and walked out with a little scratch if it hadn't been time for him to go.

Mrs. L echoed the above quotation:

> I've asked myself why but I have no answer. Why, why, why, why was it him? What did he do? But I just have no answer. I don't know, I ask myself every day.

And Mrs. B, expressing the same feelings, described the

anger that unbelieving widows could feel toward those who offered the generally unsatisfactory explanation, "It's God's Will."

> I was thinking of why it happened to him. It was not fair. I'm very angry when people say, "That's God's Will." That really makes me very angry. It's a good thing I don't believe in God, otherwise I'd be so mad at Him. It seemed so unfair.

Eventually the questions and objections lost much of their force, and the search for meaning lessened in intensity. Yet even after a widow had seemingly reconciled herself to her husband's death her questioning might begin anew, just as later, when she had apparently recovered from grief, she might unexpectedly be again seized by its pangs.

There appeared to be some differences by social class in the explanations widows considered and eventually used as bases for acceptance. To oversimplify somewhat, the more nearly lower-class widows moved toward perceiving their husband's death as having been part of some grand design, one that was for the most part beyond their grasp, or else as an expression of unspecifiable underlying forces. In either event these widows felt their lives had been shaped by powerful forces beyond their capacity to understand. Magic and superstition were sometimes part of this cognitive picture, while the accompanying emotional state included a decided note of resignation. Occasionally these widows felt that death may have been punishment for their own past misdeeds or those of their husband.

Widows of middle-class standing or higher also introduced themes of inexplicable and inaccessible forces into their explanations of what had happened, but they gave greater weight to causal factors involving identifiable agencies, including the disease process and the state of medical knowledge. They were less fatalistic, more inclined to believe that other outcomes had been possible, although if they had religious commitments they might add that God's participation would have been necessary. Sometimes middle-class widows, like less well-educated widows, did attempt to accept the death in fatalistic terms—"There was nothing that could have been done about it"—but this seemed here more nearly a statement of resignation than a reference to inexorable forces.

The death of their husband damaged the religious faith of some widows. Although seventy-three percent of our sample said that the death had not affected their religious beliefs, a significant minority said in an early interview that their faith had been shaken, and one in eight said that she was angry with God or fate for having permitted her loss.

Widows who had earlier been devout tended not to lose faith because of the death of their husband. They instead turned to the formal doctrines of their religions for explanation: fifty-nine percent of the sample as a whole, and more of the devout, said that their religious beliefs had provided a major source of comfort to them. Because they were visited by friends and family who tended to share their beliefs, widows with religious faith found support for their views in those around them. A Catholic widow who said, "If any one thing helped me more than anything else, it was my faith," described how her husband too had found solace in the Church's teachings and how this had further encouraged her to rely on the Church's teachings after her husband had died. She went on to say:

> I think you have to just accept it as best you can. God wanted it to happen and it happened. . . . I have every reason to believe that my husband is at peace. We don't know what it's like, but I do believe there's an afterlife.

Ideas of resurrection and afterlife did not seem to reduce the initial intensity of grief—the widow quoted above suffered from severe and deep grief—but did seem to help sustain morale once grief began subsiding.

In a similar way, though involving different doctrines, a widow who was a Christian Scientist found comfort in the Christian Science belief that "Death is but a moment of fear." Her husband had died from hypertension while under the care of a Christian Scientist practitioner. After his death her belief, supported by her Christian Scientist friends and by another practitioner, not the one who had attended her husband, provided her with an explanation for the death and with definitions of how she should treat it. She reported:

> It's just when you're so doubtful and the fear sets in, that's when you don't receive your healing. And that's what happened to him.
>
> I know that I am very grateful to have Christian Science. I'm very, very grateful. I think that if I didn't have it I would have collapsed. I mean, the shock would have really done me in. And I feel that in three weeks I've come quite a ways out of it.

Most widows in the sample had not been especially devout before their husband's death. Now they seemed to develop some mix of religious doctrine and independent thinking. They tended to combine personalized and rather undeveloped ideas about the death having been desired by God ("He must have wanted him very much") with skepticism regarding the immortality of the soul or the existence of an afterlife. Still, they hoped that there might be an afterlife and were unwilling to reject out-of-hand the possibility that one might exist.[1]

---

[1] Twenty-two percent of our sample expressed a deep conviction that they would one day rejoin their husbands in some sort of afterlife. Fourteen percent hoped for an afterlife but were less certain of the prospect of reunion. Thirty-four percent said that they did not know if there would be an afterlife. Four percent believed there would be something after death, but doubted reunion. Only six percent said that death was definitely the end of all interaction. Twenty percent gave no indication of their beliefs.

The very looseness of these widows' beliefs took them out of the realm of formal religious doctrines and permitted them to apply and modify their beliefs to suit their needs. Their personal nondoctrinal faith permitted them to gain much of the reassurance of religion without requiring that they submit to the intellectual discipline of a dogma. Nor did loose beliefs of this sort prevent acceptance of the support of clergy. Mrs. M's report was instructive in these respects.

> I think religion has helped me a lot. The nuns at the hospital helped me a lot. They would talk to me, in case he would die, and all this and that. And the head nun there, the spiritual leader, she was very good. They're all good, of all denominations, they're all good to me. In fact, on his bed I had the Star of David that this Jewish friend of mine gave me. I had the Protestant cross, and I had the Rosary. They were all wonderful to me, they would talk to me so that I was prepared. They more or less comforted me. They told me that death wasn't that bad.

Nondoctrinal belief was not without its difficulties. Because it was not supported by organized religion it could easily be questioned. The widow could now lose, now regain particular beliefs. Mrs. D, for example, reported:

> I don't know whether I believe in immortality or not. At times I just feel it seems fantastic and then other times I completely believe. It just depends on the mood I'm in or something. I really don't know. There are times I believe that we'll meet again in Heaven, but yet again it just seems too far-fetched that we will actually have a resurrection.

Another widow, Mrs. G, had unwavering confidence in her own rather materialistic selection from Catholic dogma:

To have faith is a wonderful thing. People have to
believe in something. I believe in God, but I don't
believe that there is a better life hereafter. I believe that
the life you live on this earth is what you make it. I
think sometimes the Catholic Church stresses another
life because you have to believe in something. But I
don't. I can't visualize another life: I feel once you're
dead, you're dead. You've lived your life.

Most widows, those who did not subscribe to particular
doctrines as well as those who did, found it helpful to be
able to offer a religious interpretation of their husband's
death to their children. They thought that a supernatural
explanation made it easier for the child to manage the loss.
Mrs. E, who did not herself hold doctrinal beliefs, offered
her daughter a rather fanciful quasi-religious idea to help
the daughter to believe in a continued protective presence:

We're not that religious. I stopped going to the Episco-
pal Mass, and now I usually go with my daughter to the
Catholic church, but three-fourths of that I don't
understand and a lot of it don't make sense to me. I
won't convert, there's no sense in going into something
I don't believe in, but I've always believed that Mike
knows and sees everything we do, and I try to teach
Laura that, too, about her father. I say, "The brightest
star in Heaven, that's your Daddy watching you, and if
you find a brighter star, *that's* your Daddy, he's
watching you."

Religious ideas sometimes eased what might otherwise
have been awkward moments when widows met other
adults. A widow might try to prevent another's embarrassment at reference to her husband's death by saying, "It was
God's Will," or "One must have faith." In the same way
religious tenets were sometimes employed by others to limit
the widows' expressions of their sadness. Widows were
reminded that the death had been ordained by God and that
it was their duty not to despair, but rather to maintain

control over their feelings and to get on with their lives.

SOLITARY MOURNING.   Once the husband's burial receded
into the past there were many moments when there was no
one to whom widows could talk, when either they were
entirely alone or they were with their children or with
strangers. The frequency of these periods depended on the
way in which the particular widow had organized her social
life when she was married, together with her present
tendencies toward isolation or participation, toward solitary
grieving and escape into fantasy or toward seeking support
in interaction with others. But taking our sample of widows
as a whole, they more and more found themselves alone,
irrespective of their wishes.

Most widows now had the experience of only incom-
pletely accepting the husband's absence. Fifty-two percent
of our sample refused to modify some practice that would
acknowledge their husband's deaths; for example, they
continued to set a place for them at dinner or they cooked as
much food as they had when the husband was alive. Some
of them were surprised to discover themselves expecting a
call from their husband or listening for his arrival home.
One widow reported hearing her husband talking to her.
Four reported briefly seeing their husbands as if they were
alive, sitting in their favorite armchair or going into another
room.

Many felt the presence in connection with experiences
they had shared, such as getting breakfast or watching
television. The greater part of our sample seemed to maintain some sense of their husband's presence, ranging from a
vague feeling through actual hallucinatory experience,
during the first two months of their bereavement.

Perhaps surprisingly, this sense of the husband's continued presence was not unwanted by the widows. They found
some comfort in not feeling entirely alone, although when

they recognized that they were in fact alone, that the sense of the husband's presence was illusory, they often began crying. Yet the crying was not unwanted either. Most widows felt that "a good cry" relieved them of "tension" or "jumpiness" or "that tight feeling I get."

Other aspects of solitary mourning, however, were more disturbing for the widows. Their restlessness in the evenings and nights made them worry about their stability, and their preoccupation began to seem to them out of their control. When they were admonished by others to return to a normal routine of life, they wondered if they would ever be able to. They were perplexed, sometimes bewildered, by their own behavior, and perhaps especially by their willingness, indeed desire, to sustain the illusion of the presence of their husband even while they mourned their loss. All this, together with occasional sleeplessness or fitful sleeping, made some of them again fear collapse as they had not since the first hours after the death, and at this point many felt compelled to ask physicians for medication.[2]

At the time of the second interview the pressures of ordinary reality began intruding in the widows' mourning.[3] Personal matters that they had been able to put off, such as automobile insurance and house repairs, began to require attention. The children's routine had to be established and managed. Decisions had to be made about working or staying home, about moving or staying put. Now some widows began to feel severely anxious for the first time and some reported somatic symptoms and acute feelings of dependency.[4]

[2] Forty percent at three weeks and twenty-seven percent at eight weeks had sleep difficulties and nearly half of these were treated with sedatives by physicians.

[3] Widows reported being anxious about more things eight weeks after their husband's death than three weeks after their deaths—an average of 3.2 items in their lives at eight weeks compared with 2.2 items at three weeks.

[4] Severe anxiety was reported by sixteen percent, feelings of dependency by another thirty-two percent.

Again they returned to the strategy they had employed when the immediate impact of the death threatened their stability. They tried to suppress or avoid or postpone their feelings if their feelings threatened to become overwhelming. They tried to keep their composure when with others. They tried in general to control their expressions of feeling. When alone they tried not to hold everything in, but at the same time not to lose control. They tried to keep busy.

Now it became important for many widows to escape seclusion, to avoid sinking into withdrawal from others and from their usual routines. Work was of enormous value. They found things to do—if possible an outside job, if not, then housework, making things, taking walks. The strategy they adopted was to distract themselves through activities that could absorb their time and energy without demanding more of their attention than they could provide. As one phrased the strategy, "The best thing is to do normal things and not be morbid; it's easy to be morbid and it's easy to feel sorry for yourself."

As an illustration of the development of this strategy of keeping busy in the first months of bereavement we can compare the comments made by Mrs. K when interviewed three weeks after her husband had died and when interviewed again six weeks later. In the first interview Mrs. K commented on the usefulness of keeping busy, but she had no specific tasks to use as resources:

> It seems to hit you more if you're by yourself than if you keep busy. At night, then I guess you think too much, then it does hit you more. You think of that last time when you saw him dying but you didn't know he was dying. I wish I had known it. I thought he was just sleeping. I keep thinking of that and I try to get it out of my mind. You try to take it out of your mind because it will start you getting sad again, and so you get busy doing something.

When interviewed five and a half weeks later, Mrs. K had

arranged for enough activities so that there were few times
in which her thoughts would be unoccupied:

> I've forced myself to go out a lot. I'm going to night
> school. The busier you keep, I think the better you feel.
> I go to night school two nights a week down at the high
> school, taking up typing and office practice. I've got
> some real good friends, girl friends, and they make sure
> I get out all the time. And getting out helps. The first
> few times I went out I didn't want to go. I forced
> myself. I didn't think it would help, but it has helped a
> lot.
>
> I think my mind was too busy to think. I was exhaust-
> ed, but at least it helped me to sleep. In fact, I had to
> push myself maybe more than I normally would, but
> when I saw it helped I just kept going that way. It's still
> a very deep feeling in you, but you know you can't sit
> around and cry all day. The children will come in and
> the busier you keep yourself, the less you have to do
> that.

It may be evident that many, perhaps most, of our widows
constantly monitored themselves. Even as they grieved they
watched themselves grieving, and evaluated the extent to
which they were dealing effectively with their grief. As they
became more able to control their feelings and to return to
normal functioning they became increasingly reassured that
they would recover rather than collapse, that they would
make it through. But, usually, there were one or two periods
when they were not sure.

Generally by about two months after the husband's death
widows felt themselves to have recovered more than they
would earlier have guessed possible, and began to see
themselves as again able to deal with the responsibilities of
their lives. Sixty-one percent agreed, at this point, that "I'm
beginning to feel like myself again." An image of themselves as widows had begun to form, and with it a new
identity that would be the basis for their return to social life.

At this point the early phase of bereavement was ending for many widows, although for others it might continue for additional months. But many widows were now beginning to recover from the traumatic disorganization of the loss, and though they would continue to have painful episodes of grief for many months to come, they would not again feel totally disorganized. They had essentially mastered the psychological shock brought on by the death of their husband, and were beginning to direct their energies to life without him.

8

THE CONTINUED TIE
TO THE HUSBAND

V ery likely a widow's attachment to her husband is never completely severed, although it may become weaker and be evoked less frequently as time goes on. In the preceding chapter we noted some of the ways in which the widows' attachment was displayed in the first months after bereavement. In this chapter we discuss the evidence of their continued attachment in more detail and describe how it changed over the course of the first year of bereavement.

Virtually all our widows reported recurring thoughts of their husband throughout the first year of bereavement. Sixty-four percent of the sample said that after a year had passed that they continued to think of their husbands "often" or "a lot." Some of them would have no thoughts of their husband for days and then would be led to think of him by a remark, a place, an article of clothing, or by their

own train of association from something apparently uncon-
nected. They might thereafter be able to think of nothing
else. Only one widow in the sample, a young woman whose
marriage had been chaotic and who was herself in some
degree disturbed, said at the end of the year of her
bereavement that she "hardly ever" thought of her husband.

Widows generally seemed comforted by immersion in
memories of their husband, in contrast to the distress that
often accompanied their review of the events leading to the
death.[1] Early in bereavement these memories were marked
by obvious idealization of the husband and the marriage.
Mrs. L, for example, fell into the following reminiscence in
her second interview, eight weeks after her husband's death.

> People talk about the dead and they say, "Oh, he was a
> wonderful fellow." But in this case everything they
> said about him is truthful because he was great, he was
> a wonderful guy. He helped everybody. He would help
> anybody that he could. Sometimes I think he overdid
> it, you know, but I let him do it because it always made
> him happy that he could help someone. . . .
>
> He was just the type that loved what he did. He didn't
> deprive his family of anything. He took care of the
> baseball team and they all got jackets and he did all
> that. And he was very well liked. . . .
>
> We had a beautiful marriage. I'm not saying this
> because he's gone. But we did, we got along beauti-
> fully. I think we were really envied by people because
> we got along so well. We were always together. We had
> a very nice social life, he took us places, he took the
> kids. He had a wonderful sense of humor. He was so
> full of fun. He was a tease with the kids. My nieces and
> nephews all loved him. His relationships at the shop

---

[1] At the second interview fifty-four percent described their memories of
their husband as predominantly pleasant, thirty-five percent as mixed, and
only ten percent as predominantly unpleasant.

were just marvelous. You'd go down there and it was just like a three-ring circus—everyone that went in there just had a marvelous time. They were always pulling jokes on each other. And he and all the workers got along very well. . . .

When we talked with Mrs. L eleven months later, her picture of her husband was more mixed and more realistic. She then recalled, for one thing, her irritation at his chronic impracticality.

But even at the eight-week point there were darker elements in Mrs. L's reminiscence, as in that of many widows. It was difficult to remember the husband's virtues without also recognizing that so many less deserving men still lived, while he was gone.

> I can look back on nothing but happy memories, whereas there are a lot of couples living together today that aren't even enjoying their married life. I know I have many friends who would have wished that it was their husband in that casket and not mine—and they told me so at the wake—who were just living a terrible life with their husbands, alcohol or gambling or women, and they said, "You've never had any of those, you never had trouble like that. And yet someone like that, so full of life, has to be taken. . . . It's a shame when someone is so full of life and something like this has to happen.

Guilt, or its obverse, defensiveness, also might enter into reminiscence. Mrs. L was one of the widows who insisted that she had no reason to feel guilty.

> I never pressed him or rushed him to do anything. There are a lot of things that he was going to do even before he died [like] he bought a new TV antenna to fix it and the antenna is still on the buffet and it didn't bother me. When he got around to it—I never pressed him or pushed him to do anything unless he wanted to do it. So I don't feel as if I overworked him.

> I always wanted him to take it easy and slow down, and always made sure that after supper he went right into the living room and rested. He never had to pick up or do anything, and then when I was through I'd go in. I put the children to bed. ... I mean thank God that I never did that, because otherwise I would say, well, I overworked him.
>
> I never wanted the best of this and the best of that. [I am] very easily pleased. I mean I had everything. I had plenty of clothes and the children, whatever they needed, we got [for them]. I never tried to live high or to compete with anybody. I never did that. And I always got up for breakfast, never stayed in bed in the morning. ... I was the first one up in the morning, started the breakfast, got the children up. And then Sundays he would always get breakfast. He loved to get breakfast Sunday mornings.

Just as the widows' idealizations usually faded with time, so did their feelings of anger and guilt. Then, usually, memories of their husband, though they remained fond and sad, became more realistic.

SENSE OF THE HUSBAND'S PRESENCE.   Almost all widows reported repeated experiences of feeling their husband was just about to arrive home, or was with them. Many reported a fairly steady sense of their husband's presence.[2] Some widows talked to their husband silently or, if they were sure

---

[2] We are unable to give reliable figures regarding the incidence of the sense of the husband's presence. Direct questions were not at first asked on this subject, since we had not anticipated the phenomenon. But even if we had included an appropriate item in our schedule of direct questions we should probably have ended with an underestimate. Rees's study ["The hallucinations of widowhood," *British Medical Journal*, Vol. 4 (1971), pp 37–41] has shown that bereaved people are often reluctant to reveal information about a matter that might easily be taken to indicate mental illness. Nevertheless forty-seven percent of our sample agreed, in the interview held thirteen months after their bereavement, that "I have the feeling that my husband watches over me."

of not being overheard, out loud. They knew quite well that their husband was not really with them but they nevertheless *felt* that he was.

Some widows occasionally experienced near hallucinations. One reported hearing her husband come to the door after work and put his key in the lock. Four others reported catching sight of their husband out of the corners of their eyes. In one case he was sitting in the living room reading his paper, in another he was standing by the door. These widows, it should be emphasized, knew better, no matter what they heard or saw. Unlike the hallucinating psychotic, they had full insight into the illusory character of their perceptions.

In contrast to most other aspects of the reaction to bereavement, the sense of the persisting presence of the husband did not diminish with time. It seemed to take a few weeks to become established, but thereafter seemed as likely to be reported late in the bereavement as early.[3]

Perhaps one explanation for the persistence of the sense of the husband's presence was that it was comforting rather than disturbing. Many widows reported that they deliberately invoked it when they were especially unsure or depressed—it made them feel less alone. They did not generally feel uneasy about having this sense of the husband's presence unless they also had other grounds for concern about their emotional stability. Then they might find that it corroborated their fear that they were losing control.

Mrs. M described reinvoking her husband's presence and noted the embarrassment this once caused:

---

[3]Similar findings are reported in Parkes *Bereavement: Studies of Grief in Adult Life* (New York: International Universities Press, 1972) and Rees, (*op. cit.*). Rees found that such phenomena occurred from time to time among thirty-nine percent of widows and widowers many years after their bereavement.

Sometimes I get melancholy and I want to talk to
somebody and then I'll go, "Well, what would *you* do
about the situation?" And it's like if he was sitting here
talking to me. I might even yell out, "What do you say,
Burt," as though he were in another room here. I know
my neighbor next door knocked at the door one day and
I was talking a blue streak, yelling out as though Burt
was in the bathroom. She says, "You got company?" I
says, "No." She says, "Who are you talking to?" I says,
"Oh, just my wandering thoughts again."

The single most important determinant of the sense of
presence of the deceased was whether the death had been
anticipated. There were nine widows in the sample who, a
year after the death, reported a continuous sense of the
presence of their husband. All nine had suffered unforewarned bereavement.[4] The lack of opportunity to prepare
themselves for the loss would seem to have predisposed
them to the development of a fantasy relationship of this
kind.

It may be that undiminished attachment at the end of the
first year was found especially among those widows who
had had no forewarning of the death and who also described
themselves as having in their marriages been unable to
function without their husband's support and guidance.
Long after other widows had begun giving a good part of
their energy to their current lives these widows remained
committed to idealizations of their husband and their
marriage. They behaved as though their husband continued
to be their closest affective tie, and as though their obligation to be loyal to their husband was in no respect diminished by the passage of time.

[4] Full details of the statistical analysis will be given in the authors'
Determinants of Grief, now in preparation. The association between
persisting sense of presence and unforewarned bereavement is highly
significant. On follow-up two to four years after bereavement, the nine
unforewarned bereaved referred to above still had a sense of the presence of
their husbands, but only two of them reported it as still being continuous.

At least momentary lapses of realism occurred with virtually all our respondents. Typically the lapses were transitory, recognized for what they were, and of decreasing frequency as the year wore on. But widows for whom this was not true, whose lapses were persistent and emotionally important, seemed to us to have special problems in recovery. It may be that continued dependence on the sense of the husband's companionship beyond the first year of bereavement may present reason for concern in this young age group.

BAD TIMES. Early in bereavement certain times of day were difficult for virtually every widow. These were the times when the husband's presence would once have been taken for granted. The evening meal, especially, became a regular occasion for reminiscence and sorrow. The later evening too, especially the hours after the children were in bed, was lonely. And so, usually, was Sunday. Mrs. L provided a description of evening difficulties:

> When the children go to bed in the evenings, if I don't have company, it's lonesome then, because we would have been watching certain shows together and talking about different things or having a cup of coffee. I don't even bother with that any more. Unless I'm having coffee with someone, I don't even bother even making anything—I may have a cup of tea about ten o'clock or so. And I get to bed earlier than I used to. I don't enjoy staying up. No sense staying up late alone, once the children are in bed. That is the hardest part of the day, the evenings.

The following comment on Sundays was reported by Mrs. J two months after her husband had died:

> I've gotten over now the feeling that he will return home at a quarter of five, but on Sunday I still

automatically put out a plate for him, which I have
eliminated during the week. ... When I find myself
doing it, it leaves a funny feeling running through me
for a few minutes. Then I'm alright. ... He'd come
home on Sunday for his meal with the children, and I
guess that's why. Sunday is still a hard day for me.

For many couples Saturday evenings had been times
when they had visited kin or friends or seen a movie. For
these widows Saturday evenings, too, were hard. In a
similar way birthdays and anniversaries and religious and
national holidays became reminders of loss and isolation.

Christmas in particular was a time of stress. Widows often
felt considerable apprehension as Christmas approached.
Their first Christmas alone was a searing experience. Christmas
is our single most important family holiday, more so
than Thanksgiving, which has undertones of patriotism and
for some a faintly commercial artificiality. It is a time when
the entire family is supposed to come together, to exchange
gifts, to celebrate their happiness with one another, perhaps
to open their home so that its warmth can be shared by
others. For our widows the contrast between their present
sadness and the happier past was starkly illuminated at
Christmas. Mrs. G reported, when seen a month before
Christmas, two months after her husband's death:

I dread Christmas Eve and Christmas morning coming
on. He made an awful lot of Christmas. He was like a
kid about it, really. We always had a lot of company
and he would invite people from work and his brothers
and his family. It was always a great deal going on, and
going and doing and going to parties. I feel this year
very bad about it. I have no desire for it at all. I have to
have it for the children, but as far as I'm concerned I
just have no desire for Christmas.

Mrs. I was interviewed just after New Year's Day. It was
then seven weeks since her husband had died.

> I went home for the week with my mother and father. It was not so good. It was the first time I really had time, not working, time by myself, and I kind of got everything out during that week that I'd been holding in for a long time. ... I broke down. It started Christmas day and I was dripping for the whole week. I think it was Christmas mainly that brought it on, and not being at work, and not having my mind taken up. I guess I remembered other Christmases and New Years with my husband. It's a sad time. It was just that Christmas was very different this year without him. And New Years was, too.

Widows were reminded of their loss not only by times when they might have expected their husbands to be with them but also by occasions of difficulty or decision that they now had to deal with alone. All widows, with the exception of those few whose marriages to alcoholic and abusive husbands had long ceased to be partnerships, missed having their husband's help in the management of their homes and families. Now they took in the car for repairs and felt helpless to evaluate the advice of the mechanics; were forced to manage their finances alone and to decide for themselves which bills to pay and which to put off; had to learn to put up their own storm windows, to check the boiler themselves, to fix a broken chair or paint the children's bedroom or put together the toy that came from the store in parts. And when responding to a door-to-door salesman, they no longer could say, "I have to talk to my husband first."

Mrs. O described some of the ways in which she missed her husband's help with chores.

> He would tell me when the car needed these things and what I should do. That I really miss because I don't know when it needs grease and oil. I have to depend on the serviceman to tell me to bring it in and all those things.

> We did everything together, even in the kitchen. If he
> didn't have to do nothing he cut up the food. If I'm
> making meat and things, he cut up the green peppers or
> onion or anything like that. Each time I make some-
> thing like meat loaf or hamburger, as soon as I have to
> cut up those things I think about him because he would
> cut up those things for me, he cut up the vegetables.
> And not only that, he would do the planning of the
> meals. Like today, we were looking around so we could
> have a quick lunch, and I just thought to myself that I
> wouldn't have had to think about it, he would get these
> things, stock up on these things ahead. He'd go
> shopping and he would buy such things for a quick
> meal, corned beef, sometimes haddock, sometimes
> herring. . . . He used to do all those things, and then
> other things, the repairing of the house and other
> things like hauling.

Of course, as the widows missed their husband's help,
they were reminded again of their husband's absence and of
their own loss. However there was throughout the first year
of bereavement a steady increase in the energy widows
devoted to their current situation as opposed to the lives
they had shared with their husbands. Though they might
not be noticeably happier, the focus of their attention
shifted steadily from the disruption of their marriages to the
reconstruction of their individual lives.

Widows' sense of themselves as separated from their
marriages only haltingly replaced their sense of continued
attachment. They alternated between holding on and giving
up, self-reliance and return to the security of reminiscence
and illusion. A year after their loss twenty-eight percent of
our respondents could say, "There are still moments when I
forget he is dead."

Yet widows did gradually acknowledge that their husbands
were dead. They did not cease yearning for their return or
cease having fantasies of the other courses reality might
have taken. But these feelings and fantasies decreased in
frequency and increasingly were replaced by a conviction

that "dead is dead," that death is irrevocable, and that its denial is pointless. Visits to the husband's grave and the setting of the stone helped establish this in the widow's mind. Now the review of the circumstances leading to the husband's death sometimes ended abruptly with the recognition that no other sequence of events would ever take place.

Religious dogma regarding death was now more apt to be accepted; one has the sense that it mattered less. In a similar fashion, if the husband's death had been preceded by a painful or disintegrative illness, the widow now permitted others to console her with the comment, "He is better off dead," or permitted herself to think it.

The first determined movement of a widow toward acceptance of her separation often was going through her husband's belongings, putting aside what was to be kept and giving away or throwing away the remainder. Only infrequently did this happen immediately after the funeral, and in the instances in which it did happen then, it seemed more to express the widow's inability to tolerate these symbolic remains than to signal the beginnings of a redefinition by her of her life. Most widows waited several weeks or even months before moving their husband's belongings from their bureaus or closets. Often this was a painful task, accompanied by reminiscence and tears. But when it was completed it became a statement that one era of the widow's life had ended and that another was beginning.

Not many of the belongings were actually discarded. This would have placed too little value on them and by implication on the husband himself. Instead they were given to those he might have wanted to have them, or to those who had shared the widow's mourning.

Widows retained the memorabilia of their marriages for themselves and their children. They kept the pictures, letters, notes, and cards that formed a history of their marriage; the gifts they had given their husband; the objects that seemed to be intimately associated with him—his pipes, for example. They also kept possessions of his that had great value or that seemed likely to have some future use, such as his tools.

The husband's brother might be given his best suits and coats, not only because the brother was often about the same size, but also because he was felt to be the closest and the most deserving recipient. The husband's father, the widow's male relatives, and the husband's closest friends might be given whatever of worth remained. The rest might go to charity.

Gradually now, the widows became accustomed to the changes in their routine, established a different way of shopping and a different shopping list, learned to set the table for their smaller family, learned to care for the car and to do their own minor house repairs, and, often hardest of all, to make their own decisions. Increasingly they sought work outside their home, were more willing to meet new people, and more capable of interacting with friends and kin as a member of the community rather than as someone bereaved. They began to function in their social worlds as widows who were no longer preoccupied with their husband's death.

As we note in Chapter Twelve, there were two quite different directions in which widows might move toward recovery, one in which remarriage might be anticipated, and one in which the widow would eschew remarriage for the foreseeable future. Each direction could produce a reasonably satisfactory pattern of life. Each could, therefore, be considered a direction toward recovery.

Often the widow's progress toward recovery was facilitated by inner conversations with her husband's presence. Paradoxically, this continued sense of attachment was not incompatible with increasing capacity for independent action. Even those widows who did not rely on the illusion that their husband was still accessible were aided in the management of their affairs by their sense of what their husband might have advised.[5] Mrs. M, interviewed about a month after her husband's death, said in relation to the problems she was then confronting:

> He talked so much about if anything happened that he wanted me to be like this and be like that. I didn't think I could, but I did. Maybe it's for his sake I did it, I don't know. But now I know I can be independent. I have to be, too. I mean I have responsibilities, the children.

In some widows' movement toward detachment from their husband's influence a kind of rebelliousness entered, in which they acted in ways they suspected he would have disapproved. Instances of rebelliousness ranged from rather trivial departures from what he might have wanted in the widow's management of her mourning, to turning for support to people he did not like, to revising plans made with him regarding the house or the children or themselves. Early in the bereavement such resistive actions occurred as isolated instances in a context of devoted adherence to the husband's wishes, but as time went on widows exhibited more and more independence in their judgments and were less and less apologetic for doing so. By the end of the first year of bereavement most widows no longer made decisions primarily on the basis of their husband's wishes.

After a year, most widows were well on their way to having detached themselves from their husband and their marriage, although the detachment might never be entirely complete. This did not mean the husband was forgotten, but rather that he was no longer felt by widows still to be a present influence on their decisions and behavior.

By the end of this first year all except a few widows whose

---

[5] A year after bereavement sixty-nine percent agreed that, "I try to behave in certain ways as he would have, or as I think he would have, wanted me to."

lives remained chaotic (see Chapter Twelve) had begun to establish new lives for themselves and their children. In retrospect most felt that they had done better than they could have anticipated.[6] Mrs. H, considering her progress over the year since her husband died, said:

> I didn't think I could do it, but I've done it. I think I've done pretty good. I joined a sewing club and I go once a week. I belong to another club—I belong to three clubs—that keeps me busy. And I suppose I'm lucky that I have the children. Like if I really don't feel like doing something, I have to whether I feel like it or not. . . . And there's always someone around.

A CASE STUDY OF ATTACHMENT AND DETACHMENT.   To further display the complex process of movement from a lingering sense of attachment to at least partial emancipation, we present excerpts from three interviews with Mrs. B. Mrs. B's husband died of cancer at the age of twenty-seven, when she was twenty-five. There were no children. They had gone together for four years before their marriage but delayed marrying because of religious differences. When Mr. B's illness was diagnosed they decided to marry despite those differences. The husband's physician guessed, at the time of their marriage, that Mr. B might have five years of life remaining. In fact, he had less than two.

The circumstances of this marriage were not at all typical of the sample as a whole, yet the feelings experienced and expressed by Mrs. B during the year following her husband's death were very much like those expressed by other widows. In the first weeks after the death she was concerned

---

[6] A year after bereavement fifty-nine percent of widows had a job outside the house and most were enjoying it. Forty-eight percent were thought to be more socially active than they had been before bereavement (although nine percent were less socially active), and eighty percent were thought by our coders to have achieved a good or very good level of functioning.

with its causes, its meaning, its impact on her marriage and on her life. Though his death had been anticipated, she could neither fully realize it nor accept it. She saw herself as still maintaining an attachment to her husband and could not conceive of relinquishing her identity as his wife. Yet his absence left her distraught and confused:

> During the first couple of nights I tried so hard to have dreams so I could see him, but all I ended up dreaming is that I couldn't find him . . . I felt that I was living in the past. When we got married, I had a very simple goal, just to try to make the best of everything, every day, to make him happy. It seemed very simple. All of a sudden I felt there was nothing more to do, there's nothing. I'm so confused, so lost, I feel so lost that I don't know . . . All of a sudden he passed away and I couldn't do anything more for him. The ambitions or hopes or inspirations I had before seem no longer important to me. . . . How am I going to live? What am I going to hang on to?

Interviewed again two months after her husband's death, Mrs. B reported that her life was becoming more structured. She had returned to work and was seeing a few friends. She feared periods of inactivity, such as evenings and weekends. Then, she said, she sometimes reexperienced watching her husband die, as in a nightmare. But she still wanted very much to keep her memories of him vivid. She reread letters they had written to one another. She thought of him when doing things he would have enjoyed, or when cooking dishes he would have liked. And she forgot at times that he had died, and would think, "Oh, I have to tell him this." But simultaneously she was learning to attend to tasks for which her husband had been responsible, even as she protested her inadequacy.

> He took care of the laundry and especially the car, which I'm not used to doing. It was his car. And the

fish tank that he used to take care of, now I have to
learn how to work the thing. And he used to pay all the
bills and take care of that part. And there's just a lot of
little things I could always ask him. But we did so
many things together, although he did most of it, that I
sort of have a little idea how he did it. With the car, like
what's wrong with the brakes and things like that. I'm
not mechanically minded at all, so I just have to trust
the garage or find a garage for myself now because he
used to take the car to a place near his work. To change
the light bulbs, I had to find the janitor to help me out.
And carrying things—I wanted to move a can of sand
from the car to the basement and had to wait until my
girl friend came so we could do it together, because I'm
not strong enough to do things like that myself.

At this point Mrs. B resisted the idea of too much change.
She decided to keep the apartment:

> I felt it was the home we made together and I want to
> keep it. We picked the things here together and I find
> that I still can't bear the thought that he's gone
> completely. Everything here was a part of him.

But she indicated greater acceptance of her husband's death,
and could say that although she was handicapped by his
absence, "I feel that I have to learn." In a moving passage
she spoke of her feelings of loss and her resolution to
recover:

> It seems that when we got married we were one, and I
> was much richer and stronger than what I am now. So I
> feel I'm in a way crippled. I have to learn to live this
> way . . . I feel like somebody that just lost their arm or a
> leg or something. I just have to live without it. I was
> quite touched the other day. I was in the savings bank,
> and I saw this girl who had lost a hand and not quite
> half an arm. And she was able to sign her name on a
> check and take the money out. I feel that she must have
> had quite a bit of adjustment to do. That is going to

happen to me, in a way. In a way, it's the same because
I just have to learn it.

Yet even as Mrs. B was resolving to adapt to her widowhood, she was reluctant to think of herself as a widow and
took offense when she was referred to as one:

> You know, they call me Marv's widow, but I still insist
> on being Marv's wife. It's just a word, but it hurts so.
> It's just very unpleasant.

A year after her husband's death, Mrs. B had not entirely
shifted her self-image. She still thought about her husband
and still felt attached to him, although she felt more distant
from his death. Her memories of him no longer were so
obsessive. Now she avoided those others who by their
sympathy made her depressed about her current situation.
She did not want to be overprotected; she was irritated to be
asked solicitously how she was doing with her car and
whether she was having any problems in maintaining it
properly.

> They make me feel that because I don't have Marv that
> maybe they want to do it for me, feeling sorry for me.
> They mean well but they just make me feel that they are
> sorry for me and I try not to have that feeling.

Although Mrs. B's social life remained restricted to a few
friends and relatives, she was clearly moving to a redefinition of herself as a single woman. She was even willing to
contemplate the idea of remarriage.

> I don't think I would get married just because I wanted
> so badly to have children. But if I should meet
> someone I figure I could like equally as much as I
> loved Marv, maybe I will. But I don't know yet.

9

THE WIDOW AS MOTHER
AND PROVIDER

Some widows said that only recognition of their children's need for them prevented their collapse. One widow said, "I have three children and I figured that if I went to pieces, where would they be?" Several widows said something like, "I don't know what I would have done without the children to take care of." Mrs. D was one of these:

> I absolutely don't know what I would do without the children. As much as Nora is a holy terror and I can't do anything with her, it has kept my mind occupied and has kept me busy.

Young widows without children sometimes thought that their grief was more severe than it would have been if they had had children. They felt themselves to have lost with their husband not only their marriage, but their entire family.

Many widows reported that the experiences and observations of other widows with whom they had had contact reinforced their belief that having had children to care for had been of substantial benefit during the first year of bereavement. Only two widows of all those in our sample who had children failed to view their presence as having been helpful.

Nevertheless in many ways their new responsibilities to their bereaved children taxed the widows' strength and resources. Despite their beliefs to the contrary, they may well not have been helped so very much by having children. In terms of our measurements of recovery, women with children recovered from their loss neither more quickly nor more surely than those without children, even though both those with children and those without agreed that children helped.

The children were frequently troublesome. They too had suffered bereavement and they too were being forced to adapt to a new set of familial arrangements. Many of them displayed behavior problems. They were disobedient, if only marginally, by being slow to respond to calls or requests; they withdrew; they were short-tempered.[1]

Widows sometimes felt confused regarding how attentive they should be to their children's distress. They wanted to give love and understanding. But they also wanted to provide structure and they shared the usual expectations parents have of children. In addition, many widows worried lest they do too much for their children and damage them by their undiluted solicitude.

As heads of one-parent families the widows had now to be

---

[1] Fifty-four percent of those with children said that the children had given rise to problems that were matters of major concern. Half of those who reported such problems dealt with them entirely alone.

the ones to decide how family funds should be spent, what rules the children should follow, how the homes should be maintained. They might in fact have made many or most of these decisions before their husband died, but now they carried sole responsibility for them. Most widows found the change unwelcome.

The widows were now solely responsible for insuring the family income; whether they worked or not, they had become the family provider. Even though, as we discuss later in this chapter, there ordinarily was no immediate want, widows were uncertain that they would be able to manage in the long run.

If the husband had suffered from a protracted terminal illness, a redefinition of familial roles may have occurred before his death. Soon after the husband's hospitalization something approaching a one-parent family may in fact have developed. But despite its actual structure, the family would have been understood as a two-parent family with one parent absent, one in which the new arrangements between the mother and children were only temporary. Not until the husband's actual death would the arrangements be seen as permanent.

One of the first tasks of a widow as new head of her family was to inform her children that their father had died. All widows found this extremely painful. But almost all felt that despite the pain it was right and proper that the task should be theirs; for another to have told the children would have appeared to them as invasive. They were the ones to perform the task, whatever the emotional cost.

Most widows (seventy percent) informed the children without delay. Others procrastinated, or found some evasion, such as telling the children their father had gone away. Two widows could not force themselves to tell their children and at length prevailed on a relative to inform them. Mrs. L. described in this way her experience in telling her children.

> All I was concerned about was how I was going to tell
> the children. But I told them. I don't know where you
> get the courage at a time like this . . . I tried not to break
> down as I told them . . .
>
> Linda came in first. She's seven. She's a happy-go-
> lucky child. Thank God for that. She's a little tomboy.
> She came in swinging her bag, "I've got no home-
> work." That was all she was interested in. Of course,
> then she looked around—the house was filled with
> people—and she says, "Why is everybody here?" Well,
> my brother wanted to tell her, and I said, "No, I think I
> better tell her." And I went in, took her in the other
> room, and I told her, very calmly. I didn't break down.
> And she couldn't believe it. Of course she's only seven
> after all, and it was a little hard for her to understand.
> But she took it very well.
>
> Then my boy came in later and I told him also. He took
> it, he was alright for a while, and then he broke down.
> Tommy is very sensitive. Then he apologized for
> crying and I said there was no apology necessary. I'm
> glad that he did cry. I wanted him to cry. I said, "After
> all, when grown men cry, you certainly have got every
> right to. I want you to cry and get it out of your system
> and feel better."

Children not quite in their teens seemed able to anticipate
their father's death and to understand death's finality.
Children between three and six in contrast, seemed
usually to be unable to accept that their fathers would not
return from the hospital. They could respond to their
mother's report with apparent understanding, be sad for a
time, but then brighten, and talk about the father as if he
were still alive and would soon rejoin the family. Their
mothers were then forced to explain once again that the
father had died. Mrs. E described the incomprehension of
very young children:

> Mary is five and Donald is three, and they still think
> their father is coming home because once before he

was in the hospital and he did. They've seen everything, but they don't understand it. They think Dad
will still be home. If I get on Donald—he was my
husband's pet—if I get on him, he says, "Well, I won't
tell Daddy, when he comes home." I say, "Well, Daddy
won't be back."

Now the seven-year-old, she'll tell him in a minute.
"Daddy won't be back no more." She understands. But
the five-year-old and the three-year-old do not. They
think he'll be home because I brought his clothes
home, and they thought it was from the hospital. But it
was from the undertaker. And it is so hard to explain to
them. They see his keys and everything. They think
he'll still be home . . . They'll hear somebody come in
downstairs and they'll say, "Mommy, is that Daddy?"

When mothers confronted the harrowing task of informing children they found themselves in a dilemma. How
could they be both protective and candid? They had to
decide, with little guidance, what the children should be
told and how much they should be told, whether they
should be fully informed or should partially be shielded,
and how much and how carefully they should be comforted
and reassured.

These issues were most acute at the time of the initial
informing but they recurred in connection with each new
ceremonial. Should the children attend the wake and the
funeral? Should they see the body? Should they attend the
burial?

In slightly different form the conflicting directives of the
desire to help the children face reality and the desire to
protect them from it produced dilemmas for the widows
throughout the first year of their bereavement. They were
unsure whether it would be better for their children if they
discussed the father's death openly or if they avoided
referring to it; whether they should encourage their children
to remember their father or to forget him; whether they
should support their children's expression of sadness, per-

plexity, and anger or, instead, discourage it. Because there were no guides for the widows to help them with these dilemmas, they acted on the basis of what seemed right at the moment.

Many widows worried that they had discouraged their children from grieving adequately. The widows by and large believed that children did better to express their grief. They thought that their children *should* cry, that crying was a natural and necessary therapy and release, and perhaps even more so for them than for adults. They were concerned lest stifled feelings express themselves later in unpredictable but assuredly unfortunate ways. Yet they described their children as not crying as much as they thought they should. They worried whether they, as mothers, might somehow have been responsible for this. And indeed they may have been: without recognizing it, they may have acted to discourage their children's expression of sadness, depression, or pining.

To begin with, the widows presented their children with the model of their own behavior, in which expression of grief was treated as private and perhaps embarrassing. Mothers dissembled rather than display their grief, not only before outsiders, but before their children as well. They may have felt that their children required that they appear strong and reliable, capable of comforting and not requiring comfort themselves. There was undoubtedly validity in this belief. Yet their display of fortitude is likely to have called forth a similar display in their children. One can see in the report of Mrs. L the pressures on the mother to keep her feelings under control:

> It upsets the children to see me sad, so I try not to be. They caught me crying the other night. I thought they were sleeping, and they both got up and they were very upset. I said, "Well, I can't do this. I can't upset them."

After a time, when the children no longer mentioned their

father themselves, mothers became reluctant to create disturbances where, superficially at least, there seemed to be none. This too played a role in suppressing discussion of the loss. Mrs. F, for example, said:

> My daughter don't talk much about him. You know, once in a while she'll say something, but otherwise she don't bother talking and I don't approach the subject with her. I'm afraid she'd get upset.

The widows did not want their children to forget their father. On the contrary, they often instructed their children to think of their father—but not as a parent who had died. Instead they tended to describe the father as somehow still present. An occasional mother told her children the father watched them from heaven. Some widows for a time encouraged their children to say daily prayers for their father or their father's soul, which in another way suggested the father's continued existence.

Usually the children's grief and insecurity could not be entirely contained. The children asked why their father had died, and some of them asked what would happen to them if their mother should also die. Some became sad and withdrawn so that it became obvious to their mother that they were thinking of their loss. Others became overactive. Although this too is in children an expression of grief, the mothers seemed not to recognize its motivation.

The widows often attempted to fend off sadness or depression in their children by offering them positive and optimistic explanations, sometimes organized around religious beliefs to which the mothers themselves did not entirely subscribe. Their aim was explicitly that of maintaining their children's faith in the goodness of their world. And so they searched for a formulation that would show that "it was for the best."

The mother might be aided in her search for a positive interpretation by the children themselves. This was Mrs. F's experience with her daughter:

> I just told her that "Daddy went to see God." And she
> said, "He won't be sick any more," because she knew
> he was always sick, either in the hospital or he was sick
> in bed. So now she says, "My Daddy won't be sick any
> more."

Mrs. M had encouraged her children to pray for her
husband when he was sick. Despite their prayers he died.
She then was faced with the problem of explaining how it
was all for the best even though the children's prayers
hadn't been answered, and also to demonstrate that the
children's prayers had had value despite their father's death.

> The oldest really was hysterical and I talked to her and
> I said, "Don't be like that. You didn't want him to stay
> the way he was," because he was just a vegetable. What
> she couldn't understand was why he didn't get any
> better because of all those prayers. I said, "That doesn't
> mean anything. Those prayers might help him [now
> that] he is dead. If he'd gotten better, all well and good.
> But . . . they're not going to waste."

The widows wanted to protect their children's religious
faith. They believed that religious dogma had helped them
present their husband's death to their children as consistent
with the picture of the world they wanted their children to
retain—an orderly place in which there was reward for
goodness and piety. They hoped that in this way religious
belief might offer not only consolation for the short term but
also a framework for continuing moral behavior.

Most widows, including those who relied on religious
interpretations of their husband's death, were uneasy about
the way they had informed their children of the death. This
was more marked among the middle-class mothers, but
apparent among others as well. They assumed that there was
a right way to have managed the task, which would have

minimized the impact of the death on the children's personalities. Failure to have found this right way might have
produced a condition that would eventually express itself in
a damaged personality. And they were not certain they had
found the right way.

There were several reasons for their anxiety. First, of
course, was their concern for their children. But also they
needed now, more than ever, to believe themselves good and
competent mothers; their functioning as mothers was now
the chief way in which they could maintain their sense of
worth. And in addition one of the few means still available
to them to express their continuing devotion to their
husbands was to give the very best of care to the children the
husbands had left behind.

There were still other worries besetting these young
widows. Like other mothers in our expert-respecting society, they were alert to the opinions of those who claimed
some special insight or knowledge regarding child rearing.
Most of them had read articles or heard discussions reviewing the deleterious effects on the development of boys and
perhaps girls that might ensue from a fatherless family.
Those who had read the articles were concerned that unless
a male figure entered their children's lives—their own
brother seemed a possibility to some, but others were quite
at a loss—their very conscientiousness as a mother might
disable their children.

While concerns regarding the children's present or future
emotional well-being were lingering uncertainties, in other
respects there was a gradual return to ordinary life. Household routine was reestablished. Both the widows and their
children required it. Mrs. D, for example, said two months
after her husband's death:

> I'm trying to get back into my old routine, doing things.
> I've always done the housework in the morning and
> then if I had to do errands they were always done the
> first thing in the morning. And then Nora and I would

have lunch and she'd go in and take a nap and I would
go in and take a nap. And then when the boys came
home from school I got up. I slept for about an hour.
I'm trying to get back into our schedules. It's going to
take a while, I think, but we'll get back there.

The widows' obligations to their children led to tasks that
nearly filled their days. They prepared the children's meals,
supervised their cleaning, cared for their clothing, saw them
off in the morning and greeted them in the afternoon,
monitored their school attendance and their choice of
friends. These were familiar chores, but now the widows
often seemed to bring to them a new determination to be
good mothers, whatever that might mean. They were at
pains to be available to their children. They spent more time
with their children than they had previously, and did more
with them and for them. Mrs. J said:

> I think it's important for me to be with them. At night
> it's their homework, and I think I should be with them
> while they're doing their homework because that's very
> hard for them. They have quite a few hours studying
> and I have to amuse the youngest one so that she
> doesn't go over and start scribbling on their homework
> or taking their books away or something like that. And
> when they come home from school I make sure I'm in
> the house and not shopping or anything like that
> because they really go looking for me. They'll go from
> neighbor to neighbor looking for me to make sure I'm
> around, and I don't want that. I want to be home when
> they come home. I don't want them to feel like they
> have no one at all, no one cares for them. So I'm usually
> home when they come home. I guess it's very impor-
> tant to them because, I mean, the loss of their father,
> something's gone there, and if they feel like their
> mother is gone too, I think it is too much for them to
> take.

As we have noted, one consequence during the early
weeks of bereavement of the widows' efforts to help their

children was to provide the widows themselves with a reason to continue functioning. Several widows used their responsibilities to their fatherless children to combat fleeting suicidal fantasies. About a quarter of them said, two months after their loss, that were it not for their children they would not want to go on living.[2] Mrs. K, responding two months after her husband's death to the interview question, "Have you felt that you didn't care whether you died tomorrow?" said:

> I think if you didn't have any children you could easily feel that way. Now I know I have to take care of them.

Widows with children sometimes worried about their own health because they saw themselves as critically important to their children's well-being. This gave them reason to eat regularly, and to attempt as far as possible to establish normal sleep patterns.

Under some circumstances having children seemed however to delay, even subvert a widow's recovery. This potential of motherhood was not explicitly noted by any of the widows, but one could recognize in their reports repeated instances in which their child-care responsibilities had prevented their resumption of an active social life. Some were hesitant about taking a job because they felt they should be at home for their children; they were reluctant to have their children attend a nursery or other child-care facility or, if the children attended school, to have them come home to an empty house. Other widows declined social invitations because baby-sitters were expensive and difficult to get and anyway they could not bring themselves to leave their children alone in the evening. Still others hesitated to leave their children alone in the evening so that they could attend evening classes. In many ways their maternal responsibilities inhibited the widows' development of more satisfactory lives.

[2]By the end of the year only ten percent felt this way.

Despite their greater involvement with their children, and despite their determination to compensate for the father's absence by being more loving themselves, widows seemed to find greater difficulty in dealing effectively with their children than they had when their husbands were alive. They were, to begin with, under tension themselves.[3] At times they worried that their physical or mental health might give way entirely, partly because of the demands of child care, leading to the social if not literal orphaning of the children.[4] Mothers of children of all ages were likely to wonder, sometimes aloud, what would happen to their children if they themselves should get sick or die. They had, of course, just learned forcefully the lesson of human mortality. One widow said, "My main and only concern at this time is being healthy for these children that I have to bring up now."

The widows were at first unsure of their ability to deal with crises, even minor crises such as the routine accidents and illnesses of childhood. Many could not visualize who might stay with their children while they went shopping. As it turned out, a number found themselves now and again forced to leave even quite young children briefly unattended. They were concerned that if one of their children suffered a serious illness or injury they might not make the right decisions about physicians or hospitals, and that if they became involved with getting care for a child in need they could not attend to their other children. In time most of these widows made arrangements with kin or friends or

[3] Among those with children only nine percent expressed decidedly angry feelings toward a child during the interview held three or four weeks after their husband's death. But in the interviews held five weeks later the percentage had risen to twenty-eight percent. By the end of the year the percentage had dropped somewhat, to twenty percent.

[4] In only two cases did the coders of our interview materials feel that there was justification for this concern. For the rest the coders felt there was little indication that the widows in fact were failing to manage competently, despite their fears.

neighbors to help in emergencies, but in the first weeks of bereavement the prospect of having to manage crises entirely by themselves frightened many of them.

The development of the children's character was not initially a source of anxiety. As time went on, however, it became a persisting concern. During the period of their husband's illness and in the first few weeks of bereavement, they had been little inclined to enforce rules of behavior. At times their emotional turmoil prevented them from much awareness of their children; at other times, witnessing the children break rules, they could not bring themselves to insist that children about to lose a parent or just bereaved should behave as they always had. They permitted bedtime hours to be suspended, allowed household chores to go undone, let the children miss school, and let them do what they wanted with their friends.

But generally after the first weeks of bereavement had passed and the widows began to reestablish their household routines they reacted against the laxity that had entered their households and reintroduced firm rules. Their rationale, often, was that fatherless children, like any children, need to know what is expected of them.

Many mothers believed that if they did not hold the line firmly their children would "take advantage" of the situation of being without a father, by which they meant that the children would display more autonomy and would have less respect for the mother and her directives. There may have been some basis for this belief. Older children did seem to feel themselves to have increased standing in the family in the absence of the father. When the father was still alive, even if the mother had been the actual disciplinarian, the father's symbolic authority and the threat of his physical intervention gave weight to the mother's directives. Without the husband's backing, the widow's authority was suspect. In addition, widows now sometimes discussed problems with their older children where previously they would have consulted their husbands; this of necessity diminished their ability to demand obedience from the older children. The movement from a two-parent household to a one-parent household unsettled many former arrangements; in particular, there was more emotional closeness to the children but a less firm basis for authority.

Some widows dealt with the situation by becoming more authoritarian than they had been while their husbands were alive, reacting against the changes required by the new structure, and accepting the increased conflict as inevitable in a fatherless household. Others instead became more indulgent, or accepted the shift in family structure in which the children became more nearly equals. Some were by turns restrictive and indulgent.

The adolescence of children is difficult for all parents. Adolescents experiment with emotional independence, as sexual maturation brings new social interests, new demands on parents for freedom and respect, and new potentials for delinquencies or mistakes. At the same time, adolescent children remind parents of their own experiences, reawakening long dormant hopes and fears. Some parents may hope they can relive and perhaps improve on their own adolescence through their children. Others may resent their children approaching maturity as they themselves age. Still others may fear their children's exposure to romantic misadventure, to drugs, or to failure as an adult.

The widows experienced all these parental problems, and had others in addition. The mothers of boys were worried because the boys had no fathers to instruct and guide them. The mothers of girls were often fearful that their daughters would develop a distorted model of the life of an adult woman. Some mothers of girls who thought they might themselves date eventually were uneasy about competing with instead of supporting their daughters. A very few widows, of working-class background, worried about the possibility of danger to their daughters from the men they might themselves see. One said: "I know for sure I wouldn't want a younger man. I mean, I've got the girls in the house that I've got to be careful of."

Widows of working-class background often seemed concerned about their ability to direct their children past the hazards of adolescence, fearing aggression and criminal behavior in the case of boys, and sexual laxity in the case of girls. They felt that commanding the respect and obedience of the children was a problem at any age, but was both more difficult and more essential with adolescents.

Mrs. J was in her late thirties, had been married for about eighteen years, until his death from alcoholism, to a quite unreliable and occasionally abusive man who was sometimes home, sometimes not. Mrs. J had always carried responsibility for the direction of the children, even when her husband was home. Nevertheless she felt that her husband's death had fundamentally altered her situation. She said:

> I used to feel more secure if he was home. If there was something real bad I could talk to him and he would listen. And then, probably, he'd walk out. But still, the idea is, he was home. It was different. Whereas today, well, I hit a problem and there's no one to come back at except myself. My oldest son wanted a BB gun and he still does and I told him flatly, "No." If in the past he had been able to have these guns and play with toys and what not, when he was younger, he wouldn't have the urge he has today for it. But his father wouldn't allow them to have any guns at all . . .
>
> The boy has had an urge for a BB gun now for the last three years. His father used to flatly say No, and that was the end of it. He's gone now, and the boy thinks he can get around me. He's made it difficult because I said No, and it still hasn't cut any ice with the fellow. He still insists he is going to have a BB gun. As far as I'm concerned, it is No, and I will not buy it for him. But it's quite tiring and aggravating to listen to him.

Interviewed ten months later, Mrs. J had been successful in withholding the BB gun from her son but her worries had not ended with this. She believed she had to keep him and her other sons under constant surveillance or they would get in trouble. She set strict rules regarding when they could go out, for how long, and with whom. She sternly required each of them to be responsible for household chores. But though she sometimes beat her boys to make them obey she still felt beleaguered without her husband's authority to call on.

> There seems to be a group around here that just can't stay out of trouble. My kids more or less stay with them, hang around with them, and get into mischief with them. It's very hard keeping boys straight. They do need a firm hand and I have to more or less be the one with the firm hand. I think it's more difficult for a woman than it would be for a man . . .

> Even though my husband wasn't home half of the time, there were times when he was sober and they would listen to him. Oh yes, they definitely would. With me, I'm a woman, and a boy can't understand a mother's attitude toward different things. You know, that they shouldn't be able to hang around with anybody they want. But if their father was here he'd be more firm with them and that would be it. He wouldn't let them get away with it.

> So far they've been very good. I've been very strict with them. I had to. They call me the old grouch. But they're pretty good. I can still get them in pretty early at night and they're not hanging around the neighborhood until nine, ten, o'clock at night getting into mischief . . .

> I don't spare the rod. I'll just as soon pick a stick up or a strap and I'll give it to them. I have had to do it. And also keep them in for a week, which they don't like at all. I had to hit them to make them listen to reason . . . They'll straighten out one way or another.

Worth noting in Mrs. J's comments is the restriction imposed on her by her responsibilities as head of her household. When we had talked with her two months after her husband died she had wanted to return to work. She said then, "I need a few hours of thinking of something else other than just the housework and the kids." Yet her decision that her sons needed her close attention had kept her at home. A year after her husband died she still had not returned to work.

Mothers of girls were more worried about sexual delinquency than about the mischief or stealing that worried mothers of boys. Like mothers of boys, they relied on close surveillance and firm rules to keep their children from going wrong. Mrs. M, the mother of three daughters, said:

> It's not going to be easy for me because they are three girls. My oldest one, she's at the age where they notice boys. She's gone to parties, but I know what they are and where she is and all that. But I told her, I said, "Don't think this summer that you're going to hang around in the park," because she's not. You've got to start when they're younger, otherwise they get out of hand. But then, I can't tell the future. I mean, you never know what's going to happen.

There is indication that some of the widows who had older daughters had reacted to the potential competition between themselves and their daughters for masculine attention by defining themselves as ineligible for new attachment. This is still another way in which the presence of children may have limited widows as they considered a new life.

PROVIDING FOR THE FAMILY. Although many of the widows had no immediate financial problems, almost all widows were concerned about family income. Whether their current income would continue indefinitely was frequently problematic, but for the most part widows found that they were able to get along for the present much better than they had anticipated—generally not much worse and in a very few cases even better than they had prior to their husband's death. Their incomes were not reduced as much as they at first had feared, and their expenditures, after the burial, were less than they had thought they might be.[5]

Few of the widows were left with hospital bills to pay. Most of the husbands had had hospitalization insurance or had been provided free hospital care as war veterans, so that little if anything remained to be paid by their survivors. The realization that they did not have to pay bills that ran into thousands of dollars, bills so large that without insurance or similar assistance they could not have begun to pay them, contributed to the widows' sense of having avoided financial disaster. Funeral and burial expenses were often partially covered as well—not as fully as hospital costs, but still to a substantial extent—by Social Security benefits, veterans benefits, or insurance. In some cases the cemetery plot had already been owned and paid for by the family, so the widow was charged only for opening the grave. Fairly often the parents and siblings of the dead man contributed to whatever costs remained.

Funeral bills were high. Few cost less than $800 and most cost considerably more. There was nevertheless almost complete acceptance of the validity of the fee. As has already been observed, widows felt that the undertakers performed valuable services for them. This judgment did not change with time. As we pointed out, widows wanted a

[5] Although fifty-five percent of our total sample said their financial situation had deteriorated after their husband's death, only one widow found it truly difficult to make ends meet through the first year and most—eighty-three percent of the sample—said they had managed their finances through the first year without undue difficulty. As noted further on, two widows reported that their financial situation had improved.

funeral that would display their continued devotion to their husbands. Having purchased an expensive funeral was not without its value and most of the widows reported the cost of the funeral proudly rather than resentfully.

Some widows found themselves in receipt of a good deal of money. Contributions from the husband's kin, friends, and co-workers could be substantial. Most husbands either had life insurance or were members of pension plans that had life insurance provisions, which meant that after their death their widows had enough cash to meet current obligations, with something left over. Some widows were able to bank a good part of the policies after having paid all the bills connected with the funeral and burial.

Social Security payments and veterans benefits assured most widows of a continuing income, never more than barely adequate and in some cases not even this. But where there was a discrepancy between what widows received and what they needed, it was small enough so that in every case but one it could be managed by withdrawals from savings or by borrowing from kin.

The widows who were making up the difference between income and expenditure by withdrawals from savings might in time come to the end of their bank accounts. And even those widows whose current income was adequate to their immediate needs might in time find that they had consumed major capital investments when a new car had to be bought or the house needed repair. These widows might have only been postponing financial troubles. But at least in the first year of bereavement the Social Security check, augmented in many cases by a pension or insurance payment, went a long way toward relieving them of financial concerns.

One problem, it might be noted, was that widows often had difficulty working out how to obtain their Social Security or pension or insurance check. Penetrating the commercial and governmental bureaucracies was difficult and troublesome, especially for the poorer widows, who were of course likely to need the money the most.

The nature of the widow's financial problems was dependent on the various aspects of her situation: the number and ages of her children, whether she had savings, whether she worked, and her ability to call on her kin for temporary help. In addition, social class made a difference not only in the intensity of financial concerns but also in the manner in which they were likely to be handled. At least temporary absence of financial concerns seemed characteristic of the situation of upper-middle-class widows, such as Mrs. I:

> I don't have any financial problems at all. I have my salary and then my husband left some insurance. I was able to take care of everything. The health insurance didn't cover everything, but we had Blue Cross and Blue Shield and Major Medical and it covered a great deal of it. Then the rest of the bills are being paid from the estate, from bank accounts and things like that. There's no financial problem . . .

In contrast to this multiplicity of resources, widows whose husbands had earned more nearly lower-middle-class incomes were just about able to manage with the help of Social Security benefits. Mrs. M was perhaps unusual in that she had received a good deal of money as a gift from her husband's co-workers, but otherwise was not atypical.

> The hospital bills were large but I have a very good insurance plan and they paid for everything but twenty-five dollars.
>
> I had the insurance to pay for the funeral. I'm going to get Social Security for my children. We'll never be in great hock. And I plan to continue working as much as I can . . . I will be getting about eighty dollars a week, which I think I'll be able to manage on. And . . . if I don't I can always go to what the people gave me. I put that away so if I need anything I can go right to it. But

I'll try to get along on what I make, which I think I'll be able to do because my expenses aren't as high as they used to be. I had a very big loan which I was paying and I was worried about it—I didn't know how I was going to pay it. But fortunately my husband had it insured so that when he passed on, it just automatically dropped. So I don't have that to worry about. It's just my everyday expenses, the insurance and the telephone, which I think I'll be able to manage.

It was only among widows who had always had severe financial difficulties, where there had been little savings and at best inadequate insurance, that the situation in the period immediately after the husband's death was complicated by worries about money. But even here Social Security benefits and pension checks or gifts or paid employment kept the widows afloat. One such widow, Mrs. N, in her late thirties and with four children, was employed in a clerical position. She reported:

The hospital wanted $300 so I told them I didn't have the money. They said, "Well, you have to pay it," and I said, "Well, I can't pay it." I gave it to this friend of mine—he's not actually a lawyer but he knows the law and everything—so he said, "Don't worry about it. They can't press you for that bill. How can you pay it?" So I haven't heard no more. For the funeral my brother-in-law paid half, $500 or something, and then Veterans paid something, $250. They've already paid—I got the notice. And we're waiting for the Social Security, they will pay $250. When they send me the check I'll give it to the undertaker.

I'm getting veterans disability. That's been approved. I get that at the end of the month. And now I'm waiting for the Social Security. That should come in another month or so. The pension will be $83 a month. I don't know how much they allow for each child or anything. The man from the government said if I wanted to quit work or work part-time or something like that I could go and collect widows benefits for myself. But he says

> while I'm working, if I make $3,000, I can't get nothing
> from Social Security ... Well, I'm getting my salary
> and if I keep working and get another raise I'll be
> alright.

In very low income families a husband's death can
conceivably result in an improvement in his widow's
financial situation. This happened in two families where an
alcoholic husband had been a drain on the family's
resources rather than a contributor to them. Mrs. J's husband was one of them:

> My Social Security has come through and I'm waiting
> for the Veterans which will be here soon. Social
> Security is $204 a month and the veterans pension is
> going to go according to that. They said if I wasn't
> getting enough they'd give me $140 a month. I have to
> wait on that and that takes another week before I hear
> from them, so I don't honestly know what I'll get from
> the veterans widows pension ... I think that once the
> veterans pension comes through I'll be all right.

> This way I know I'm getting a certain amount and my
> husband will not be taking it for drink. I'll spend it the
> way you're supposed to spend it. I'll have so much for
> food and so much for bills and things like that, and so
> much for clothing. And I'll know the money is in the
> house and he won't be taking it.

Mrs. J at another point suggested the essential role
insurance sometimes played in very low income families, as
a kind of forced savings against a possible future need to
pay funeral and burial expenses. Insurance maintained in
this way is not intended to replace the husband's income, as
it is in more nearly middle-class settings, but rather to make
it possible, should the husband die, to bury him decently.

> The funeral is paid for. I had some insurance on him
> and I paid off the full amount of it. I don't have to think

of it any more. The insurance always came out of the
household budget. Whatever he gave me every week it
used to come out of that. Even when I was on welfare I
used to pay his insurance all the time. I paid for it since
we've been married, over sixteen years . . . I could have
dropped his insurance any time I wanted to, but I
figured it was better to keep it up because I could never
tell when something would happen and I've never had
any money in the bank or anything like that.

Many widows—and not just very poor ones—found that
their husband's death produced unanticipated financial
benefits. They might be surprised and relieved to discover
that their car no longer required monthly installment payments, as a consequence of the mandatory insurance provision of most such loans. In addition, some—those whose
husbands had been better off—were able to put much more
insurance money in the bank than they had counted on. But
no widow could feel any great gratification because of these
financial boons. They meant, at best, that financial disaster
was not to be added to the other assaults on their lives.

10

CHANGES IN RELATIONSHIPS
WITH FAMILY AND FRIENDS

As the year went on many of our respondents felt that they no longer occupied the same place in society that they had when they were married. With good reason they felt that their standing in their community and their relationships with others had changed.

The specific ways in which widows' relationships changed appeared to depend in large degree on their age, social class, and life style. Change was more evident in the lives of the younger and wealthier widows, especially those whose social life had been organized around their husband's activities or had required them to participate with their husbands as members of couples.

In some cases the changes were initiated by the widows, in others by their friends. Many widows reported disappointment that friends who earlier had sworn steadfast solicitude later withdrew. Twenty-nine percent agreed with the statement, "Everyone was helpful at first, but they don't have time any more." Friends were not the only source of such distress: some felt neglected by kin as well, although others felt oppressed by what seemed to them to be kin's unwarranted attempts at invasion.

Some widows blamed themselves for the changes they perceived in their friends' attitudes. They described their friends as having continued to be receptive and solicitous as they had been at first, but said that they themselves had felt uncomfortable with them and had withdrawn from them. The temporary or permanent disruption of relationships with friends was a painful aspect of the period of reorganization of widows' lives. Although none of our respondents was at any time totally isolated, and each was able at every point to draw support and occasional aid from family or others, all had to deal with relational change.

In this chapter we review the changes that occurred in three sectors of their lives as the widows moved toward recovery. We deal with widows' relationships with their own families, with their husbands' families, and with their friends.

THE WIDOWS' FAMILIES. Bereavement brought most widows close to their own families. Although this was especially true during the first few months after the death, the closeness continued throughout the period of readjustment. They spent more time with their parents, sisters, and brothers, and they asked these immediate kin for help more often than they once had. At the end of the first year forty percent of the sample named a member of their family as the person who had been most helpful to them.

Once the first weeks of bereavement had passed, widows' relationships to their own families might take one of several courses. A small minority of widows—five in our sample of forty-nine—made relationships with one or more of their kin the central bonds of their lives. We discuss them at somewhat greater length in Chapter Twelve, in our review of the different reorganizations of life to which widows eventually come. The majority of widows seemed to establish relationships that were close, but not too close, and as time went on, their families accepted without question their return to relative independence. An appreciable minority of widows, however, encountered some difficulty with family along the way.

In the weeks immediately following the husband's death, widows were grateful to their kin and usually had no complaints about their behavior. In this period whatever latent animosities might have existed between the widows and other members of their families were overwhelmed by the awesome significance of the loss or suppressed in deference to sorrow. Twenty percent of widows reported isolated incidents of recrimination or brief tension among their kin at the time of our first interview, less than a month after the death; but at such times uninvolved family members or friends had quickly stepped in to establish family solidarity.

With the passage of another month, when grief had abated and the widows had begun to settle into their new routines, twenty-eight percent reported having developed angry feelings toward members of their family. A few of them had reevaluated the behaviors and contributions that families had made during the earlier period of deep mourning. Behaviors they might then have seen as protective or solicitous they now began to reinterpret as officious or overly demanding. Some felt that their families had done entirely too little for them. Some were resentful that their families were now doing less than they had promised, or at any rate less than they had led the widows to anticipate. And a few felt oppressed by familial solicitude that conflicted with their movement toward greater independence.

Tension arose most frequently in the relationship of the widow and her mother, less often in the relationship of the widow and one or more of her sisters, and only infrequently in the relationship of the widow and her brothers. Fathers seemed relatively uninvolved in widows' lives; when they were talked about at all, they were likely to be described as distantly benign. However they were described, the relationship was felt to be unproblematic.

Some widows hoped that their brothers might serve as a male presence in their families, partially replacing their absent husbands. In these cases it seemed that the brothers may at first have indicated that they would attempt to do so, but then discovered that other obligations, especially to their own families, made active participation in the widows' families difficult. The widows may then have been disappointed, but seemed to understand and accept the reasons for the failure.

Sisters proved the most helpful of kin members. At the end of the first year of bereavement, twenty-four percent named a sister as having been most helpful to them through the year. Only ten percent named their mothers. (It should be remembered that all the widows were relatively young and most had living mothers.) A good many widows felt that their mothers had attempted to be helpful, but had instead displayed woeful insensitivity to their needs and strivings. A very few widows criticized their mothers for not having been helpful at all, or for not having tried to be more helpful.

Maternal insensitivity to their current state seemed to remind a number of widows of their mother's earlier failings. For example, Mrs. G felt compelled to reproach her mother with what she felt to be her mother's persistent minimization of a wife's obligations to her husband:

> I have a terrible resentment against my mother and I
> don't know why. I argue with her all the time. I have
> brought up things of the past that she had done wrong,
> that I felt she could have done differently, although it is
> from the past and I should leave it there. But now that
> she is trying to tell me I should do this or I should do
> that, I bring up to her what she's done in the past . . .
> She will tell me that I shouldn't discuss things with the
> children, that they won't remember [their father] . . .
> We had a very bad argument over Don and the
> children. She felt I was neglecting myself and I was
> neglecting my children and catering to Don, and that
> while he was in a semicoma and didn't know whether I
> was there or not, I should be with my children. I said,
> "Mother, this is your viewpoint, this is the way you
> lived. You catered to us children and your husband
> came last and you lost your husband [through divorce]
> for this reason."

What may have happened in the case of some of these
widows was that their new need for their mothers made it
more difficult for them to suppress irritations that had
previously been latent in their relationships. At the same
time they may have felt increased need for their mothers
and, in consequence, new vulnerability to their opinions
and values.

Some widows said that their parents had invited them
openly or by hints to give up their own homes and return to
the parental home, or alternatively to set up some sort of
joint household. A few widows agreed to this, but the great
majority were unwilling to give up their own homes or to
risk their autonomy by bringing their mothers into their
homes.

One of our respondents, Mrs. D, felt that she had never
gotten along well enough with her mother to make the idea
of rejoining her parents plausible. Her mother had hinted to
her that she and Mrs. D's father were keeping their own

house, even though they no longer had need for so large a
place themselves, so that it would be available for Mrs. D
should she want to return. Mrs. D said about this:

> My mother said something about how she doesn't want
> to sell her house in case I'd ever went to come back to
> live there. I said, "Mother, if I ever come back I would
> bang yours and Dad's heads against the wall. Don't feel
> that you have to keep the house for me because I very
> definitely will not come back." I have no intention
> whatsoever of going back to live there. Absolutely not.
> It wouldn't work out. My mother and I have never
> gotten along that well. She is a very nervous type of
> person and even just to have the children down for
> dinner, well, the minute supper is over, out I go, and
> take the kids with me. I mean, there is just no point to
> it. They make her nervous, which in turn makes me
> nervous ... I'm too independent anyway and no
> kitchen is big enough for two women under most
> circumstances.

One area in which conflict with mothers seemed likely to
erupt was that of management of the children. There the
widows' mothers sometimes suggested that their superior
experience should be deferred to by their daughters. Had
the widows actually moved in with their mothers, continuing conflict over direction of the children might have
occurred; even when the children were only left with the
mothers briefly, conflict might arise.[1]

Mrs. F's mother cared for Mrs. F's ten-year-old daughter

[1] In one case, reported in a follow-up interview three years after the
husband's death, a widow had formed the practice of leaving her children
with her mother so that the widow could more easily stay out on late dates.
Her mother became furious at what she interpreted as the widow's
irresponsible behavior. Because her mother was caring for her children the
widow had to listen passively to her mother's harangues. Once, when the
widow left the children overnight, the mother greeted her with a sharp slap.
Here, even though the widow had not moved in with her mother, her
unusual reliance on her mother had made her subject to maternal discipline.

mornings while Mrs. F was at work. Mrs. F and her mother frequently fought over how her daughter should be treated. The specific issue in dispute, often, was one of permissiveness.

> My mother takes care of Lauri after school and during the summer when I'm at work. My mother lives right here—if you go out my back door you can go through the yard and go into my mother's house . . . I discipline Lauri and my mother yells at me for doing it. She always thought I was too strict with her. I said, "Ma, if I'm not, she's going to walk all over me. She'll talk back to me." And my mother will yell, "She's only a baby. Let her talk." I fight with my mother more than I do with my daughter.

The attempt by these widows to retain their autonomy sometimes appeared to their mothers to be rejection of them. Widows reported that at times their mothers seemed to expect that they would now become their close companions. Until a new balance could be established in their relationships, these mothers and their daughters might find themselves engaged in chronic misunderstanding.

The following report by Mrs. G suggests how a relationship that might have had its tensions when a widow was married could become almost unmanageable in her new situation of widowhood. When Mrs. G was married, her mother respected her daughter's obligations to her husband. But with Mrs. G widowed, her mother could expect to come first.

> Christmas Eve the girls I bowl with are going out, getting together to play before Christmas. They asked me to go with them. Before I had said No, because I was going to ask my mother to spend Christmas Eve and Christmas morning with me. But she gave me a very curt answer that with all my friends wasn't there someone I would rather have than her. . . .

> I think my mother resents the fact that I do have a lot of
> close friends, and that there might be someone here
> when she does come. My mother is the type that you
> have to give her your undivided attention. It just struck
> me the wrong way for her to say this to me. I thought
> she really should be here with her grandchildren. She
> is their only grandparent. I think after she said this she
> knew she had done wrong, because she said it to my
> sister that she doesn't know why she came out with
> that.

We should emphasize that only a minority of the widows
experienced the conflicts and tensions we are now describing. Most widows moved toward independence and established what they felt to be entirely satisfactory relationships
with their kin. They accepted their own need for help, but
limited their requests and made clear their desire for
autonomy. If their mothers saw them as having returned to
an earlier status as unmarried women and so as again
appropriate recipients of maternal guidance, they were able
tactfully to insist on their continued maturity.

Mrs. L was among the majority who found their way to a
satisfactory relationship with their kin. Her approach was to
limit her requests for help and so demonstrate her continued
competence:

> I can feel I can call on my family . . . I don't make a pest
> of myself; I only call if it's absolutely necessary. But I
> think that I can call on them if I need any help . . . I
> wouldn't be on anybody's back to do anything. In fact,
> they bawl me out because I don't ask. "Why didn't you
> call me?" I did it myself. It was some little thing.

THE HUSBAND'S FAMILY.   Insofar as widows experienced
conflict with members of their own families, the conflict
often seemed only a false step on the way to establishment

of new understandings. Not so the disturbances in widows' relations with their husband's family. Disturbances here were rather more common and also more intense. There was more often pervasive disappointment and disillusionment. There were fewer inhibitions to the expression of anger or resentment, and dramatic breaks in contact were not infrequent.

Again, the majority of widows did not report such disturbances. Some, indeed, became even closer to a sister-in-law or parents-in-law after their bereavement. But the minority of widows who did report conflict was a larger one. In our first interview with widows, three to four weeks after bereavement, twenty-six percent reported feelings of anger toward members of their husband's family. A month later it was forty-two percent, more than two in five.

Disturbances seemed to arise primarily in widows' relationships with the other women in their husband's family: with their mother-in-law, and, to a lesser but still noticeable extent, with their sisters-in-law. Fathers-in-law had little contact with widows, and when there was contact it was rarely troublesome. Brothers-in-law, with some exceptions, had few conflicts with widows.

The helpfulness of brothers-in-law decreased over the year. In the very early period after the loss, they were by far the most helpful members of the husband's family. But then, as with widows' own brothers, the competing demands of their wives and children forced them to withdraw. A year later only two widows in the sample named a brother-in-law as the person who had helped the most. Some widows suspected that their husband's brothers had been forced by their wives, because of jealousy, to relinquish whatever closeness with them had developed. In one instance this was clearly true—the brother-in-law was obliged to phone the widow from a public booth to avoid his wife's anger.

It appeared that where there had been latent antagonisms between widows and their in-laws, death provided the opportunity for their direct expression. A widow who had, during her marriage, minimized friction with her in-laws to avoid conflict with her husband was now more willing to be angry at what she felt to be insult or injury. Relationships with in-laws that had once been somewhat strained now became precarious.

An instance of the surfacing of previously suppressed antagonism toward a husband's family was offered by Mrs. H, whose husband had left her once or twice, with at least the tacit approval of his family. After his death she believed that her husband's family felt guilty and wanted to make amends. Two months after her husband's funeral, Mrs. H said:

> Well, I wasn't getting along too good with his mother and father before. They couldn't stand me all these years. So I said now that he's gone, why should I bother with them now? We were together in the funeral car and then they drove me right home and that was it. My mother-in-law has called me about three times and we were there for Sunday dinner. She said, "Don't be so cold now."

> The kids go up and visit her but—I don't know—I feel kind of funny. I suppose out of respect for the children I said, "We'll drive by once in a while." But I'm not going to make a habit of it. It will be the same thing over and over: they keep bringing it up [the husband's desertions]. I don't want to listen to it any more. I've listened to it too long and I've done a lot of crying and carrying on for a whole year and it never did me any good. So why start the whole thing all over again?

A year later the break was almost complete. Mrs. H said then:

> I haven't heard if my mother-in-law had an anniversary

> Mass. I haven't heard from them since before Christmas [two and a half months earlier]. And I haven't been up there ... If they can't stop in and say hello, why bother? I never see my husband's brothers either. I never got a Christmas card from them, none of them. In September my sister-in-law had a baby and I went down for the christening. And nobody even seemed to know who I was when I walked in. So that was that.

Widows who became angry at in-laws tended to locate the critical events as having occurred at the time of the husband's death or even before. Typical complaints were that the in-laws had shown little concern for the husband during his illness, that they had made few if any offers to help at the time of his death, that they had not offered to share the expenses of the funeral and burial although they could well have afforded to do so, that they had interfered with the funeral or burial arrangements the widow had made, and that they had been critical of the widow at the time of the husband's death or soon thereafter. Often widows said that the issue had seemed transient and unimportant at the time and they had wanted to maintain familial solidarity in the face of their shared loss and so they had resisted responding; and besides, they did not then feel up to quarreling. But later, the widows continued, when they had more time to reflect, and especially when further slights occurred, they reinterpreted what had happened earlier, felt themselves aggrieved, and began withdrawing from the relationships. They telephoned their in-laws less frequently and virtually stopped visiting them.

Some of these widows felt that their in-laws had been the first to withdraw. They complained that their in-laws, after initially being extremely solicitous, had failed to keep in touch with them and had shown less interest in their children than they thought proper. The very fact that the in-laws had been so solicitous to begin with exacerbated their feelings of disappointment. In self-protection, perhaps with some unnoticed desire for retaliation, they might decide, like the widows who felt they had been actively injured, "I'm not going to call them. Let them call me."

In several instances, widows reported disputes over their husband's possessions. Mrs. E did not drive and so her brother-in-law wanted to take her husband's car. Mrs. E, however, recognized that even if she could not use the car, it had a cash value. She said:

> My husband wouldn't want to take something from me and the children and give it to somebody else. It's his money even though it is his brother ... I told my brother-in-law and he hasn't been over since. It don't worry me because me and the children will make it even if they [the husband's family] never come over.

In another instance a mother-in-law was believed by the widow to have invited her to come live with her as a way of gaining possession of the widow's furniture.

> They just bought a nine-room house and they don't have the furniture to put in it, so she figured I was going to take my furniture and move in with her. I was saying to myself, "Gee, I'll be there three weeks and she'd throw me out and I wouldn't have no furniture." So I said No, we wouldn't come.

Invariably the widows felt themselves to have been the aggrieved in these frictions. If they were the ones who withdrew, their response was justified; if it was their in-laws who withdrew from them, it demonstrated their callousness and indifference to the widows and to their children. Many widows suggested that their husband's family should have been considerate of them not only as an expression of family feeling and in recognition of their loss, but also because it was their son or their brother who had authored their widowhood, and so they had some responsibility to help. This unvoiced feeling that in-laws bore special responsibility may account for the more than ordinary resentment that was displayed toward those who showed what was felt to be little concern.

One notes in the following report, made by Mrs. L, anger as well as disappointment that her in-laws had not been more attentive and understanding of her needs, and more aware of her distress.

> My in-laws have completely ignored us, so I'm ignoring them. They just turned their backs. Sometimes it bothered me. They have done this for no apparent reason. One of them told me, "You think all you want is your mother." I said, "Who do you turn to in times of distress if you have a mother still living? You turn to your mother." But they can't understand my feelings of what I've been through. They just think I don't want to bother with them and I've explained it to them, all of them, that I haven't seen anybody. I just feel they're not interested, so I just don't bother seeing them. Because if they can't feel what I've been through the last year and they can't ignore some of the things I may have done or may have said, well, I just don't want to bother with them.

Mrs. L then described how her resentment finally expressed itself after having been nurtured for much of the year.

> I had the anniversary Mass and everybody came. I mean, both families came. I was very, very friendly with them [her in-laws]. I talked to them at the Mass. But they couldn't look me straight in the eye because they know they're wrong. It was seven in the morning and naturally everybody went without breakfast. My sister said to me, "Where are you going?" "I'm going home, naturally." She said to me, "Aren't you going to ask everyone to come back?" So I said, "What is it, a party?" She said, "Well, I think you should ask your in-laws." I said, "No. I'm not asking them. If they couldn't come down to see me for one whole year, I should ask them to come today to my house? No, I'm not asking anybody."

There were still other reasons for friction with in-laws, besides the emergence of latent conflict or the development of feelings of being misused on the part of widows. Some widows felt burdened by the apparent unwillingness of in-laws to recognize their need to develop new independent lives. Some were put off by what they felt to be ostentatious or self-indulgent displays of grief by their in-laws, especially by their mother-in-law. In each case there were differences in understanding or in values that led to friction or withdrawal.

Mrs. I was among the widows whose relationship with her in-laws became disturbed. One of the issues was the mother-in-law's insistence on idealizing Mrs. I's husband. Mrs. I described her feelings in this way:

> I think I've become irritated sometimes with my husband's mother because of the way she talks to me, the way she expresses her grief. It isn't the way I express mine and I just wish she wouldn't say things to me that she does say. I think it's just her attitude in general. Of course, it's awfully hard to have a son die and she's very grief-stricken, as we all are. But it's just a little dramatic, the way she carries on. She talks about him in a way that she's almost making him out to be a saint. And I don't think of him as a saint; he was very human and warm. It's almost as if he was perfect and never had any faults, and I think this annoys me. I don't know why it annoys me, but it does, because I don't think of him like that. I think of him as being very funny and full of life and I think of the fun we had together. She talks about talking to him; she goes to his room and feels that he's there; and she talks about going to the cemetery a lot . . . I think it's kind of phony —maybe it isn't, maybe it's just the way I feel—but this is how she is.

Ten months later, Mrs. I reported diminished contact with her in-laws and added that she did not find the contact especially gratifying.

I call his mother and I go out there. I do it for my husband because I feel that he would want me to do this and he's not here to do some of the things that I can do for them. And it's hard. It's kind of depressing going out there because they're so sad. You call her on the phone and you ask, "How are you?" And she'll say, "Well, pretty well." It's never, "Fine." It's always, "Pretty well." I think of what he would say: "For God's sake, Mother, will you stop that. Don't be so morbid." I want to tell her that, but of course I can't, because I'm not her son. I'm her daughter-in-law, and there's a different relationship.

An underlying issue in relationships of widows and their in-laws is the unclear basis for continuation of the relationship. Widows are not tied to their husband's family either by bonds of consanguinity or mutual choice. Their relationship was based essentially on their ties to the same man, now dead. In-laws and widows also shared ties to the husband's children, but with the husband gone, that bond sometimes proved thinner than might have been anticipated. Much depended on whether there was in addition mutual concern, common interests, and feelings of respect, admiration, and liking.

Conflict might develop between widows and in-laws after the husband's death over any number of issues. In a few cases there was dispute over whether the widows or their in-laws should have greater voice in deciding particular funeral arrangements. In-laws sometimes claimed possessions of the husband as "belonging to the family", without the widows' agreement. And some in-laws wanted the widows to become living memorials to their husbands when the widows had begun to move toward acceptance of the reality that they were now alone.

Widows generally wanted their children to continue to know their husband's family. Most widows felt strongly that their husbands would have wanted the children to continue seeing their grandparents, aunts, and uncles. They felt that the children could benefit from the continued contact. They also often felt that they were obligated to permit the family to maintain contact with the children, that it was only right that "blood relatives" should maintain relationships. Often, as time passed, their own relationships with their in-laws were maintained only "for the sake of the kids."

We have not yet spoken of the appreciable number of widows whose relationships with their in-laws remained good through the first year of their bereavement. These included two widows who reported that their brothers-in-law had continued to be wonderfully helpful to them through the first year of their bereavement, and one widow who became heavily dependent on a sister-in-law. This group also included a good many widows whose relationships with their in-laws remained pleasant, even gratifying, without being intensely important. This group of widows, whose relationships with their in-laws remained good through the first year of their bereavement, was smaller than the group whose relationships faded or soured as time went on. But given the difficulties inherent in widows' relationships to in-laws, what may be remarkable is not how large a number reported the relationships to have been disturbed, but rather how large a number did not.

FRIENDSHIPS.   Changes in the intensity of widows' friendships in some ways paralleled changes in their relationships with in-laws. But while one could withdraw from kin or in-laws, but not replace them, it was possible to make a new set of friends. This may be why, although anger toward family members (including in-laws) was expressed by an increasing percentage of the widows as the first year of their bereavement progressed, the percentage expressing anger toward friends (thirty percent) remained constant throughout the year. This is a large proportion, to be sure; but while it is larger than the proportion of widows initially expressing anger toward in-laws, it is smaller than the proportion who eventually expressed anger toward in-laws.

There was a marked difference between widows' experiences with married couples who had been friends both to them and their husbands, and married or single friends whose bond had essentially been with them alone. For the most part, the first were eventually lost; the second were retained.

Typically what seemed to happen in relation to "couple" friends is that while, at first, they rallied to the widow's support to offer condolence and whatever aid they could give, a period of decreasing contact followed, during which widows came to recognize that the relationship had changed. Some widows reported that eventually they virtually lost their membership in what had been the social network made up of married friends. Individual couples, or more often individual wives within that network might remain friendly to them, but they were no longer included in evening gatherings. Nor, often, did they want to be; one or two experiences as a "fifth wheel" might be enough to dissuade them from attending further gatherings of married couples.

Friends of the widow herself, women she had known before her marriage as well as women she had come to know through work or the neighborhood or even through her husband who were *her* friends, rather than friends of the couple, were likely to be retained. Even here, however, major changes in the widow's concerns could weaken the basis for the friendship.

By the end of their first year of bereavement most widows had established a very different sort of friendship network from that which they had maintained during their marriage. They had withdrawn to a greater or lesser extent from relationships with married couples, from relationships with those who had been known for years as well as from those recently met. A few married couples might continue to be seen, but in general friends made during the widow's own marriage were permitted to drift away. More and more widows spent their leisure hours with women who, like themselves, were on their own. Until nearly the end of the first year of their bereavement most widows had few contacts with men.

It appeared that their friendships, like their relationships with their in-laws, might be permitted to fade as the widows attempted to reorganize their lives. There were fundamental differences between these relationships. There was no bond to friends, as there was to in-laws, through the children; nor was the latent tension of relationships with in-laws observed in friendships. But the relationships were similar in that each was liable to disruption during bereavement.

At first widows were eager to maintain their friendships. They were grateful for the appearance of friends at the wake and funeral, and grateful again to those friends who let them know directly of their willingness to help. During the first weeks trustworthy friendships appeared to be islands of security in what often appeared to be a hostile world. Despite their grief, widows were careful to respond to friends' telephone calls and notes of sympathy, and when they could they accepted friends' advice and assistance, at least in part to assure continuation of the friendship.

During these early weeks widows sometimes turned to their friends for help with problems they could not take to their families, including problems with their families. The solicitude of friends seemed more nearly disinterested, and therefore more to be trusted, whether the matter was the way the death should be explained to the children, or the advisability of the widow returning to work, or the proper time for the widow to end formal mourning. Kin often seemed only too willing to give advice, but the fee might be diminished standing in the family, and the advice could be suspect since kin might consider not only a widow's well-being but also the family reputation. Friends were less likely to be invasive or overbearing, and their advice less likely to be concerned with the proprieties.

Despite the early importance of friends, most widows found that with time most of their friendships faded. One or two close friends might remain as close or closer than they had ever been; at the end of the year twenty percent of widows said a friend had been the individual most helpful to them. But in general, friends did not call as often as they once had and now rarely came to see them. Here, as elsewhere, widows tried to be realistic. Although they might at times feel their friends had failed them, they could recognize that their friends had their own life routines and preoccupations and might no longer be able to make special efforts on their behalf. And they might recognize, perhaps not without bitterness, that they themselves were no longer as valuable as friends as they had once been, that their situation in life had changed and with it their capacity to engage in favor exchange and to reciprocate for sociability. Furthermore, their concerns were now somewhat different.

With the fading of friendships, widows began to feel themselves no longer appropriate members of their former friendship networks. They had become outsiders, odd members of the group who were difficult to relate to and uncomfortable when attempting to relate to others. They felt no longer able to contribute to the matrix of social understandings maintained by their friends and, once by themselves, they no longer felt similar to their friends in their concerns. Their friendships, they might feel, had become remnants of outdated loyalties.

There were other reasons as well for the fading of former friendships after the first months of bereavement. The widows now had no one to escort them. For this reason, and also because they were reluctant to leave their children with a baby-sitter, they minimized outings. In any event they were in mourning, and although social participation was important for them, they felt it should be limited. Yet the most important reason for the fading of friendships was that the friendships had stopped working for the widows, and very likely for the friends as well.

All the widows in our study reported experiences with former friends that made them aware of a change in the friendships. Friends might be oversolicitous and at the same time inattentive. Sometimes widows suspected the friends of extending invitations to them out of pity. As Mrs. M said:

> I've been going out more socially and I see everybody, but although they accept me I do feel kind of funny, as though I'm a fifth wheel. Or I feel that they feel sorry for me and that's why I'm there. Although they say I shouldn't feel that way.

Chance encounters with friends and acquaintances were apt to be uncomfortable. The widows felt awkward in their new status, and were perhaps oversensitive to the attitudes of others. Mrs. A reported:

> Some people avoid me. I've noticed that. I was walking down the street one day with a friend and a couple of fellows that worked with my husband were coming down the other way. At first their faces were—I mean, they didn't know what to say or what to do—they kind of were talking to each other and all of a sudden they got this, no expression at all kind of a look, a blank expression on their faces. And I smiled at them and said hello, and they said, "Oh, hello." And I think they were shocked to pieces that I had a smile on my face. I think they expected me to be crying or something. They didn't know how to react.

After having been accustomed for years to relating to friends as a married woman, widows had to learn to relate as women without husbands. This was much less significant an issue during the daytime when neighborhood friends were also alone. But evenings and weekends, the times when widows were most lonely, their friends' husbands were home and the friends were available only as members of couples.

Mrs. F worked during the day. Her work for her was a substitute for the occasional neighborhood sociability available to nonworking widows. But she, like them, was isolated after dark. This is what she said about her situation:

> The girls at work are all married, and they like to spend time with their husbands. When I was married I didn't want to go out at night either. You work all day and you don't want to leave the house, believe me you don't. My girl friends once in a while come over, but most of them are younger than I am. Like that girl that I went with to a party, she's ten years younger than I am. The girls that are my age are married and they got two or three kids and they want to stay home with them at night.

It is important to note that widows felt uncomfortable with married couples, and were in part responsible for the inaccessibility to them of married friends. A year after their bereavement, fifty-one percent of the sample agreed with the statement, "I feel uncomfortable in groups of married couples." This was primarily because they themselves felt out of place, marginal, and in consequence insecure. But there were occasional reports of discomfort stemming from a sense of themselves as sexually vulnerable. Most husbands of friends appeared to be distinctly courteous and helpful, but nevertheless widows occasionally feared the latent sexual possibilities of such attentiveness. Even a fleeting fantasy of sexual involvement was distasteful to them, and in addition they feared the antagonism of their friends, the wives. Some imagined that the wives already harbored false suspicions.

For all these reasons many widows discovered that they

could not sustain former friendships. A few widows did continue to attend gatherings of the friends and neighbors of their married years, but only in the company of an unmarried sister or another widow. In this way they protected themselves against feeling isolated within the group and provided themselves with testimony to their sexual inaccessibility.

Most widows proceeded slowly to acquire new friends. At work, through their children's school, or through a church or other interest group they met other women in situations like their own. When asked to describe the process of making new friends, they pictured it as casual and haphazard, but actually they seemed to have been actively alert to anyone with whom they might now and again get out of the house and away from their children and their memories.

Eight weeks after her husband died, Mrs. G, although still preoccupied with her feelings of loss, realized that her old friends no longer were adequate:

> I don't want to lose my old friends, but I think I will
> have to get out and get into different things other than
> being with the same group all the time. I don't think I
> really will enjoy it.

Mrs. G joined a singing club for women and eventually formed friendships with a number of other women she met there—women who, like her, were without husbands.

In similar ways and with similar goals, other widows became more active in church groups, joined adult education classes, or simply became friendlier and more accessible to other women who lived in their neighborhood. At the end of the first year of their bereavement, forty-eight percent felt themselves to have become more sociable since the illness and death of their spouse. Only nine percent felt themselves to have become withdrawn and less sociable.

Many of the widows seemed to be rather careful in

choosing close friends from among their new acquaintances. Some reported having met other widows much older
than they with whom they could not form friendships
because of the age difference, although they found their
example of self-possession to be heartening. In other cases
widows were anxious to form relationships with women
who were not themselves widowed. A few of the younger
widows did not want to identify themselves with a community of widows; they felt themselves to have much in
common with women who had not yet been married and
could not bring themselves to accept the social niche of
widowhood so early in their lives.

Widows still in their twenties when their husbands died
could not entirely accept the label "widow," which they felt
implied age and seclusion. Indeed, almost one-quarter of
our sample expressed a strong dislike of the term "widow."
Among the younger women, three had no children and for
them the solution was to drift back to their single crowd.
One who began dating about eight months after her husband's death defined herself essentially as a young single
woman. A second who began dating before the end of the
first year of her bereavement remained unaccepting of any
definition of her status. She felt that she was neither a
widow nor a single girl; indeed, she felt that she belonged
nowhere. A third continued to define herself as a married
woman for a longer period than seemed typical. This was
Mrs. B, whose insistence, two months after her husband's
death, that she was still her husband's wife and not his
widow, has already been referred to. At the end of the first
year of her bereavement she felt herself to be neither wife
nor widow, like the second woman we have just described.
She had attempted to retain her married friends and said
that she was uncomfortable among the unmarried. But in
fact she was uncomfortable among the married as well. She
said:

> My friends are married couples. I'm not quite comfort-
> able with single people. . . . they seem a bit—I shouldn't
> say immature—but their interests are entirely different
> from mine. So I don't fit in that well. Maybe I'm trying
> to say I don't have a sense of belonging . . . [But] I feel
> uncomfortable if everyone is in couples and I'm the
> only girl, and especially if other people try very hard to
> be nice, like opening the door and pulling a chair or
> something like that.

Mrs. B's marginality suggests the dilemma of women who
lose their husbands while still young. If they are young
enough to return to the world of single people, their having
been married may be almost forgotten, and a most important
era of their lives and a most important relationship may be
treated as if they had never happened. But if they reject that
world, they have available to them only marginal membership in a network of married couples or, possibly, the
uncongenial and age-inappropriate company of older
widows.

11

THE RECOVERY PROCESS

The period of deep and continued grief described in earlier chapters seemed usually to last only a few weeks or at most a few months. By the time of our second interview, about two months after the husband's death, sixty-one percent of widows agreed with the statement, "I'm beginning to feel more like myself again." Further recovery seemed to progress more slowly, and was not yet fully achieved by the end of the first year of bereavement. Indeed, some widows seemed just barely to have stabilized their lives when we saw them three or four years after their loss. Failure to begin to move toward recovery during the first year seemed to signal continued difficulty thereafter.

By the end of the first year of their bereavement most widows believed that although they had not yet arrived at a new stability, they had done well. They felt more in control of their lives and themselves. They were, significantly, much less likely suddenly to give way to tears.[1] A few widows seemed to have recovered very little, however; they were still given to despair and their lives continued to be chaotic. The reasons for their failure to recover seemed varied and we consider them later, but it is useful to note here that although movement to recovery was the most frequent pattern, it was not the only one.

Most components of the grief syndrome—feelings of shock, of abandonment, and of loss of a part of the self, for example—seemed to be a response to the loss of the husband, and so to have faded as the loss receded into the past. Loneliness, however, seemed to be a reaction to the husband's absence, or rather to the absence of any figure who could bestow security.[2] It did not fade with time. The percentage of widows who agreed with the statement, "I'm so lonely," dropped comparatively little during the year: seventy-eight percent agreed with the statement three weeks after bereavement, seventy percent a month later, and sixty-five percent a year later.

By the end of the first year of their bereavement some widows were dating, generally without the emotional reliance on the man or men they were seeing who would have allayed their loneliness. The follow-up interview, held two, three, or four years after the death of their husbands, revealed however that a good many were engaged to remarry or had already remarried. None of these described themselves as still lonely, although most continued to sorrow for the loss of their first husband.

---

[1] When we talked with widows three weeks after their husband's loss, about one in three cried during the interview. Five weeks later only half as many cried. In the interview held after the end of the first year only two widows cried.

[2] See Robert S. Weiss, *Loneliness: The Experience of Emotional and Social Isolation* (Cambridge, Mass.: M.I.T. Press, 1973).

THE COURSE OF RECOVERY. Let us review the usual course of recovery once the widow has passed the period of deepest grief. The very first evidence of the beginning of recovery seemed often to be the widow's own sense that she was emerging from grief, and beginning to feel better. It might be possible now for the widow to begin to take interest in activities and in being with others.

Sometimes when widows looked back on the first year of their bereavement they could single out events they felt had special significance for their recovery. Some spoke of incidents in which they asserted for the first time that their lives must continue and that they must look forward and not back. One widow, for example, described her recovery as beginning in a conversation with her mother-in-law in which she first made explicit her intention of building a new life. Others described sudden eruptions of intense emotion. One widow described an outburst of tears, almost unprovoked, that continued uncontrollably for much of an hour. When it ended she felt at peace, and able to set about reconstructing her life.

Widows' relations with others now began to undergo change, as we have already described in some detail. Now the widows were less reluctant to take the initiative in entering social situations. At the same time they began to value their independence more and the advice or support of friends and kin less. They less often sought such advice and support, and some became impatient with sympathetic friends or relatives who volunteered undesired assistance.

Widows now confronted the fears of helplessness and vulnerability that might earlier have impeded their functioning. Many widows began to develop new respect for themselves as they recognized their ability to cope with their new situation. Mrs. L, for example, overcame a long-standing fear of being alone in the house. She said:

> I never would go to bed until he was home. I couldn't

sleep unless he was in. If he had a meeting or
something, he always said, "Go to bed, you don't have
to wait up for me." But I never would go to bed. I'd
always wait until he came home. So I thought that I
would be frightened being alone with the children. But
truthfully I haven't been, surprisingly. I know he's not
going to come home, and the children are in, and I lock
the doors, and that's it.

Developing confidence in their ability to manage helped
the widows to resume planning for their future. Some
decided to return to school to become self-supporting.
Those already working gave new importance to their job.

At first almost no widow was willing to contemplate the
possibility of remarriage. The very suggestion of remarriage
early in the bereavement might have been seen as a
suggestion to be disloyal to the memory of her husband.
Later about one in four began moving actively toward
remarriage.

The course of recovery was interrupted by a good deal of
retrograde movement. Periods of optimism and energy gave
way to periods of grief and despair. The first visit to relatives
living far away as a single woman unaccompanied by
husband, or the return of the time of the year in which the
husband had died, might be enough to return the widow to
desolation. But gradually, as more of the widow's energy
was given to her current situation, she was less affected by
reminders of the past. By the end of the first year of
bereavement most widows felt that they were well on their
way to recovery, though still not their old selves. They had
more energy, could once again be spontaneous with others,
and felt more hopeful about the future. They were functioning again. There were now long stretches in which they felt
relatively free from grief—though, in many cases, not from
loneliness.

At this point most widows reflected proudly on how far
they had come. About two widows in three agreed with the

statement: "I feel more positive about the future than I would have thought possible a year ago." Mrs. L, for one, said:

> I never thought I could take what I have had to take. I thought I would fall apart. But I fought my way back. So maybe I'm stronger than I ever realized. I always leaned on Phil. I always felt that I leaned on him. But now I've got to stand on my own two feet. I just never thought I could do it, but I have. I found out I was a bit stronger than I thought I was.

Three themes repeatedly appear in many of the widows' accounts of their recoveries: keeping themselves occupied, developing new skills, and returning to active social participation. Let us consider each more closely.

KEEPING ONESELF OCCUPIED. In the first weeks of bereavement widows often sought respite from their grief in distraction. They attempted to occupy their minds and hands with chores within the house, or, if none could be found, with busy work. Almost uniformly they felt that keeping busy was therapeutically valuable.[3]

There were a number of ways in which continued activity was beneficial, in addition to its usefulness as distraction. Widows found reassurance in continuing to function, despite their grief; staying active reduced their concern that they might succumb to the disorganization that they felt to be threatening to them. Friends and kin, as they recognized their determination not to let go, expressed approval, and this too increased the widows' self-respect and belief in their own capacity to recover.

In the first weeks after their bereavement many widows

---

[3] In the first interview, forty-three of the forty-nine widows thought that advising widows to keep busy was helpful to them. Only one widow thought it might be detrimental.

could not concentrate their attention or accomplish disciplined thought. Forty-four percent of the total sample reported major failings in either concentration or memory. During this period some widows found it difficult to understand television programs. To give their attention to newspapers or books was beyond many of them. They could manage only the most routine and mechanical of activities. Eight weeks after bereavement their capacity to concentrate had in large part returned—only twenty-two percent reported difficulties in concentration or memory, and most were able to consider more demanding ways of keeping themselves occupied. Instead of busy work whose merit was that it made it possible to briefly forget, and which tired the women enough to bring on relaxation if not sleep, they began undertaking more meaningful tasks. A few began painting the interior of their home. A good many accepted part-time or full-time employment.

Movement from concern only with keeping occupied to concern with purpose was illustrated by a report made by Mrs. K. Just after her husband's loss she had thought of joining a sewing class as a way of getting out and keeping busy. A month later she changed her mind, saying:

> Why sew? I won't have time to if I have to go to work. So I decided to take something to give me more confidence if I go look for a job.

And so Mrs. K registered in night school to learn typing and office procedures.

This is not to say that work did not also function as a distraction. Indeed, as a distraction work appeared unmatched. It required a major segment of the widow's time, and it demanded her attention during that segment. Mrs. O, for example, two months after her bereavement, suggested how going to work might effectively fill the hours:

> I've just kept busy. I've gone back to work. And the rest of my time is all occupied—when I come home I have

housework to do and everything—so my time is really used up. I don't have much time for thinking. It helps. I found out that working and keeping busy helped a lot.

Work sustained the spirits of the relatively unskilled as well as of the professional and the manager. Mrs. S, a blue-collar worker, said:

I finally got off the tranquilizers the doctor gave me. I had to get off of them—they were worse than having your nerves because you depend on them too much. Every little thing that went wrong, I took one. But since I went back to work I feel a lot better since I haven't got time to think, because I'm working all day. If I was home I would go crazy, but since I've been working I'm feeling pretty good.

Work had a variety of values for widows. It assured them that others respected their ability to contribute. It provided them with an opportunity for productivity, accomplishment, and—not least important—independence. It integrated them into a social network, and made it possible for them to escape the house and the dulling and stressful monotony of child care. And last, it provided a setting in which they might form a new identity, distinct from their marital status. As an indication of their sense of work as a different milieu, widows felt it less appropriate to wear somber clothes to work during the first weeks of their bereavement than when meeting kin or friends.

DEVELOPMENT OF NEW SKILLS. All the widows in our sample, with the exception of a few whose husbands had been alcoholics or invalids for years, had depended on their husband for tasks that they felt were beyond their own capacities. The husband had been responsible for minor repairs in the home, for lawn and car care, and in many instances for management of family funds. Bereavement forced widows to assume responsibility for these tasks, and in many cases to learn the skills necessary to perform them. Although some widows made a practice of calling on a brother or a tradesman, most widows learned to do what was necessary themselves. They learned to change light fuses, to balance a checking account, to mow the lawn. Widows who had not known how to drive now took lessons, and virtually all of them learned to keep their car serviced and in repair.

Mrs. L was one of the widows who had not known how to drive. Now that she was alone, she felt that without that skill she would forever be dependent on others, and was determined not to let this happen. Just after her husband's death she said:

> I'm going to have to learn how to drive because I have the children. And after all, everybody has their own problems. People are going to be helpful for a while, then time passes and they're going to go along. They all have their own families. They have to live their own lives. I can't depend upon who's going to drive me here and who's going to drive me there.

A month later Mrs. L obtained a learner's permit, registered in a driving school, and was soon driving with confidence. Recalling her husband's skepticism of her ability, she wondered how he would have reacted:

> Even when I'm driving the car I say, "He must be laughing up there. Look at his wife driving a car, taking all his family out for a ride."

Many widows were at first uncertain about their ability to manage the new tasks. Nevertheless they were determined, because they saw no other way to independence. Once they had mastered one skill they knew they would be able to master others as need arose. Mrs. M, another widow who had not driven before her husband's death, said at the end of the first year of bereavement:

> Learning to drive was important for me. I thought it would be difficult when I started, but the first time I got in the car the instructor said, "Go ahead and drive," and I did. I didn't do too badly ... I didn't think I could drive, but I did. I passed the learner's permit and then passed the test ... When you have to do something, you do it.

With the sense of competence and independence that mastery of necessary tasks gave them, some widows began exploring activities that might earlier in their lives have seemed inappropriate or too difficult. One learned to ice-skate, several attended school, and several planned summer travel despite little experience of travel. Widows found their abilities and interests more extensive than they might have guessed, and though they were at first forced to learn new skills just to manage, they continued to develop their capacities far past the point of necessity.

THE RETURN TO SOCIAL PARTICIPATION. Our society seems to assign widows to a special and peripheral role, one that may elicit respect but that is essentially marginal.[4] This ascription of marginality must be unattractive to widows of any age, but to the young widows who constituted our sample it seemed strange, anomalous, simply wrong. They

[4] Lopata, on the basis of her study of older widows, noted that only sixteen percent of her sample agreed with the statement, "Women lose status when they become widows—they lose respect and consideration." Nevertheless she concluded on the basis of her interviews that "the general impression left by the interviews is that many widows consider the role of wife to have been a very important one and that they lack another major role upon which to focus their current personality." See Helena Z. Lopata, *Widowhood in an American City* (Cambridge, Mass.: Schenkman, 1973), p. 92.

disliked the implication that they had entered a form of early retirement—that although they might be protected, deferred to, and understood as entitled to special consideration, they had lost standing as full members of society. About a fourth of our sample said spontaneously and emphatically that they disliked being referred to as a widow. Because being a widow was so repugnant to them, a few of these women lied about their marital status. Mrs. S, for example, said:

> Being a widow is just something extraordinary. You don't belong. You're a widow, you know, as if you were a freak or something . . . I wear my wedding ring all the time. I don't tell people I'm a widow. Strangers, they say, "You're married?" And I say, "Sure." It's easier. You feel better that way.

Widows sometimes felt that widowhood was interpreted by others as a kind of handicap, like loss of a limb, and that its recognition embarrassed strangers and made them feel awkward. They might hide their status out of consideration for others. Mrs. D illustrated how being forced to admit that one had lost one's husband could make others feel they had blundered into a sensitive area.

> I think the hardest thing is when someone says, "Well, why can't your husband do such and such a thing?" And then you have to say, "Well, I don't have a husband." And then, of course, they're ready to crawl under the table. Like I bought a new bedroom set and when they brought it in—I had him bring it into my room—the guy said, "Why don't you have your husband do this?" I said, "My husband died." And they felt bad.

This is not to say that there is no secondary gain in widowhood. The status effectively supports dependency claims. Widows in our sample sometimes seemed to feel a special claim on the help of parents, siblings, older children,

friends, even our interviewers. Nor were fantasies of martyr-
dom entirely missing among our sample. Some widows
described their suffering and struggle in terms that might be
called heroic. But taken all together, these gratifications of
widowhood had only fleeting appeal; for the most part the
role of widow was uncomfortable and uncongenial.

It was almost impossible for widows to avoid having their
personalities and behavior affected by what they thought
others expected of them. For the first few weeks of bereavement they chose clothing and entered activities with some
attention to what others might think appropriate. Even later
they were concerned lest failure to mourn appropriately be
interpreted as absence of love for their husband or of loyalty
to his memory. Some widows questioned the extent to
which they were expressing genuine feelings in their behavior rather than responses to the expectations of others. If
they became more quiet and withdrawn than they once had
been, they were concerned that they were simply conform-
ing to expectations, and if they behaved as they always had,
they were concerned that they might be only rebelling
against what they felt to be demands for change.

Despite these complex difficulties most widows began
fairly early in their bereavement to reestablish social link-
ages. They attended gatherings of old friends, and somewhat more hesitantly invited others to their own home. They
joined choral groups, sewing groups, and bowling clubs.
Many, as we have noted, worked and participated in the
social networks their jobs provided.

By the end of the first year of bereavement, most widows
had returned to fairly active social participation. Seventy-
eight percent of the sample reported that they saw friends or
kin on many occasions. Forty percent attended parties at
least now and then. Some widows reported that some of the
friendships they had made when they were married now
were fading. But other social networks seemed available and
few widows had succumbed to social isolation.

MEETING SOMEONE NEW. Our society maintains inconsistent expectations regarding appropriate mourning behavior of widows. Widows are at the same time expected to
display loyalty to their dead husband by single-minded
mourning and to deal realistically with their loss by beginning to build a new life. By the second month of bereavement many widows in our sample had experienced these
contrary expectations. While some friends seemed to expect
them to withdraw from active social participation, others
more or less tactfully suggested that they make themselves
available for dating or plan eventually to remarry.

The same inconsistent expectations seem to exist in
relation to widows' accessibility to new relationships. Even
in the first months of a widow's bereavement she might be
encouraged to recognize that she had many years yet to live
and might remarry. Yet if the widow were to adopt this as
her own view she might well be censured for displaying too
little grief for her loss.

Widows invariably found early suggestions that they
consider remarriage unpleasant and even jarring. When
asked by our interviewers two months after bereavement
whether they expected to remarry, only eight of the forty-
nine widows said that they hoped that they might. About
half the remainder rejected the suggestion, saying that they
did not expect to remarry. The other half said that they could
not know. The question itself appeared to be unwelcome.

At this early stage of bereavement widows who were
reentering the social world were concerned that they might
be censured for frivolousness. Some felt required to defend
innocent sociability as therapeutically necessary. Mrs. F, for
example, noted that she might be criticized for having gone
to a party, but defended her attendance in these words:

> Going to that party, I'm afraid people were saying,
> "Gee, her going to a party only after seven weeks. He's
> only been dead seven weeks." But I felt relieved when
> I went that night. When I came home I felt awfully

good. I had a good night's sleep. Usually I wake up
every two or three hours, but I had a good night's sleep.
I don't think it was the drink I had. It was just that I
had a good time.

Willingness to accept male companionship developed
gradually over the year. By the end of the first year, nine
widows of the forty-nine had entered into a fairly serious
relationship with another man and five widows dated
occasionally. Of the remainder, some might have accepted
an invitation from a man, though perhaps with ambivalence.
Many, however, continued to define themselves as inaccessible to new relationships.

Continued loyalty to the dead husband was not the only
impediment to forming a new relationship. Several widows
were concerned that remarriage might burden their children
with an unsympathetic stepfather. Others felt that because
of their age or their children they would be unattractive to
men, and did not want to expose themselves to rejection.
Some were afraid they might experience another loss. But at
the end of the first year of bereavement continued loyalty to
the husband remained the most prominent reason for
reluctance to consider new relationships.

Mrs. M was one of the widows who became fairly active
socially but avoided serious involvement with men. She was
suspicious of the men who seemed interested in her, and
perhaps uncertain regarding her own vulnerability. But
most important, she could not conceive of replacing her
husband with someone new. She said:

> As long as my husband is not around I guess I'll always
> feel lonely. I don't think there is anybody that can take
> his place. I'll just have to live with it . . . I could never
> think of anybody to put in his place . . .
>
> Going out helps me a lot. It helps me forget. They are
> mostly parties, because I really haven't gone out on any
> dates that I could call them dates. When I go to parties I
> meet some of the men. They sit down and they ask me

to dance or buy me a drink or something. But that's all. That's enough for me.

Early in bereavement more than half our sample said that although they constantly and painfully missed their husbands, they did not especially miss the sexual aspect of the relationship. They suggested that their despair and grief had suppressed all sexual desire. Many widows continued to define themselves as uninterested in a sexual relationship even after they had in other ways returned to normal functioning. Perhaps this was in part an attempt to present to the interviewer what they felt to be an acceptable image, but there was every indication that for the most part they truly felt themselves to be without sexual desire.

Some widows may have projected suppressed sexual interest onto the men they met. Certainly widows who continued to report their own absence of interest in a new relationship sometimes pictured men as motivated primarily by predatory sexuality.[5] One said:

> I think they know you're a widow and a lot of them might want to take you out just for sex. They feel, well, "Gee, I've got a lonely widow and, you know, maybe I can help her or something." And that's all that is on their minds. A couple of fellows I've been introduced to have said, "You're a widow, so you go to bed." So I said, "I'm sorry. I'm not going out with you if you just want to go out and have a good time." I'm not going to go out with someone just for sex.

Some of these widows may have found the projection of sexual desire useful as a way of dealing with a painful dilemma. While they felt intensely the need for a male figure

[5]Lopata reports that low-income widows and especially those who are black are disproportionately more likely to agree that "Widows are constantly sexually propositioned, even by the husbands of their friends." It may be that in low-income circumstances men who are helpful are more likely to make sexual overtures. But it also may be that those widows who have fewest resources are the most threatened by the possibility of loss of respectability. See Lopata, *op. cit.*, pp. 85, 202, 203.

in their lives, they rejected the idea of sexual relations outside of marriage, and at least for the time being rejected the idea of remarriage.

Of those widows who did form sexual ties, a few felt guilty about the new involvement. Others found a way of making their continued commitment to their dead husband consistent with their new commitment to another man. Their husband would have wanted them to go on living, they might say; or, perhaps, the new man was somehow very much like the husband and so in a way recreated him, or was very unlike the husband and so did not compete with him. What is remarkable is not so much the form their justifications took as the invariable need for justifications.

A CASE STUDY OF RECOVERY. Many of the themes identified earlier in this chapter are illustrated by the experiences of Mrs. I. Mrs. I and her husband were both thirty when they married, and were both schoolteachers. After their marriage Mrs. I's husband resumed graduate work and, two difficult years later, earned an advanced degree that shortly brought him a good job with a promising future. After about a year in the new job it was discovered that he had cancer. Mrs. I's husband attempted to help her to accept his coming death. Later Mrs. I said that his courage had helped greatly. The husband's death came little more than two years after the first diagnosis.

Mrs. I's first reaction was to feel, in her words, "numb, blank, empty." Her husband was constantly in her mind. At night she slept fitfully. The ceremonials of wake and funeral almost shattered her, but somehow she managed to get through them. Because she and her husband had no children she felt totally bereft.

Eight weeks later, she had emerged from her initial shock. She was still depressed and had some difficulty concentrat-

ing, but was able now to focus on reading, which she had
not been able to do before. She now looked for ways to fill
her time. She registered for an evening course at a nearby
university and planned a summer trip to Europe. She
described her state of mind this way:

> I think I'm being realistic—I've accepted the fact that
> my husband is dead. I think what has helped me more
> than anything is to know that I made my husband very
> happy and that we had five very happy years together
> . . . Some nights I can't get to sleep right away, but I do
> sleep alright, and I make myself eat . . . I think I could
> concentrate on things now. I don't think I could have a
> month or so ago, but I could not, probably. I still feel
> nervous, but perhaps not to quite such a great extent.
> It's not as bad as it was.

Mrs. I forced herself to take over those tasks that had been
her husband's. Because she lived in an apartment and had
no children she may have had fewer new skills to learn than
most widows. But she did have to learn how to take care of
the car.

> I never knew you did anything but drive a car. Now I'm
> more conscious about it. I've run out of gas several
> times and I've forgotten to have it oiled. I have to
> remember to do these things. When my husband was
> alive he'd do these things. He'd say, "Well, it's time to
> get the car oiled. You'd better bring it down and I'll
> pick it up." He'd take care of the car all of the time and
> it was just one of the many things that I didn't think of,
> but I do now.

Mrs. I's work sustained her morale. After her husband's
death she took a week's leave and then, after the funeral,
returned to her class. She said:

> I like the people I'm with and I enjoy contact with the
> kids and they kind of keep me going. I don't know what

> I'd do without going to work because it keeps my mind occupied. I think I'd probably go out of my mind if I weren't working. I'd be thinking about my husband's death all the time. I think my job is a lifesaver.

A year later Mrs. I was still occasionally depressed, but she kept herself busy and tried not to think too much. She appeared to others and occasionally to herself to have returned to normal.

> I think I'm feeling more like myself than I have during the year. Time does help . . . I'm not numb any more. I'm more realistic . . . my family said to me, "You seem like yourself again. You don't seem as preoccupied as you did." . . . I try very hard not to sit around feeling sorry for myself. I realize that life is worth living, that everything isn't over . . . I notice I'm happier than I was. I'm more cheerful. People tell me—I don't remember—that I was terribly quiet all last winter. I wasn't as bouncy as I usually am. I would sit with people and just not say anything. I don't remember being like that, but people tell me I was off in a world by myself.

Mrs. I recognized that she now was less often gripped by depression, but she felt that sorrow was nevertheless always near the surface. She felt time would help but would never cure; her loss was a permanent part of her experience.

> I don't think you ever get over it. I think time takes care of lots of things, probably, and I imagine as time goes by it won't be quite so painful. But I don't think you ever do really get over it. I don't think you will ever be like you were before . . . I don't think I'll ever be like I was before.

Four years after her husband's death, Mrs. I told us that beginning about two years earlier, one year after the comment quoted above and two years after her husband's death, she had begun dating. She had briefly dated two men, both widowers, before meeting a third widower whom she liked immediately. She said about him:

> He's very much like my first husband in many ways, which is very strange. He has the same kind of personality. And he looks like him. He's very bright and kind and considerate. It's very strange in many ways. Because he is so much like my husband was.

When we talked with her she and the man were planning to marry. They spent much of their free time together. They had already begun looking for a house. Nevertheless Mrs. I said she thought about her first husband every day and assumed that she always would.

> I don't know what makes me think about him. I pray for him all of the time and I suppose that's what makes me think of him. Even though I don't think he really needs it ... and just through the course of the day things will happen that might make me think of him. Or, you know, I'll look at his picture or something like that.

Mrs. I was able to reconcile her forthcoming marriage with her continuing commitment to her first husband by assuming that her first husband would have approved. She said:

> I think he'd be very pleased because he talked about it before he died. It was very difficult for me, but he used to joke about it and tease me.

Because of the new man in her life, Mrs. I was no longer lonely. In other ways too, she would seem to have recovered completely from her loss. Yet her loss had changed her. Her personality was different—she was more independent and somewhat less outgoing. But more than this, the memory of her husband and of his death was never far from her thoughts. Even though she was about to remarry, her first marriage continued to be part of her life.

12

PATTERNS OF RECOVERY

By the end of the first year of bereavement most widows reported that their energy levels had returned to about what they had been before their husband's death. Some widows, whose grief had earlier caused them to appear drawn or stressed, were being told that they once again looked their old selves. Some were dating. One was engaged to be married.

Not all widows were doing well, however. Twenty-eight percent agreed at the end of the first year with the statement, "I would not care if I died tomorrow." A few reported that their grief had continued unabated and was as intense at the end of the year as it had been at the beginning. And still other widows, though they claimed partial recovery, seemed compelled to dissipate in frenetic activity feelings that might otherwise have been expressed as fear or anxiety or

intense sorrow. Three widows seemed to be using alcohol as
a device to fend off distress. Two of them seemed well on
their way to becoming alcoholics at the time of the follow-
up interview.

THE FOLLOW-UP. To obtain our original sample of widows, we had contacted over a period of two years all women
in the appropriate age categories whose husbands had just
died. We had our thirteen-month interview with the last
widow we interviewed about two years after the thirteen-
month interview with the first widow we interviewed. A
year after our last regularly scheduled interview we
obtained funds to conduct follow-up interviews with the
proviso that we complete them within six months. These
follow-up interviews were therefore conducted anywhere
from two years to four years after the husband's death.

We were able to reach forty-three of the forty-nine widows
who participated in our study. The sample with whom
follow-up interviews were held included sixteen women
whose husbands had died four years previously, seventeen
whose husbands had died three years previously, and ten
whose husbands had died only two years previously.

One of the six widows with whom we did not have a
follow-up interview had herself died just after the first year
of her bereavement—of cancer, the same disease that had
killed her husband. We were unable to locate the five others.
They had included one who had apparently been doing very
well at the end of the first year of her bereavement, partly as
a result of the contribution of her warm and protective
family; two who had presented a more mixed picture; and
two who had seemed to be doing poorly. Of the last two, one
had been disturbingly withdrawn and depressed at the end
of the year. The other, a woman who had been hospitalized
for mental illness earlier in her life, had seemed at the end of

her first year of bereavement again to be moving toward severe disorganization.

In the sections that follow we describe the patterns of life organization widows had established at the time of our follow-up interview. With these patterns in mind, it was also possible to decide the direction being taken by each of the widows who did not give us follow-up interviews: that is, to decide the kind of life these women seemed to be in process of developing. We can therefore report what proportions of our total sample were moving to or had firmly established one or another pattern of life.

The pattern of life widows eventually established was closely related to whether or not they had been able to anticipate the death of their husband. We will discuss this issue at length later in this chapter.

ALTERNATE DIRECTIONS IN LIFE ORGANIZATION. The widows in our sample reorganized their lives along one of two fundamentally different lines. The first of these was toward remarriage and integration into the community based on being a wife. The second was away from remarriage, toward the establishment of a life in which remarriage was seen as undesirable or impossible.

This second direction, away from remarriage, resulted in three patterns of reorganization, not always clearly distinct one from another. The first was reorganization of life about an intimate nonmarital relationship with a man in which the woman's social independence was understood as permanent. It involved no anticipation of marriage, nor did the woman define herself as a quasi-wife with wifely responsibilities. The second was reorganization of life about a close relationship with one or more kin, ordinarily a sister or the widow's mother, although in a case encountered in another study a widow took as the central supportive relationship in her life a tie to a brother. The third pattern among those assuming permanent widow status was one of virtual independence from close relationships with other adults. Some women who adopted this pattern were extremely close to their older children, but others seemed relatively isolated. All told, we can discern four patterns of life reorganization. (1) The reestablishment of a marital relationship and a return to the married pattern of life. (2) The establishment as a central commitment of a nonmarital relationship with a man. (3) The organization of life around close supportive relationships with kin. (4) The establishment of a life independent of any very close relationships except, possibly, with the widow's own children. (5) In addition some widows were unable to establish a satisfactory life organization, nor were they moving in that direction. Their lives appeared chaotic, and seemed likely to continue so.

Forty-seven of the forty-nine widows in the study could be associated with one or another of these five patterns. The two remaining widows themselves became cancer victims; one, as we have noted, succumbed after one year of bereavement; the other, when we talked with her in the follow-up, believed herself to have entered upon a terminal course, and had resigned herself to dying.

The patterns of recovery that seemed to have been adopted by the remaining forty-seven widows are described below. The frequencies we give for these patterns are based on reports made two to four years after bereavement. In the few cases without follow-up the assessments are based on reports made at the end of the first year. Since our sample underrepresented widows whose husbands died without forewarning, it may also underrepresent widows who were less likely than others to move toward remarriage.

MOVEMENT TOWARD REMARRIAGE. At the time of follow-up fourteen widows had either remarried, were engaged to remarry, or were moving toward remarriage in the sense of dating actively with the intent of finding someone to marry.

Four of the fourteen had already remarried at the time of follow-up: three had remarried about three years after their husband's deaths; the fourth had become engaged before the first anniversary of her husband's death and had remarried not long after. An additional five widows reported definite plans to remarry within a few months. Three of them had been bereaved for four years at the time of their engagement, one had been bereaved for three years, and one for two years.

Five widows appeared to be moving actively toward remarriage although they had not yet become engaged. All were dating. Two of them were currently going with someone with whom they hoped marriage might eventually prove possible. The three others said that they would like to remarry if they could find the right man. Of this group, three were three years beyond their bereavement, and one was only two years beyond her bereavement at the time of follow-up. We did not have a follow-up with the fifth.

It would appear that widows who move toward remarriage begin dating about a year after losing their husband. A few in our sample began dating earlier, although none dated earlier than six months after the husband's loss. A few used Parents Without Partners as a transitional experience to help them return to life as unmarried women, and met men whom they dated within that organization. Most of these widows had reported by the end of the first year of bereavement that they hoped to remarry.

It is noteworthy that by the time of the follow-up, of the fourteen women who appeared to us to have directed themselves toward remarriage, four had already remarried, five were engaged, and two had serious relationships that might lead to marriage. Only three still were looking. It would seem that most of those widows in our sample—which, of course, was limited to widows no more than forty-

five years old—who definitely wanted remarriage were able
to achieve it.

The widow who remarried after her first husband had
been dead only a year was Mrs. G, whose experience of loss
was described in Chapter Three. She met the man she later
married only five months after her husband's death, and
began seeing him on a romantic basis not long after. Perhaps
because of the long period in which she anticipated her
husband's death, Mrs. G. had already moved rather rapidly
toward recovery from her initial deep grief. She had
returned to social participation in the fourth month after her
husband's death:

> The first three months was really a very lonely, lost
> period. I wasn't going out, I wasn't doing anything.
> Which wasn't good. Then in the fourth month I started
> to go back bowling.

Married friends then had invited Mrs. G to accompany them
to a movie or to come to a party, but Mrs. G had had the
usual experience of feeling marginal when with them:

> I had been asked to go out twice with my girl friends
> and their husbands. But I felt very much alone, not a
> part of this group at all, and I didn't enjoy it. Because
> people that I was friendly with were all married, so
> there weren't girls that you could go out with. I just
> found myself very much on my own, very much
> alone ...

Mrs. G also had the usual experience of friends, after having
rallied around, returning to their own lives and their own
concerns:

> I found that people weren't helpful at all really.
> Everyone had their own life and that was it. Everyone
> went their own way. I would have liked it if people
> were more helpful or had a little more time for me.

Mrs. G became a close friend to her next door neighbor who was also a widow. The neighbor was engaged to be married, and also knew a widower who might be suitable for Mrs. G:

> About five months after my husband died the girl next door—who is also a widow, she's engaged to be married—called me up one evening. Her girl friend had died just after Easter. She said, "I'd like you to come over for coffee." I said, "Well, all right." . . .
>
> I went over and her girl friend's husband was visiting. I had met the girl friend once or twice, but I had never met him. She said, "I'd like you to meet him." Well, then I felt very funny, really, because I realized she deliberately had me come over to meet him.
>
> We had a nice evening and then a few weeks later he called her up to ask if she thought I would go out. She said, "Well, I really don't know. Why don't you call her and ask her?" So as it worked out we did go out with the girl next door and her boyfriend, the four of us, and we had a very nice evening.

Mrs. G and the widower began seeing each other regularly. In talking about what was good in this new relationship, Mrs. G inevitably compared it with her marriage, identifying similarities and drawing contrasts.

> Bryan [the new man] and I found out we had a lot in common. We have the same backgrounds, we are practically the same personality. Usually opposites attract, and in both cases in our first marriages we married people completely opposite from ourselves . . .
>
> Bryan is a very outgoing person and he has a marvelous personality and he enjoys people so much. His wife, like my husband, did not enjoy a lot of people . . . We're both the same age and we both graduated the same year from school. Jack [husband] was seven years older than

> I was. He'd been in and out of the services and when I
> met him I was only seventeen, and he always treated
> me like I was a child . . .

> I feel very close to Bryan. He can—well, it's something
> you really can't explain. If you have not had a good,
> close, relationship the first time, I think you look for
> this the second time. I am much closer to Bryan than I
> ever was with Jack.

Because Mrs. G met Bryan so soon after her loss of her
husband, it was extraordinarily difficult for her to reconcile
her new commitment to him with the loyalty to her husband
that she continued to feel, despite her belief that her marital
relationship had not been close. Her conflict was not
lessened by the response of her mother to the news that she
planned to remarry: "What will people think of your getting
married so soon?" But her grandmother and also her first
husband's family reassured her. The reassurance of her in-
laws was important to her. Mrs. G undoubtedly would have
proceeded with remarriage in any event, but the support of
her husband's family helped allay her guilt. She said:

> Jack's brothers, they think Bryan is terrific. They are
> pleased. At first I didn't know what their reactions
> would be. I called them and told them that I was
> planning to be married and they said they thought it
> was wonderful.

Friends, too, were supportive:

> All of my friends have been pleased. One had a party
> for us. She invited all of my girl friends and their
> husbands, and it was a complete surprise to me. I
> didn't know anything about it. It was to meet Bryan
> before we got married, which was wonderful . . .

> All of my girl friends think it's wonderful. In fact they
> took me out to lunch just last week, about twelve of us.
> Rather than have a shower, which I didn't want, they

figured this way we could all get together. I know they
all think it's marvelous.

Despite the support of those close to her—her mother, to
an extent, excepted—Mrs. G was in some conflict because
she did in fact have commitments to two men: her dead
husband and her husband-to-be. She tried to sort out these
competing commitments in this way:

> Sometimes you say first love is the most important one
> or the one that will mean more to you. But I haven't
> found that to be so. I don't think you can ever recapture
> first love. But I have more in common with Bryan and
> he with me than both of us did in our first marriages.

Of very great importance to Mrs. G was her feeling that
she had her husband's permission to remarry. She felt she
did *not* have his permission to have her children adopted by
her second husband, and "would not go against his wishes."
It is doubtful that so soon after his death she would have
been able to go against his wishes in relation to remarriage if
she had felt he would have been opposed.

> I have the advantage of having been able to discuss
> these things with Jack when he had been sick for so
> long and he knew that he was eventually going to die
> from the disease he had. He said he would want me to
> remarry, for the children to be brought up in a normal
> family atmosphere with a mother and father. He said
> that he thought I was the type that needed to be
> married. We discussed this, plus the idea of our son
> changing his name and being adopted by someone. He
> definitely did not want this. He wanted his son to keep
> his own name. Bryan at first wanted to adopt the
> children and have them all have the same name, but of
> course I told him that Jack didn't want it and I would
> not go against his wishes on this.

Mrs. G, it may be noted, did not begin moving toward
remarriage until she met the man who would become her

second husband. She was still early in the course of her recovery when she was introduced to Bryan. But it seems likely, because of her husband's permission—almost commission—to remarry, as well as her own desires, that she would have moved toward remarriage in any event. The appearance of Bryan seems only to have hastened the process. Mrs. G seems to have needed remarriage to regain her balance and to have had few resistances to accepting it:

> Until I met Bryan I was terribly depressed, terrible crying spells, very short with the children. I shouldn't say I hadn't any thought for the future—you always have thought for the future—but you just take each day as it comes. No plans, nothing to really look forward to. Very depressed, terribly much so. After about two months I came out of it a little, but I just felt alone, terribly alone and lonely. It's a funny thing—you're in limbo almost, you are neither here nor there, you're in the middle. People still consider you married, yet your married friends don't invite you to go because they feel, well, you're by yourself . . .

> My sisters, my friends, even my mother, have said to me that since I met Bryan and during the past several months I am myself.

We interviewed Mrs. G again three years after her marriage. She said the marriage was wonderful. She noted, in passing, that she and her husband had each adopted the other's children. How she reconciled this with her first husband's wishes we do not know; perhaps after her remarriage her second husband's wishes took precedence.

Since many seem to assume that a widow's second husband is forever being compared, to his disadvantage, with an idealized first husband, it may be worth noting that this is not necessarily so. Mrs. G, like widows in general, did compare her second husband to her first, but in her case it was to the advantage of the second husband:

My whole life has changed. I'm much happier. I have a
much happier marriage. I've become more easygoing. I
probably don't notice it as much in myself but so many
people say to me that I've changed, they can see it more
than I can. I'm more relaxed. I'm not as tense as I
always have been. Jack had a very domineering personality and I was constantly on guard that everything
would go smoothly. Everything had to be just so and
just right. Then everything would be fine and the
children wouldn't annoy him. My whole way was so
that he wouldn't get upset about anything. But Bryan's
the type that he's very easgygoing and he's made me
that way. If things don't get done, if everything isn't
just right, well, it'll be better tomorrow.

ADOPTION OF THE WIDOW ROLE. The patterns of life organization described below are variants of the major pattern
in which widowhood is treated not as a transitional stage
between marriages, but as a potentially permanent status.
We identify three variations of this pattern: relative independence of other adults, dependence on kin, and involvement in a non-marital fashion with a man. The variations shade into one another, however; many of the women
we consider independent nevertheless maintain relationships of varying degrees of closeness with kin or with
men, although they do not organize their lives around
these relationships.

*Relatively Independent of Close Relationships with Other
Adults.* Seventeen widows had organized lives relatively
independent of close relationships with other adults and
seemed likely to maintain this pattern. We should emphasize
the word *relative* when we refer to their independence; most
in fact did maintain some fairly close relationships. Eight
of the seventeen were keeping company with a man; one
had had an illegitimate child with her boyfriend. But all had

reasons of varying degrees of plausibility for not contemplating marriage. More generally, all defined themselves as functioning on their own and resisted attempts by others to infringe on their autonomy.

It is interesting to consider the reasons given by widows for refusing to consider remarriage despite an intimate relationship. The widow who had the illegitimate child explained that she wouldn't marry the child's father because he might favor the new baby over her children by her first marriage. A second widow explained that she would not marry her boyfriend for fear she might die after remarrying and her children would then be stuck with a stepfather. Another simply maintained that a two-year intimate relationship with a man her children sometimes called Daddy "was nothing serious." Two confided that they would have been willing to marry a man they had been seeing for a year or so, and would in fact still be happy to marry him, were it not for the objections of their children; in one case an older child objected, and in the other case all three of the children objected. Their placid acceptance of their children's objections strongly suggested that they were themselves less than determined on remarriage. They may well have fostered the children's objections to provide themselves with a reason for avoiding remarriage. Widows who moved toward remarriage invariably managed to reconcile their children to the prospect; indeed, their children desired their remarriage.

Other widows who established autonomous life organizations were close to kin or friends rather than to a boyfriend, and a very few maintained a good many relationships, including a boyfriend and women friends as well as reliable kin ties. A few others seemed more nearly isolated except for close ties with older children.

Most of these autonomous widows appeared to be managing, some of them rather well. Many appeared to devote much or in some cases almost all their energies to their children. None seemed to be entirely happy—not nearly as happy as Mrs. G seemed in the follow-up, for example. Many of these widows, even some with close relationships with men, said that they were lonely. At least two chose to work some evenings to reduce their loneliness. Some, although not all, continued to pine for their husband two, three, and four years after his death.

To suggest the nature of these widows' lives, we give excerpts from follow-up interviews with two of them, one who had a boyfriend, though she disclaimed the seriousness of the relationship, and one who was more nearly alone, although her husband's brother was a permanent boarder in her home.

Mrs. P was the widow who, four years after her husband's death, had been going with someone for almost two years but nevertheless described the relationship as "nothing serious." She was thirty-five when her husband died of lung cancer rather soon after having recovered from a hernia operation. She was furious with his physician and with her husband himself for having treated lightly, at the time of the hernia operation, a shortness of breath that was in fact an early symptom of cancer. When the cancer was finally diagnosed, Mrs. P's husband had only a few months to live.

Mrs. P's sister moved in with her after her husband's death. At the end of her first year of bereavement, Mrs. P was dependent on her sister's help with the children, but there were conflicts, especially over what Mrs. P felt to be her sister's sloppiness. When we saw Mrs. P three years later the sister had left for her own apartment, much to Mrs. P's relief.

A year after her husband's death Mrs. P was working and making new friends, but wanted to withdraw from her former social circle. She cried when she was alone, was lonely, and felt unsafe and insecure. Nevertheless she was afraid of remarriage. Three years later Mrs. P had established a stable life relatively independent of other adults. She maintained a fairly close relationship with a younger sister—not the one who had lived with her—and occasionally saw her two other sisters. She had remained fairly close to her mother-in-law. But she guarded her independence:

> That's the kind of person I am: I don't like to be dependent on anyone. I don't like to feel I'm imposing . . .
>
> In the beginning, I felt if I started to impose on people and I got to depend on them, they'll get tired of me, and then where would I be? I mean, you can only ask for help for so long and then they feel, listen, you'd better get on your own two feet. And by this time you may be so used to them helping you, you can't help yourself. So I don't like to bother people.

Mrs. P had a number of girl friends, some of whom she had met through her job as cashier in a local restaurant, and in addition there was a man whom she described, with some diffidence, as the man she dated. At first, talking about this relationship, she minimized its importance, saying that she saw the man only once a week, perhaps even less often. But then it became evident that the man was more important in her life than this suggested. The children called him, not entirely jokingly, "Dad." Nevertheless Mrs. P insisted, "There's no big heavy romance." Here too she wanted to guard her independence. Asked how she would feel about remarriage, she said:

> I wouldn't like to get married again. Because I feel the responsibilities are great, and I feel they are my responsibilities. You might find a man that might want the responsibility of five children, but for him to come in and live in the home, there's always going to be some kind of friction. And I don't want to be between him and my children or side with my children against him.

Mrs. P's boyfriend had asked her to marry him. The children, too, wanted Mrs. P to remarry, and they very much liked Mrs. P's boyfriend. Still, Mrs. P found objections:

> He hasn't been married and I feel he doesn't really realize what it's like to live in a house with five kids! They *can* get on your nerves. I mean, this is how I feel.

Mrs. P offered still another objection that seemed to express her fundamental fear. The husband who had died had been her second husband. Her first husband had deserted her when the oldest children were very young. Now she was afraid of still another loss for the children and perhaps for herself.

> Then, I feel, to be sincere, why should they—my oldest —get themselves involved with a third father, and have something happen to him?

Mrs. P's boyfriend had met her sisters, and had attended with Mrs. P family ceremonies, such as a son's graduation. He gave her advice on management of her financial affairs, which she invariably followed. Mrs. P indicated, though not without ambiguity, that the two maintained a sexual relationship. Nevertheless she was determined not to remarry.

Mrs. P continued to feel linked to her dead husband. She visited her husband's grave about once a month. Asked why she went so often, she said:

> I can't explain it. I really think people go for their *own* satisfaction. I bring him flowers, because he loved flowers. But—I really don't think they *know* that you visit the grave. Or that you're going to get some special reward because you've been going. And I don't feel I go because I have to go. I go because I want to go.

Mrs. P also talked about her dead husband with her children:

We talk about him quite often. Not every day, but I
would say most days something will come up, like
"Daddy used to like that," or if you cook something,
"Do you remember Daddy liked this?"

Mrs. P was rarely happy. Four years after her husband's
death she continued to grieve for his loss and to feel bereft.
Her life, at times, seemed to her to be meaningless and she
had fleeting thoughts of rejoining her husband in death:

> There *are* some times you do feel is it really all worth
> the struggle, getting up every morning, going to work,
> coming home, same thing day in, day out. Who really
> appreciates it? Even if I did die, the kids would
> manage. As much as I would like to be here for the
> younger ones, they would manage. So you do feel—I
> don't know, I can't explain . . . You might say you just
> are feeling sorry for yourself. This is when I think you
> do most of your crying . . .
>
> I could be sitting in there and the kids out here, but
> sometimes you just can't come in with them because
> they're talking about *their* music and *their* friends. And
> you're pretty much by yourself. And a lot of times I ask
> myself if I were, you know, to die, well, this is how
> they would get along if I should die . . . I look around
> and I say, well, they really don't *need* me outside of
> financially, but if I die their money would still be
> coming, things would go along.

Three themes seem evident in Mrs. P's report: unwillingness to depend on others for fear she would then lose her
capacity for self-reliance; unwillingness to permit herself
again to be vulnerable to loss; and continued attachment,
despite the passage of years, to the husband. The result is
determination to go it alone, despite the deficits in her
chosen life, despite the urgings of all those around her, and
despite her own recognition that a different life, with less
loneliness and less despair, is available:

I would imagine if I got married I wouldn't be lonely.
But for me that's not the answer.

Let us turn now to a widow whose independent life had
no place in it for a boyfriend. Mrs. R was forty-three when
her husband died suddenly of coronary occlusion. He had
had no previous heart attacks; his death was entirely
unanticipated. The attack came while Mr. R was about to
replace a flat tire. He had apparently opened the trunk of his
car to get the jack out, and then feeling himself becoming
weak had sat down on the edge of the trunk floor. His body
was found still sitting in the trunk space, slumped against
the side. A neighbor rushed him to the hospital, where he
was pronounced dead on arrival.

For years the younger brother of Mrs. R's husband had
lived with them. He continued to live with Mrs. R and her
three children after the husband's death. But his relationship with Mrs. R became more uncomfortable and more
distant. When we talked with Mrs. R in our follow-up
interview three years after her husband's death, she said she
would be pleased if her brother-in-law would get married
and move away, but she saw little likelihood of his happening.

Mrs. R was fairly close to her sister and her sister's
husband, who owned a house in the country and the
preceding summer had rented a nearby house for Mrs. R.
The summer had been fun for the children, but only a
relocation of the same lonely life for Mrs. R. Mrs. R was by
no means socially isolated—she had girl friends, her mother
lived near to her, and she had joined a diet club. But despite
these social ties and a living situation that seemed stable and
manageable, Mrs. R was often despairing. The days just
before her menstrual period were likely to be especially
difficult.

I notice sometimes I tend to get blue like around the

time I get my friend ... Or sometimes I feel like, "Oh,
if I could just have a darned good fist fight with
somebody." Really and truly get angry with somebody
you didn't care about, and really give it to them
good ...

I used to have crying jags more than I do now. I'd go up
and I'd be doing something and all of a sudden—just
like when you get pregnant—all of a sudden doing the
dishes, water would pour out of my eyes ... And once
in a while, just before I get my friend, if the kids say
something to me ... I get blue.

Again, as in the case of Mrs. P, there was evidence of
continuing attachment to the dead husband. Mrs. R did not
think of him every day, but now and again she would be
startled by the feeling that he was about to return or by the
momentary belief that she had seen him.

Sometimes at night if I'm out looking for the kids at
supper time—he used to walk up from the square—I
think of that [that he might be about to return]. One
time I saw a guy coming up who looked so much like
him at a distance. When you saw him close it wasn't,
but it almost brought my heart into my mouth for a
minute, as if to say, "Oh, gee, he's coming back."

The only man in Mrs. R's life was the brother-in-law with
whom she lived but with whom she did not get along. To
some extent, at least, the absence of men seemed to be Mrs.
R's choice. She seemed to avoid contact with men to spare
herself the pain of recognition of her husband's absence.
Asked by the interviewer if she missed her husband sexually, she said:

Not as much now as I did. But if I went out, if I went
out dating or to a dance or something, I probably
would. But I don't—I more or less keep away from it.

Life Organized Around Non-marital Relationship with a man. Five of our widows appeared to have developed a stable life pattern organized around a nonmarital relationship with a man. Unlike the widows just described who had boyfriends, they did not protect their independence from the men in their lives. Indeed, their relationships with their boyfriends were central to the organization of their life. Nevertheless—and despite the birth, in two cases, of an illegitimate child—they were determined to avoid remarriage.

To suggest the quality of the relationship with the boyfriend that characterized these widows' lives we will report from the follow-up interview with Mrs. S. Mrs. S, a woman in her early forties, had been married for twenty years, a relationship she described as having been beautiful. Her husband had become ill with pneumonia, was hospitalized, and died five days later, without any warning that his illness was potentially fatal.

When we talked with Mrs. S four years after her husband's death she had become a member of a religious sect in which resurrection and eternal life were prominent concepts. She also had begun keeping company with a man who was not as devoted to her church as she. The relationship was central to her life, though. This is how she described it:

> We go together all the time. Everywhere I go, he goes. Everywhere he goes, I go. Different places—church and dinner, something like that . . .
>
> Things I need, he'd do for me. Anything went wrong with my car he'd help me. He'd fix it, you know . . . He helped me around the house. If there was anything I'd need he'd help me with money. He'd lend it to me or give it to me—most anything.

But when asked what were her plans for the future so far

as this man was concerned, Mrs. S laughed and said, "Nothing."

> I'm not planning to get married no more. I don't want to. Don't misunderstand. Married is a beautiful life. But I want my husband. That was a beautiful life in the world to me; I wouldn't have had another life in the world. But I don't think I'd ever get another husband in the world like he was, and I don't want to mess my life up.

At this point Mrs. S was asked whether she didn't feel that her boyfriend would make a good husband. She hesitated, and then said:

> He'll make a good man, but I'll never replace my husband. I guess that's what I'm looking for. But I'll never get anyone to touch him.

Mrs. S was pressed further to explain why she wouldn't marry the man with whom she was so deeply involved. She said:

> My reason is just what I said. I really won't ever find a husband like he was. I have my own ways and I don't want to be buckled under no one any more . . . I don't want no one telling me when to go to church and when not to. He's not as religious as I am, and I want to go to church when I want to go and I don't want nobody telling me don't go to church, because that's my whole life . . .

Mrs. S suggested that her dead husband had spoiled her for other men, and also that she was unwilling again to have to accept the restrictions of marriage. But in addition, the sudden unexpected loss of her husband may well have left her unwilling again to become vulnerable to loss.

Establishing a Life Pattern Around Relationships with Kin. Five widows had in some measure organized their lives around a relationship with a mother, sister, or group of close family members.

Mrs. T was in her early thirties. Her husband, who had been a chronic alcoholic unable to maintain a regular job, died unexpectedly of cirrhosis a few hours after a sudden collapse.

Even while her husband was living, Mrs. T had been unusually close to her mother and two sisters, all of whom lived in the apartment below hers. She also had been close to her only child, a girl. The bonds to her mother and to her daughter, then twelve, were still extremely close when we talked with Mrs. T four years after her husband's death. When Mrs. T was upset, she would call on her mother for help. And sometimes when she was lonely she shared her daughter's bed. To suggest the quality of Mrs. T's relationship with her mother, the following response to a question about how she managed her depressed moods is revealing.

> I just start yelling and complaining loud enough to anyone that will listen to me. It's usually my family downstairs. Then I get over it. After I yell and scream and holler for a few minutes, my mother will say, "Well, gee, what can you do? These things just happen." And that's what I mean by her giving moral support. She's right there to encourage you. "Things will be better," you know. And then she'll find ways to help solve my problems. I was in a car accident, not a serious one . . . The car was parked in front of the house and one morning I come out and the side of the door was all scratched. And those things just infuriate me. She'll call a brother-in-law of mine, "What do you think Donna should do? She was in a car accident."

> I'm just so worried everything is going to be alright with her. She was very sick last summer. She had lost a lot of weight and we were back and forth to the hospital almost every day for treatments—radiation treatments. At times the doctor would say that there wasn't too much hope for her. But now she's come a long way.

She's doing very well and the treatments have been successful . . .

But I feel unsure about my future. I don't know whether I'm going to be spending it by myself or what.

Mrs. T's report suggests one of the risks for widows in a life organization built around a continuing relationship with their mothers. When the mothers become ill and die, as is likely to occur in the widow's middle age, the widows are left alone.

Mrs. T was twice invited on dates by girl friends who had arranged with their boyfriends to bring along an extra man. She rather enjoyed these evenings, but had no further interest in the men she met. Asked if she would like to go out on dates in the future, she said she would, but only as a member of a foursome.

FAILURE TO RECOVER AS INDICATED BY CHAOTIC LIFE ORGANIZATION. Six widows were categorized as having failed to move toward reorganization of a stable life pattern. Of these, four were seen in a follow-up interview, two of them three years after their husband's death, and two only two years after their husbands' deaths. Although it is possible that one or more of these widows eventually moved toward stable recovery, in our last contact with them they had not.

Only one of the widows in this group had anticipated her husband's death. This widow had been hospitalized for depression during her marriage. She displayed an unusually high level of guilt after her husband's death.

Indication that things were not going well seemed to be present in this group by the second interview. At that time, six to eight weeks after the husband's death, most widows in the sample had begun to show the first signs of recovery. Three of the widows in this group felt as bad or even worse at this point than they had at first. The other three, however, displayed an inappropriate absence of mourning. One went to a party three weeks after the funeral and had a "gay time." A second was entirely controlled and realistic about her husband's death but gradually increased her intake of alcohol. By the end of the first year of her bereavement she suffered both from depression and incipient alcoholism. By the time of follow-up two years later, the depression had receded, but the alcoholism seemed well advanced. The third widow also moved toward alcoholism and, indeed, later lost her children for fourteen months on a charge of neglect.

In what follows we describe briefly the experiences of the four widows in this group for whom we have follow-up interviews.

Two of these displayed severe personality disorganization. The first was a woman of about forty-five, one of the two who became alcoholic. She had been hospitalized for depression before her marriage and possibly during it as well. The marriage, however, appeared to be mostly happy and sustaining. After her husband's death the widow began to fear a return to hospitalization. By the end of the first year of her bereavement her fears had been realized and she was an in-patient in a mental hospital, diagnosed as schizophrenic. Her explanation was that she had been brooding on her husband's death, had begun drinking to forget, and then lost her bearings.

Three years after her husband's death this widow continued to dream of him. Asked whether she awoke after dreaming of her husband, she said that she did, and added that she then tried to return to sleep so that she could again dream of him. She believed that her husband watched over her, and felt she could almost see him. She continued to be obsessed by the reason for the death. In fact, the diabetic coma that had led to death had been produced by overconsumption of alcohol. The widow sometimes blamed herself for not having somehow obtained a doctor who might have given her husband insulin in time to save him. The second of the widows who displayed severe personality disorganization was a woman in her late twenties whose husband had been killed in an automobile accident. This widow and her husband had maintained a most unstable married life, with many separations. Her husband's loss was nevertheless intensely traumatic. But within a few months, still grieving over her husband's loss, she became involved with another man and by the end of the first year told us that she was engaged to marry him, though it appeared that the engagement was in good part fantasy. She also told us that she disliked the man. When we saw her two years later there had been no marriage, and the man had disappeared. The widow had been chronically depressed for over a year and had attempted suicide several times.

It is difficult to say what was most important among the contributing factors in these widows' unhappy outcomes. The preexistent instability undoubtedly played a role. The unanticipated deaths of their husbands might then have introduced immense emotional stress while removing the important stabilizing figure.

A third widow in this group, the one who had anticipated her husband's death, was in her late thirties, of Catholic background. She had been married for many years, and hers too had been a stormy marriage. At one point in it she had been hospitalized for depression and had had a course of shock treatment. She was the widow, referred to earlier, who had been involved with another man during her husband's hospitalization.

This widow, in our follow-up interview two years after her husband's death, was riddled with guilt regarding her husband and his death. Her affect in early interviews had seemed inappropriate, with deep grief alternating with a kind of indifference and even humor regarding her loss. When seen in the follow-up interview, she was hardly managing at all. The interviewer reported that when she called on the widow the house was a total mess, unmade beds were visible in the bedrooms, dishes were on all flat surfaces, and everything was in disarray. A sister lived upstairs and sometimes helped. The widow was seeing a psychiatrist, but for the time being seemed totally unable to function.

The fourth for whom we have a follow-up was the widow who had become alcoholic or nearly so. She was a woman in her late twenties whose husband had died of a heart attack after having had a single mild earlier attack. This widow reported that she began drinking after her husband's loss in order to get to sleep. About four months after her husband died she began drinking heavily, days as well as evenings. When interviewed at the end of the first year, she said that her drinking had dropped off, partly in response to the urgings of a boyfriend she then saw regularly. When we saw her two years later, however, she told us that she had been hospitalized for alcoholism for several months in the preceding year and had had her children taken from her on grounds of neglect. She now again had her children, but only on probation.

ANTICIPATION AND SUBSEQUENT LIFE ORGANIZATION. Of our forty-nine widows, twenty-one anticipated their husband's death, twenty-two did not, and we cannot be certain of six. In the first category we put those who were entirely aware that their husbands were on a terminal course, whether or not they had any sense of when his death might be expected. In the category of those who did not anticipate the husband's death, we put those whose husbands were killed in an accident, whose husbands died of heart attacks when there had been no reason to consider them ill, or whose husbands died of illnesses initially understood as not fatal. In the category of uncertain anticipation we put those who could have anticipated the husband's death on the basis of the information available to them, but who denied in the interview with us that they had recognized that the husband was on a terminal course. In this group we include four widows whose husbands had suffered one or more heart attacks before being stricken fatally and one widow whose alcoholic husband had been told that if he continued to drink he would die.

The new life organizations constructed by widows or in process of being constructed by them corresponded remarkably well to whether or not they had anticipated the death (see Table Two). Among those who had anticipated their husband's death, and setting to one side the widow who was herself overtaken by fatal illness, sixty-five percent—thirteen of twenty—moved toward remarriage as the direction of their recovery. Of the remainder, six moved toward

TABLE TWO.   ANTICIPATION AND SUBSEQUENT LIFE ORGANIZATION

	Anticipated Husband's Death	Did Not Anticipate Husband's Death	Uncertain
Moved toward remarriage	13 (65%)	0 (0%)	1
Moved in other direction toward reorganization	6 (30%)	17 (77%)	4
Failure to move toward reorganization	1 (5%)	5 (23%)	0
	20	22	5
Incurred fatal or potentially fatal illness	1	0	1
	21	22	6

Total sample = 49

reorganization of their lives on bases other than remarriage and only one was among those whose lives continued to be unstable. Of those who did not anticipate the death, *none* moved toward remarriage, seventeen (seventy-five percent) moved toward some other basis for reorganization of their lives, and five (twenty-three percent) failed to move toward a stable reorganization of their lives.

Finally, of the five widows for whom anticipation was uncertain, setting aside the widow who incurred a potentially fatal illness herself, only one moved toward remarriage, while the remaining four moved toward some other basis for reorganization of their lives.

Evidently the possibility of anticipating the husband's death is of extraordinary importance in determining the direction taken in recovery. As we shall point out in another report from this study, anticipation of the husband's death is one of the most important determinants of the *adequacy* of recovery. Here we see that it is an extremely important determinant of the *nature* of recovery.

Why should this be so? What is it about anticipation that could account for this finding? We should first note that it does not seem to be the case, or at least not only the case, that anticipating the husband's death permits the widow to begin her grief earlier. That is, it does not seem to be the case that the same process of recovery took place but was begun earlier where the death was anticipated. Evidence against the occurrence of this sort of "anticipatory grief" was reviewed earlier.

Nor does it seem an adequate explanation that where the husband's death was anticipated it was possible for the widow to free herself from her commitment to him, while otherwise the widow was eternally tied to her vows. This idea has some support in that it seemed to facilitate acceptance of remarriage if widows felt that their husband would have approved. But all widows continued to feel loyal to their first husband, and those who remarried had first to reconcile the remarriage with their obligations to their first husband. Nor did those who did not anticipate their first husband's death show greater loyalty to them by a greater aversion to new sexual relationships. On the contrary, most of the widows whose husbands had died without forewarning, like most other widows, established new sexual relationships of some importance, and some organized their lives around these relationships.

The one critical difference among widows was that those who did not anticipate their husband's death did not move toward remarriage. Indeed, they rejected the idea of remarriage even when pressed to remarry by a boyfriend, by their children, or by their immediate kin, even in two cases when they had a child with the boyfriend. Why should this have been so?

A frequent comment among those who did not anticipate the death was that they did not want again to risk unanticipated loss or to place their children in a situation where they too must risk another such loss. We are led to think of survivors of unanticipated disaster, of hurricanes or floods or fires, who cannot again enter the situations they associate with catastrophe. These widows whose husbands died without warning are like survivors of a fire who forever after are uncertain in a house at night, or like survivors of an automobile crash who can never again enter a car with equanimity. They have become phobic toward marriage.

If this interpretation of our finding is correct, it would appear that the process of recovery from anticipated death is different from the process of recovery from unanticipated death. In the anticipated death, there has been a period preceding the death during which the wife and husband have together gradually given up hope as they were progressively failed by therapies and regimes. The death, when it came, was traumatic, but its cause was understood. But when the death happened unexpectedly there might be no such sense of the death having resulted from what had become a familiar, if hated, process. Now the widow might not know what to fear.

Our surmise is that where the husband's death was anticipated and could confidently be ascribed to a disease process, then it was cancer or emphysema that was thereafter feared. But where the death was unanticipated, could not have been anticipated, where a marriage that had seemed entirely reliable had suddenly and inexplicably ended, then danger might seem everywhere once one was in marriage, and marriage itself would be feared.

13

WIDOWERS AS A
CONTRASTING GROUP

To this point we have given our attention to our sample of widows, to the way bereavement affected them, and to their struggle toward recovery. Bereavement for our sample of widowers was in some ways a similar experience, in some ways quite different. This chapter is concerned with these similarities and differences.

Initially twenty-two widowers agreed to work with us and we completed at least two interviews with each of them. A year later, when we returned for our thirteen-month interview, we were unable to locate two of our sample, and a third had left the country. We therefore had third interviews with only nineteen widowers. We returned for follow-up interviews from two to four years after the widowers' bereavement. At that time one widower refused this further interview, apparently because he did not want to be required to review painful memories, and an additional widower could not be located. We therefore had follow-up interviews with seventeen widowers.

It may be worth repeating that our sample was restricted to men no more than forty-five years old, living in the Boston area. As we noted in Chapter Two, many of the widowers whom we invited to participate declined, and as with widows, we did not press those who were reluctant. The sample therefore cannot be argued to be representative on statistical grounds, even if its small size did not disqualify it from so presenting itself. Nevertheless our respondents reported occupations ranging from college professor through laborer, and included members of every major religious group and of every major ethnic group.

THE IMPACT OF LOSS.   We can summarize our data regarding the reactions of men to the loss of their wives by saying that insofar as men reacted simply to the *loss of a loved other*, their responses were *similar* to those of widows, but insofar as men reacted to *the traumatic disruption of their lives*, the responses of men were *different*. Men and women appeared to have been similar in the affective bond they had maintained with their spouse, and therefore were similar in the impact of the loss of the loved other. But men and women organize their lives differently in our society, and react to attack on their lives in different ways. Therefore insofar as the men in our sample were not so much expressing the emotions of loss as they were dealing with these emotions and also with the other life changes associated with bereavement, their experiences and reactions were different from those of widows.

Expressions of grief were reported by rather similar proportions of men and women, with minor variations. A somewhat greater proportion of men than women reported yearning for the dead spouse (fifty-eight percent compared with forty-seven percent). A somewhat smaller proportion of men reported feelings of pain or grief (thirty-eight percent compared with forty-five percent). A somewhat smaller proportion of men than of women cried in the interview we held three weeks after the loss of the spouse (twenty-five percent compared with thirty-two percent).

Although painful grief seemed as regular an occurrence among men as among women, men tended to interpret their loss somewhat differently. More often than women, men tended to define what had happened to them as a dismemberment rather than an abandonment. That is, men more often than women spoke in terms of having lost a part of themselves; women more often than men tended to speak of having been left. Although similar expressions were used by both men and women, there were apparent differences in the imagery each sex felt to be more appropriate. One man said: "When my wife died I lost a part of myself." Another said, "I feel like part of my body was cut down." A third said that his first reaction when he saw his wife's body was that it was "like both my arms were being cut off." Widows, in contrast, were more likely to speak of having been deserted, abandoned, left to fend for themselves.

Speculatively, one might explain the different imagery used by men and women by supposing that men, more than women, saw their spouse as a necessary component of the functioning system they captained, whereas women more than men saw their spouse as providing protection and comfort, and thus as necessary to their continued well-being. Support of this assessment may perhaps be found in the difficulty men had in giving attention and energy to their work after the death of their wives, whereas women tended to find in work at least temporary surcease from pain. For men it appeared that marriage had sustained their capacity to work; for women marriage and work seemed more nearly alternate spheres for engagement.

Men, much more than women, were unable or unwilling

to display their grief; a third of the men reported that they were unable to cry, but "choked up" instead, something reported by only one woman in eight. As the year of bereavement progressed, men more quickly than women ended emotional display; by the end of the year only forty percent of the men said they continued sometimes to cry, compared with seventy-four percent of the women. Many women, like most men, viewed self-control as "strength" and preferred not to cry in front of others, but men tended to be more successful than women in achieving this self-control. Indeed, they maintained self-control even when alone and even when they felt, as did many women, that it would be better for them to let their grief find expression in tears. One said:

> Every time I cry it is going a little bit away from my body and I feel a little more comfortable. But because I'm a really tough guy I didn't cry too much.

One man was self-condemning because he had cried despite his determination to control himself for the sake of others. For him tears were unmanly. He said:

> My expectation was that I would be brave but I actually wasn't. I didn't want to cry but I did. You never see a man cry at a wake, only women.

Insofar as their emotional state became an issue, men wanted to be permitted to move toward greater control rather than to be encouraged to greater emotional expressiveness. They were quite different from women in this regard. For example, asked whether they would find it helpful or annoying if someone encouraged them to express their grief, less than half the widowers compared with two-thirds of the widows said they would find it helpful, and half the widowers compared with somewhat more than a fourth of the widows said they would find it annoying.

Asked, however, how they would react to someone remind-
ing them of the need for control, half the widowers,
compared with a fourth of the widows, said they would find
it helpful. Only a third of the widowers, compared with over
half the widows, said they would be annoyed.

Along with wanting to maintain control over their feelings, men, more than women, tried to maintain a realistic
outlook. This greater commitment to realism displayed itself
even before the spouse died. About the same proportion of
widows as widowers had forewarning of the spouse's death,
but forty-two percent of the men had given up hope before
the spouse's actual death compared with only fifteen percent
of the women. In other ways, too, widowers continued to
display greater realism. Only one of the twenty-two with
whom we had early interviews reacted to his wife's death by
saying something like, "It's not fair," whereas almost one
woman in four said something like this. And whereas more
than one-third of the women were rated by coders as
displaying generalized hostility three weeks after their
husband's death, none of the men showed this reaction.
They simply did not blame fate or become angry with those
who had not had similar misfortunes or in other ways
express anger that could not be justified rationally.

A few men did report fleeting feelings of unjustifiable
anger in an early interview. In two cases this was expressed
toward the spouse for having left the men with the care of
the children. In one case a man said, eight weeks after his
loss, that he was furiously angry, but he didn't know at
whom. But these men recognized, half humorously, the
inappropriateness of their anger, and did their best to return
to the male sense of the proper reaction to loss: realism and
control.

Men were not as successful in managing guilt as they
were in managing anger. Four of twenty-two men (compared with only three of the much larger sample of women)
blamed themselves for having in some way contributed to

their spouse's death, and another five (compared with seven women) felt guilty for having failed their spouses in some other way. Men blamed themselves for such failures as not having been sufficiently sensitive to the spouse's illness, not having required the spouse to see a physician, or not having prevented the accident that led to the spouse's death. Two men who had lost their wives in childbirth blamed themselves for having made their wives pregnant, although one of them also blamed the stillborn child.

This greater prominence of guilt among men is true only for the period immediately after the death of the spouse. Within the first two months after their bereavement, most men who had felt guilty at first no longer did. Indeed, the proportion of men who continued to brood on how they might have prevented their wife's death decreased (from forty percent to thirty percent) between the first and second months after the death, whereas the proportion of widows having such thoughts increased (from twenty-eight percent to forty percent) during the same period. Widowers exhibited less guilt as time went on; widows more.[1]

Men's greater concern for control extended to recall of the spouse. Men, more than women, tried to control the occa-

---

[1] Our coders appraised forty percent of the sample of men as feeling less guilt at the time of our second interview than they had at the time of our first. In contrast, the coders appraised only seventeen percent of the women as showing less guilt in the second interview than in the first. The coders believed that twenty-five percent of the women showed *more* guilt at the second interview than at the first, whereas in their judgment *no* men showed more guilt at the second interview than at the first. It was almost typical for men to feel guilty at first and then less guilty as time went on and for women to feel little guilt at first but *more* guilt as time went on.

The coders felt that *both* men and women displayed increased anger toward family, friends, children, or others, as time went on. The coders believed that forty percent of the women and thirty-two percent of the men displayed more anger in the second interview than in the first. In the second interview women tended to express anger toward the dead spouse and also toward at least one child, and both men and women tended to express anger toward their own family and toward their children as a group.

sions of recall. They were more apt to look at photos (forty-five percent of men reported this as compared with twenty-six percent of women) or to read old letters (ten percent of the men, compared with none of the women). At the same time they might try to avoid reminders of the spouse, to avoid thinking of the past (forty percent of the men compared with thirty percent of the women), or to avoid places that evoked memories (twenty percent of the men compared with six percent of the women).

Almost half of those in the sample reported having had involuntary visualizations of their dead wives. Slightly more than a quarter of the widows reported involuntary visualizations. But the widows were much less likely to seek control of their perceptions and therefore to characterize fleeting visualizations—which most of them experienced—as "involuntary."

On the basis of their responses in the second interview, eight weeks after the spouse's death, all but two widowers were appraised by coders as having fully accepted the reality of the death. Fully half the widows at that point were judged as still at times acting as if their husbands were still alive. About the same proportions of men and women had at some point felt the presence of their spouse during this early period of bereavement. (Twenty-five percent of the men and eighteen percent of women reported feeling their spouse's presence by the third week.) But men's greater commitment to realism displayed itself in a greater unwillingness to believe that the spouse might actually return—over half the widows reported such feelings compared with fewer than a fifth of the men.

Men seemed not to engage in intense and prolonged obsessional review of the circumstances of the spouse's death. There was such a review, to be sure, in the early weeks after the wife died. But the men attempted to shake it off, to recognize it as ultimately pointless, and to return themselves to their immediate concerns and to planning for the future.

In the eight-week interview only thirty percent of widowers, compared with fifty-three percent of widows, said they talked with family or friends about their loss. Differences in relation to tendency to review the loss were especially marked in our one-year interview. Widowers, in contrast to widows, appeared to find little value in again rehearsing the events that had led to their spouse's death. They would do so when pressed by our interviewer, but even then they did not display the recall of small detail that widows did. More than widows, they appeared uncomfortable when asked to return to the past.

MANAGING IN THE FIRST WEEKS.   Friends and kin rallied to the aid of widowers just as they rallied to the aid of widows. But they saw the widowers as needing something different. Widows were seen as needing relief from their daily duties so they could attend to their feelings. They were understood as overwhelmed, perhaps prostrated, with grief, and as needing sympathetic attention and emotional support. Widowers were seen as needing help with their new responsibilities for the home and children. It was apparently assumed that they could deal with their feelings themselves.

A few widows had felt that the sympathy and solicitude they had received from others had not been helpful, although the great majority were grateful to those who rallied around. All widowers, without exception, reported that others had been helpful. The help others gave to these men, help in their homes and with their children, was clearly useful.

Since the kind of help men were understood to need was replacement of the wife's functioning, most of the help was furnished by women. And since early in their bereavement widowers had few female friends, all but three reported that they had been helped more by family than by friends. In contrast, about thirty percent of the sample of widows said that they had been helped more by friends, or helped equally by each.

Widowers were helped often by their mothers-in-law (twenty-five percent reported this), or their sisters-in-law (reported by thirty percent). The helpful brother-in-law was almost solely present in the case of widows; with men the brother-in-law had no role. (Thirty-six percent of widows reported their brothers-in-law to have been helpful to them, but only one man reported being helped by a brother-in-law.)

Widowers were more likely than widows to try to make their own way without asking help of others. By the end of the year seventy-five percent of the widowers (compared with ninety-two percent of the widows) had asked for help from others, and only four widowers, as compared with forty percent of the sample of widows, had sought help from a social worker, physician, or other professional. Indeed, twenty percent of the men were judged to be insistently independent in that they actively refused help; only eight percent of the widows were so judged.

In general, although the widowers were more concerned than the widows with how they would manage household tasks and child care, they were more confident of their ability ultimately to recover from their loss. Only twenty percent of the widowers reported at any point being afraid of nervous breakdown, compared with fifty-two percent of the widows. By the end of the second month of their bereavement, only two men displayed what coders felt to be nonspecific anxiety, compared with forty-four percent of widows at that point in their bereavement.

Men less often than women were upset by the funeral and burial rituals such as seeing the corpse, or by attending the wake, funeral, or burial. They did not seem to have to mobilize themselves as did many widows to manage their roles in the ceremonies, nor, in general, did they seem to give to these ceremonies the emotional importance given them by widows. They wanted to express through the ceremonies their love and respect for their wives; but they were more concerned with how they would manage in the subsequent months than with the management of the ceremonies. Widows tended to see each ceremonial almost as a milestone, but widowers wanted to get through with the ceremonials so that they could get on with reestablishing their lives.

Associated with their lesser investment in ceremonials, widowers gave much less attention to details such as the kind and quantity of flowers at the funeral, the length of a service, and even who attended. Perhaps this was the inexperience of most widowers in arranging social events since for most of them responsibility for social arrangements had long been left to their wife. But also it seems to be a masculine tendency to care less about how things look, about the face the family presents to the community; responsibility for these matters, too, would ordinarily have fallen in the wife's domain.

Because they needed help less—and would, in any event, have accepted it less willingly—and because they cared less about the details of ceremonials, widowers seemed to be less praising of undertakers. They were appreciative of the undertakers' helpfulness and manner, but did not express toward them the gratitude that was so frequently expressed by widows. More often, too, they questioned the expense of the funeral. Although they were not outraged at the undertakers' bills, they often felt that they were too high.

GRIEF, MOURNING AND RECOVERY. If we compare the emotional state of widowers with that of widows at the end of their first year of bereavement, we might at first glance say that widowers, as a group, seemed somewhat further along the road to recovery. Widowers were less likely to report themselves as having felt depressed or very unhappy within the preceding weeks (forty-two percent of widowers compared with fifty-one percent of widows). And widowers were more likely to agree with the statement. "I feel like myself again" (seventy-one percent of widowers agreed with the statement, compared with fifty-eight percent of widows).

Yet there are reasons for suspecting that despite these data our widowers proceeded no more quickly in recovering from the trauma of marital loss than did our widows. When we examine the responses made by our comparison group of nonbereaved men and women we find that in this comparison group the men were less likely than the women to give indication of depression. (This may be either because the men less often felt depressed or because they were more reluctant to admit to it.) Comparing bereaved and nonbereaved, the bereaved men seemed to differ more from the nonbereaved men than the bereaved women did from the nonbereaved women. From this standpoint one might say that men showed the impact of bereavement slightly longer than did women, and if at the end of the year the widowers reported less emotional distress than did the widows, they nevertheless reported a good deal more than did nonbereaved men.

Widowers seemed to be distinctly less likely than widows to be worried about how they would manage their financial situation. Widows, even though they might be financially secure at the moment, recognized that they would in the future have to manage on a severely reduced income. But widowers seemed to have the same increment in indicators of stress—including tension and restlessness—when compared with nonbereaved men, as widows did when compared with nonbereaved women.

In sum it appears that widowers did not move toward emotional recovery more quickly than did widows. Widowers did, however, move more quickly toward reestablishing a stable life organization based on remarriage, and thus toward social recovery.

Men withdrew from their normal roles and functions to a much lesser extent than had widows. In an extreme but instructive instance, a professional man met appointments the same day his wife died. We felt that his behavior resulted from a sense of obligation to which was added a kind of stubbornness: he would not permit himself to give way to the weakness of grief.

We have noted the disinclination of widows to accept a protracted period of mourning. Yet widows did change in dress and behavior, and withdrew themselves for months, even years, from full social participation. Widowers, in contrast, displayed few outward symbols of their grief. None wore mourning, nor did any seclude themselves as a kind of ceremony.

Most widowers saw no point in observance for the sake of observance. One widower, asked in the thirteen-month interview whether he had done something to recognize the anniversary of his wife's death, said:

> If I do something about the anniversary of my wife's death it doesn't make any difference any way. My wife is dead. She doesn't know anything if I do something good or if I do something bad.

Women and men seemed to define somewhat differently the nature of their continuing obligation to their deceased spouse. Widows tended to feel that loyalty to their deceased spouse required circumspect and proper behavior; widowers appeared to feel that restricting their behavior could do their deceased wives no good. In the third interview both widows and widowers were asked if they would agree with the statement, "I try to behave as (my former spouse) would want." Some sixty-nine percent of the widows as compared with fifty-three percent of the widowers said that at some time they had felt that way, and sixty-three percent of the widows, compared with forty-eight percent of the widowers, said that they felt that way now.

One more reason for men moving more quickly toward social recovery may have been the special difficulty men had in working and keeping a home together. Women might have had somewhat less commitment to a job. A few men tried for a time both to keep up their work and simultaneously to run their home themselves. They rose early, fixed breakfast, sent the children to school, went off to work themselves, shopped on the way home, fixed supper, cleaned up afterward, prepared the children's clothing for the next day, and went to sleep exhausted. If there were older children they might rely on them for help. But when all the children were younger, as was true in many cases, most soon found it necessary to ask the aid of a female member of their family or their wife's family. One man had his two unmarried sisters come to live with him. Another relied on his mother-in-law, who lived nearby; he left his preschool daughter with her every morning and had her care for his school-aged children after they returned from school.

There were other possibilities. One man arranged with a woman friend, herself recently divorced, to care for the children during the day. He had already shifted jobs so he could be with the children more. Another had neighbors care for his children when he was at work. One of our respondents was unable to make other arrangements and had to send his four-year-old son to live with his sister in another city.

Widowers were apt to find new problems at work that might force them toward social recovery. Work was often therapeutic for widows, because they could see it as something extra, a respite from their major concerns. But widowers cared more about maintaining their highest level of functioning, and were dismayed by the inevitable reduction bereavement produced in their energy and competence.

The aim of returning to functioning at their previous level became one among many motivations for remarriage. In addition to wanting to regain their capacity for work, many men desired to reestablish an intact home, and to regain the role of husband. They wanted to reestablish an orderly life in which their children would be cared for; they would have a structured routine and they would have a home.

The pressures of loneliness and of sexual desire played a large role in pressing men toward social recovery. Whether these motivations were greater for widowers than for widows we cannot be sure, but they did seem to be reported by widowers with greater frequency. Widowers seemed to deal with sexual desire and loneliness in a way which differed from that of widows. They were less likely to deny their existence, and they were more likely at least in fantasy to plan for remedies for their situation. Early in bereavement sixty-eight percent of the widowers said they would miss sex, compared with forty-seven percent of the widows. And in the year-end interview almost all widowers who were not remarried or seriously involved said they were lonely, compared with perhaps half the widows in this situation.

Widowers moved far more quickly than widows into dating and eventual remarriage. Whereas most widows were unwilling to begin to think of the possibility of remarriage in the early period of their bereavement, a number of widowers made comments like the following after two months:

> There is no question in my mind about remarrying. The problem is finding the right person again . . .

> I certainly want to find another wife and rebuild the kind of environment I like to have in which to live.

A few widowers began dating only two months after their wife's death. At least one talked about his grief with his new girl friend. Her understanding helped him cope with it.

We do not mean to identify social recovery with remarriage. Yet remarriage would seem one way of establishing a stable new life organization. By the end of the first year of their bereavement, fifty percent of the widowers had remarried or were associating with someone on a basis that could be considered premarital, as compared with eighteen percent of the widows. At the end of this first year about a third of the widows would still not consider remarriage compared with about a tenth of the widowers. Thirty-one percent of the widows had no current interest in *anyone* of the opposite sex, compared with only ten percent of the widowers.

Yet it must not be forgotten that despite the more rapid movement of widowers toward social recovery, their movement toward emotional recovery was if anything slower than that of widows. To suggest how rapid social recovery accompanied by slower emotional recovery might appear, we may consider the case of Mr. T, an engineer in his late thirties. His wife became ill in the spring and a cancer was diagnosed. Fourteen months later she was dead.

Among Mr. T's first reactions to his wife's death was relief that the terminal phase had been brief and that she was now released from pain: "I felt that her suffering was over and I think for the first week after it happened that sort of carried me." But then Mr. T experienced the full force of grief. He was nearly overwhelmed by his sorrow; he just barely was able to maintain his self-control. He kept busy, avoided talk, and took sleeping pills to get him through the night. He cried now and then.

As the weeks went by Mr. T reestablished a routine, but despite it became increasingly lonely and depressed. Now instead of crying only occasionally he cried once or twice a day. He blamed himself for not being able to control his feelings more successfully, but he could not. He had no children and so was free in the evening. He began trying to find activities that would keep him out of his home after work. He spent a good deal of time in bars, drinking steadily through the evening.

Seven months after his wife's death Mr. T began dating. He soon found a girl he wanted to marry. Eleven months after his wife's death he remarried and brought his second wife to live with him in the house he had occupied with the first. He stopped drinking. He had new energy for work. Gradually he became happy.

When we saw Mr. T fifteen months after his first wife's death (we had trouble arranging this interview and so held it later than we had planned), Mr. T's first wife was still very much in his thoughts. He spoke of her often to his new wife. His new wife accepted this; she talked with Mr. T freely about his loss and visited his first wife's grave with him. Mr. T remained close to his first wife's parents and sometimes brought his new wife to see them.

Two years later, when seen in the follow-up interview, Mr. T had a two-month-old son. He appeared to be in good spirits and described himself as happy. He continued to idealize his first wife and at times to grieve for her. His second wife continued to accept this.

ANTICIPATION OF THE DEATH AND LATER LIFE ORGANIZA-TION. We do not find with widowers the neat correspondence of anticipation of the spouse's death and movement toward remarriage that appeared among our widows. Rather what we find is that failure to anticipate the wife's death produced a more difficult emotional situation for the widower, not always relieved by remarriage.

Remarriage and Anticipation. Nine of our nineteen widowers had remarried by our last contact with them. In four cases, including the two in which we were unable to obtain a follow-up interview, this was before the end of the first year of their bereavement. Still another widower, when seen in a follow-up interview, had all but decided to marry a cousin who had been caring for his children.

Of the nine widowers who had remarried by the time of our last contact, four had been able to anticipate their loss. About another it is difficult to be certain: his wife had been diagnosed as having a brain tumor but he said that he was not told until the end that her condition was fatal. All five seemed to have established satisfactory lives after remarriage. One was described by his interviewer as "completely reconciled to the loss of his wife and happy with his future prospects, which are indeed bright with a new home in the suburbs and a new young wife; the new family couldn't be happier." Another was described by the interviewer as "in good spirits, friendly, happy." A third was described as "an exuberant, self-satisfied man." Asked whether his first wife's death had affected him, this widower said, "The effects were all changed by the remarriage." A fourth also reported that he had completely recovered from his loss and felt fine. The fifth, the man whose first wife had the brain tumor, was also described as happy.

Only one of these five married widowers whose first wife's death had been forewarned (including here the fifth widower who may well have known subconsciously) appeared to have put aside the memory of his first wife. Two with whom we spoke three or four years after the wife's death gave the same report. Each said he still thought of his first wife frequently and sometimes talked about her to his new wife.

The widower who was planning marriage to a cousin, although he had had forewarning of his first wife's death, afterward had a slow and difficult recovery. When we talked with him thirteen months after the loss of his wife he said he sometimes contemplated suicide; he wanted somehow to die. But three years later much had changed. His cousin, an attractive younger woman, had come to help him care for his children and a close bond had developed with her. Now, with his cousin as a prospective new wife, the man seemed reasonably content.

Four widowers without forewarning had remarried by the time of our last contact with them. One of these widowers refused a follow-up interview and so was last seen only a year after the first wife's death. He had remarried by then and appeared quite happy. He said that he often called his second wife by his first wife's name, although the two were dissimilar people. Nevertheless he had no dreams of the first wife, no feeling of her presence, and did not think of her. He felt he had begun a new life; he felt confident about his future.

A second widower had also remarried happily despite a sudden and unforewarned loss. He had been in his early twenties when his wife had died as a result of a pregnancy complicated by a physical malformation. He was convinced that her death was due to a surgical blunder and seemed never to have felt guilty for having made her pregnant. By the end of the first year of his breavement he had returned to living with his parents and was dating actively; essentially he returned to the status of a young single man. About a year later he remarried. When we saw him after he had been remarried two years he said that he had almost put his first wife out of his mind, although he could still feel angry at the doctors and now, for the first time, could also feel guilty that he had initiated the chain of events that led to her death.

The other two remarried widowers who had no forewarning did not seem to be doing especially well when we saw them some four years after the loss. One, a writer and entertainer, had gotten involved in a major project that had failed, through what he believed to have been no fault of his own. He said his marriage had helped him a great deal both with his earlier grief and with his present reverses. He still missed his first wife, however, and still worried that he might have prevented her death had he been able to get her to a hospital earlier. (His guilt would seem to have been unjustified; his wife had died of what was described to him as an inoperable cancer.) The interviewer felt that even though it was now four years since his wife's death, this man continued to have a good deal of underlying depression.

A second remarried widower whose wife's death had come without forewarning also seemed to exhibit underlying depression. He too was seen four years after the death. This man had by then married an acquaintance whom he had employed for a time to help him with his children. During the first year of his bereavement he had encountered a number of serious business reverses, some of which may well have resulted from his distraction. At the time of our last contact he had three new children by his second marriage, in addition to four by his first, and felt that his business was getting along. He felt that his first wife would have approved of his remarriage: "How proud she'd probably have felt if she could see her family growing." But at the same time he wondered if he should not obtain professional help for himself, saying: "I think at this point I'm tight on a string and the string is very thin and could break."

Independence and Anticipation. Five of our widowers had organized their lives in a way that made them relatively independent of other adults. Three of them kept house for their children without help, one paid a woman to come in and keep house for him, and two of them had a neighbor take care of the children.

Four of these five men had lost their wives without forewarning. Two of these, who refused follow-up, were seen just one year after the death of their wives, one three years after, and one four years after. All four appeared depressed and disconsolate when we last saw them.

One of them had briefly married, an impulsive marriage that he described as having ended three days after it began. He insisted that he did not want to marry again, yet he could not tolerate being alone. Two of the others occasionally went out on dates, and said they hoped to marry. But one of them added that he was frightened of marriage even as he wanted it.

The widower in this group who had forewarning of his wife's death found a girl friend with whom he maintained a relationship of some depth, but preferred, for the time being at least, not to remarry. His life appeared to him to be reasonably satisfactory.

Kin Dependence and Anticipation.   Three of our widowers had brought one of their female kin to live with them. Two brought in sisters, and one his wife's mother. In each case the female relative took responsibility for maintaining the house and caring for the children. One of these men had had forewarning of his wife's death; two had not. The forewarned widower had by the third interview established a new cross-sex tie of some intensity. When we saw him three years later that relationship had ended, but there were several girls whom he dated regularly. His sister continued to live with him and keep house. His life appeared to him to be relatively satisfactory.

The two widowers in this group who had had no forewarning did not seem to be doing well. The one whose mother-in-law was caring for his children had become alcoholic after his wife's death. By the time of our follow-up interview, four years after his wife's death, he had joined Alcoholics Anonymous. He dated occasionally, generally as a result of friends' arrangements, but nothing worked out. He seemed discontented and lonely, although otherwise he seemed to function reasonably well so long as he avoided alcohol. The other widower was also extremely lonely. He had not dated at all when we saw him four years after the death. He said that sex was indeed a problem, but that he didn't want to get mixed up with the women he met in bars. His one social activity was to get together with other lonely men for a beer or two.

Continued Chaos. Finally we come to the one widower whose life remained chaotic four years after his wife's loss. He had been in his late twenties when his wife of eight years died suddenly of a heart attack, with no forewarning. The marriage had been happy. There was one child, at that time four years old. The man had had a nervous breakdown before his marriage. During his marriage he had been fine, but now he began feeling upset again. (This history of early emotional instability, combined with absence of forewarning, seemed among widows also to give rise to failure to recover.) As time went on this widower became less and less able to do his work. He had to give up care of his child, and sent his son to live with his parents. Four years after his wife's loss he was considering bringing his son back to live with him. But he was not working well, and had not since his wife's death. He dated a good deal, but found it difficult to become involved with any of the girls he saw. He was deeply depressed and said that his life had been destroyed by his wife's death.

SUMMARY. As we review the relationship of anticipation and eventual life organization for men, we see that anticipation plays almost as important a role in relation to the recovery of widowers as it does in relation to that of widows, but it is a somewhat different role. The unexpected death of the spouse seems as difficult for men to recover from as for women. But there does not seem to be the quite general phobic response to marriage among men that was displayed by women who had lost spouses without forewarning. Rather, at least some widowers suppressed whatever anxiety they felt and moved toward remarriage. But they, as well as other widowers whose wives died unexpectedly, seemed to have some area of life in which stress was exhibited. Two widowers whose wives had died without forewarning established satisfactory marriages but had severe problems in their work.

Some widowers who had anticipated the death, as well as some who had not, adopted nonmarital life organizations— independence of other adults or the establishment of a household with a female relative. But virtually every widower who had had forewarning managed to maintain a dating life that provided him with adequate gratification, whereas virtually every widower whose wife had died without forewarning was unable to establish a satisfactory dating life.

In general it appears that with widowers as well as with widows the loss of the spouse without forewarning affected the nature of eventual recovery. Although widowers without forewarning might again remarry they seemed likelier than other widowers to harbor tension or anxiety, perhaps expressive of a generalized distrust of fate, that resulted in troubled relationships or in personal discomfort.

14

DEALING WITH LOSS

In contemporary Western society we tend to share certain basic assumptions about people. We assume that people are "individuals," essentially separate one from another. We assume that people are "free," by which we mean that they have the right to choose their own place in the world. And we attach to such separateness and freedom so high a value that we often ignore the extent to which people require one another to sustain their own functioning. It is to this society that the widows and widowers whom we studied belong and it is this context which must be taken into account if we are to understand the nature of their reaction to bereavement and suggest some of the ways in which it might have been mitigated.

Bereavement, which entails the severance of a bond, presents a challenge which all are reluctant to face. Even as we rally around to help, we may not know what to say and so end by saying almost nothing. Grief, we may decide, is a "private matter," like an infectious illness for which social withdrawal and the passage of time are the only treatments. And so, as soon as we can, we may leave the griever alone, to deal with his or her grief in isolation.

Yet many bereaved for some time need the reassuring presence of others, though they cannot act in relation to them as they normally would. C. S. Lewis, in the midst of deep grief for the loss of his wife, wrote:

> I find it hard to take in what anyone says. Or perhaps, hard to want to take it in. It is so uninteresting. Yet I want the others to be about me. I dread the moments when the house is empty. If only they would talk to one another and not to me.[1]

More understanding of grief is required both by those of us who serve as supports for individuals experiencing grief, and by those of us who will experience grief ourselves. Most of us, it may confidently be asserted, will fall into both categories.

This study has shown clearly the importance of previous warnings of bereavement to come. Yet can people be prepared or prepare themselves for bereavement? At once we run into a difficulty. To prepare for something is to anticipate it, to rehearse it in advance, to create in imagination the world that will one day exist in reality. But this preparing for a possible future comes near in our minds to *willing it* and we are then only one step removed from that most dangerous of wishes, the death wish. The only hypothesis we can offer that adequately explains the observation

---

[1] C. S. Lewis, *A Grief Observed* (copyright 1961, N. W. Clerk). Used by permission of the publishers, in the U.S.A., The Seabury Press, New York, and in England, Faber and Faber Ltd.

that we all avoid preparing for bereavement is that we fear the magical power of wishes or plans to come true, and we feel uncomfortable with ourselves if we discover our thoughts turning to the possibility of the death of others. Because of this, formal preparation for grief—such as classes on the nature of grief for those about to be bereaved —seem hardly likely to work, even if we could identify prospective widows and widowers.

But it seems not to be the case that there is nothing we can do to lessen the trauma we will feel at the death of someone we love. It does seem to help if we have gained as much acceptance of death as we are able to achieve, so that the death process, when we finally encounter it in someone we love, is not an absolutely inexplicable malign force.

When should preparation start? Since all are mortal it is reasonable to suggest that preparation for bereavement should begin in childhood. Sometimes we can help our children to some mastery of their natural fear of death. For many children the first contact with death is the death of a pet. If the children are permitted to touch the dead pet, and to bury it with due reverence, they may recognize both the finality of death and its naturalness. And if they can express openly their feelings of sadness in an appropriate manner, they may establish an outlook that will make it easier for them to cope with later bereavements. Children can be frightened by death too, of course. But we would think that most children will gain from being able to deal with a manageable reality in addition to their fears and fantasies.

The element of "play" in the death games of children is not to be regretted; play is, after all, the principal means by which children prepare themselves for the realities of life. "Death games" seem fairly popular with children. If adults share in such games they may find opportunity to educate the children to an acceptance of death as a sad part of life which, though unwanted, can be examined and accepted.

Even those parents who lack a religious or philosophical explanation for death may be able to teach children to tolerate the uncertainty of death, and, like a corrective experience of reality, may be able to modify if not entirely dispel whatever grotesque and horrific fantasies the children may have developed.

"Death games" are not confined to childhood. A great deal of public entertainment takes advantage of the fascination we continue to have as adults with themes of death. Such entertainment allows us to externalize our fears and fantasies, though at the cost of distorting the true nature of dying. Most deaths occur peacefully and without violence or undue suffering, quite unlike the picture of death that we obtain from the mass media.

If entertainment vehicles give central place to violent death, they push grief to the periphery. The detective, having interviewed the murdered man's widow concerning the circumstances of his death, moves swiftly on; we may wonder briefly at her emotional state, but our attention is called away to other, more important filmic events. We are not so concerned with grief, it would seem, as we are with death. And the death we are concerned with is one that comes unexpectedly, and perhaps with savagery. This is what our films give us the opportunity to master.

Recent attempts to deal with death and grieving at a more realistic level illustrate both the difficulties and the possibilities of the mass media. In Britain a German television team spent a week working with the nurses in a hospital in which many but not all patients were receiving terminal care. Once patients, families, and hospital staff had got used to their presence the team introduced their cameras and filmed the day-to-day life of the ward, they did not film the actual death of a patient. Although the film was neither shocking nor sensational, its showing on a German television network provoked widespread criticism. Charges of intrusion and sensationalism were made. The film is unlikely to be released for general distribution. In contrast, both a British and an American film of interviews with dying patients have been well received by viewers; so has another British film in which bereaved people described their experiences. Apparently the actual dying of real people is more than an ordinary audience can deal with, but the confrontation with the imminence of death of a dying individual and the experience of bereavement of those left behind can be accepted.

In the world of books there are many accounts of death and bereavement. Perhaps the best known are James Agee's *A Death in the Family* and Louisa M. Alcott's *Good Wives*. But there are also some excellent autobiographical accounts of grief such as Susan Beck's *Diary of a Widow* and the book from which we quoted above, *A Grief Observed* by C. S. Lewis. The best of this genre are not little books of comfort with easy answers and glib assurances of reunion (which rarely seem to convince), but rather accounts that relay the experience of bereavement and somehow allow a message of hope to arise from the simple fact that to be able to look at the awful together with another—even though that other is only the author of a book—makes it less awful.

There are several serious studies of death and grief by psychologists, sociologists, and others, though perhaps not yet enough to deal with all the issues of bereavement. This book is an example; others are Elisabeth Kubler-Ross's *On Death and Dying*, John Hinton's *On Dying*, David Sudnow's *Passing On*, C. Murray Parkes's *Bereavement*, Peter Marris's *Widows and their Families*, and Geoffrey Gorer's *Death, Grief and Mourning in Contemporary Britain*.

Is there anything we can do to prepare individuals for loss whose spouses have illnesses that carry a high probability of ending fatally? Typical would be the wife of the cancer patient whose doctors have decided that no further surgery or radiotherapy is likely to stem the course of the illness. Our findings give no certain indication how she might be prepared; but issues that need to be considered include the information she is given about the illness, the advice and assistance she receives in communicating such information to her husband or discussing its implications, and the opportunities she can be given to contribute to his care in the later stages of his illness. In relation to these issues this study and others lead us to the following recommendations.

Since individuals who have been given timely warning of the likely fatal outcome of a spouse's illness cope better with bereavement than those who have had no such warning—and despite the anxiety these warnings evoke—we think that doctors and others who are in a position to make reliable predictions usually should pass them on to the patient's spouse. But it should be remembered that it takes time and courage to absorb the implications of the news of a loved person's coming death. Wherever possible some hint of the possibility of bad news should be given in advance; it is better for the patient's spouse to be appropriately worried than to be unprepared. Excessively optimistic reassurances at an early stage of treatment, often given to save the recipient anxiety and the giver embarrassment, are likely to be reinterpreted in an even more optimistic light, so that the total distortion of information can be considerable. When eventually it becomes clear to the doctor that a fatal outcome is highly probable he should be prepared to take as much time and trouble over imparting this news as he would over a delicate surgical procedure. He is inflicting a wound upon the recipient's psyche as surely as he would be inflicting one on that individual's soma should he incise his or her abdomen—but here it is without the benefit of anesthesia. He must be prepared to sit through the tears or anger that may need to be expressed, to answer whatever questions there may be, and to provide whatever comfort he can in an intolerable situation. Few physicians are entirely comfortable with the task. Perhaps hospitals should develop supportive structures for physicians so that they can, in turn, provide support to the bereaved.

Too often now the unsuspecting wife or husband is called away in the middle of a hospital visit and led into a forbidding office or treatment room to be confronted with the white-clad presence of a doctor who is obviously embarrassed and ashamed of what he must say. Anxious to get the unpleasant business over as quickly as possible the doctor blurts out the news that there is nothing more to be done, that the patient has an incurable cancer and will not live very long. The doctor may advise that the fact should be concealed from the patient, to save the patient unnecessary distress, and then return the spouse, in shocked condition, to the patient's side.

Obviously there are better ways. When conditions are ideal and the spouse has been kept fully informed of the progress of the patient's disease there need not be a single occasion on which "the news" is told. Rather the spouse can be kept in close touch with the doctors and nurses who, over a period of time, can accustom him or her to the idea that the patient may not get better. By providing the spouse with frequent opportunities to talk with them, by taking the initiative in reporting the patient's progress to the spouse, and at the same time by showing understanding and respect for the spouse's feelings, they can help the spouse to move gradually toward a full understanding of the situation.

When conditions are less ideal because the illness is progressing very rapidly or an unexpected biopsy report has been received, it may be necessary to break the news without adequate preparation. We think it important, if possible, that more than one member of the family should be present, so that feelings can be shared. The meeting should be timed so that those just informed do not have to return to the patient's bedside unless the patient too has been informed. Facts should be given simply and directly;

where knowledge is uncertain no attempt should be made to conceal this fact. The physician must constantly remind himself that he is imposing a shock on the recipients of his news; he must be as supportive, as responsive to their needs, as he can be. Precise estimates of expected survival should be avoided; they are bound to be taken literally and sometimes assume the significance of a death sentence, with everyone waiting for the date on which the patient is expected to die. Quite apart from the psychological burden they impose, most such predictions are inaccurate.[2]

Even when the patient is believed to be near death it is seldom enough to rely on a single meeting between doctor and family for the communication of vital information. The distress evoked by such interviews is sometimes so great that it is necessary to interrupt them to give those present time to gather strength to proceed. Even when this has not been the case it is important that the family be given an opportunity to return for further discussion. It is easy for misunderstandings to arise that reflect the hopes or dreads of the family members. For example, one woman who had been warned that her husband only had a short time to live thought that this meant he would be with her for two or three more years. In fact the physician intended by his statement to warn her that her husband was unlikely to survive more than a few months. His attempt to provide her with forewarning was undone by his reluctance to be definite and the widow's unwillingness to consider that the time might be as short as it was.

Should patients know they are going to die and be

_____

[2] In a recent study estimates of survival were made by doctors and nurses on patients with incurable cancers who were thought to have a short prognosis. Although most patients died within twelve weeks, confirming the short prognosis, forty-four percent of the estimates exceeded twice the actual survival time and nine percent were less than half the survival time. (C. Murray Parkes, "Accuracy of predictions of survival in later stages of cancer," *British Medical Journal,* Vol. 2, (1972), pp. 29-31.

encouraged to talk about this with their spouses? This is an extraordinarily difficult issue.[3] When circumstances have made open communication possible between a dying patient and his or her spouse, the chances of successful recovery of the spouse seem to have been enhanced. But there seem to be many reasons why patients who to at least some extent recognize the seriousness of their illness may prefer to maintain a social fiction that they will eventually be well; for one thing they may feel that otherwise they would assume a peculiarly marginal and disagreeable status in their family, that of someone poised on the edge of departure. It might be good for patients to have some control over the degree to which they are required overtly to recognize their condition.[4]

One other issue should be discussed before we consider the care of the bereaved: the extent to which husbands and wives should be encouraged to contribute to the care of the dying patient. It is now usual for most people to die in hospitals whereas, in former times, they would be more likely to be nursed by their family at home. This change is partly the consequence of the high technical standard of medical and nursing care that can be achieved in a hospital and that causes many severely ill patients to feel safer in a hospital than they do at home. But it does mean that the spouse now has almost no role in the care of the patient. The spouse of a dying patient is apt to be treated by the hospital

---

[3] See Ruth Abrams, *Not Alone with Cancer* (Springfield, Ill.: Charles C Thomas, 1974).

[4] One hospital of which we know tells all patients that they can learn the exact nature of their condition if they ask the doctor responsible for coordinating their treatment, but that no one else can say. Some patients assiduously avoid asking that doctor for their diagnosis. Their implied wish not to know is thus respected, while at the same time the arrangement makes it possible for them to find out. Most observers agree that the majority of terminal patients recognize the seriousness of their condition, though they may not admit this to others.

staff as at best a guest, and at worst as an inconvenience, perhaps an intruder.

One reason nursing staffs do not share care of a patient with the spouse is awareness of the spouse's emotional link to the patient. It is easy for a spouse to become possessive of the patient or to collude with the patient in criticism of the staff or the treatment. But by keeping communication open doctors and nurses can prevent distortions and misconceptions from reaching levels that sometimes cause a dying patient to leave the hospital, or the patient's spouse to become belligerent.

We have emphasized the support that family members and friends can give to the individual whose energies are absorbed by the need to visit and be with, if not actually care for, a dying spouse. When it is the husband who is dying the wife's normal responsibilities to care for the children and home continue despite her attendance at the husband's bedside. Indeed, many of the roles formerly performed by her husband now fall on her shoulders. Anyone who will share these responsibilities—help her about the house, come in to look after the children when she is at the hospital, see to the servicing or repair of her car and drive her to the hospital while it is out of commission—is not only setting her free to fulfill her new obligations but is reassuring her of the care and concern of the world in general.

Some writers on the topic have suggested that the anticipation of a death enables grief to start in advance of the event and that one aim of preparation should be the expression of this grief. We are unconvinced of this. Although it may be possible for a person to grieve in advance of a death, we suspect that this can only be done by the person so far withdrawing from the dying patient that the patient is treated as effectively dead. To do this to a living person might well later give rise to corresponding feelings of guilt in the mourner.

Moreover, there is no evidence that the expression of feelings of depression before a death is associated with diminished grief afterward. Rather it seems that the opposite is the case. A study of feelings of depression reported by widows of all ages in Cincinnati found that those who reported being depressed prior to bereavement were *more*, not less, likely to be depressed afterward.[5] Our findings seem to confirm these observations: those of our widows who were most upset by their husband's illness were likely to be most upset by his death.

It is important for the spouse of a dying patient to face the facts, to turn toward the problems posed by the illness, and to confront them realistically. At the same time it is probably unwise for the spouse to begin too soon to worry over and to plan for the life that will follow bereavement. Rather it seems to work out better if the spouse and the dying patient together focus their attention on making the married life that remains to them as worthwhile as it can be. Having faced the worst—the patient perhaps only tacitly—they can regard each day that remains as a bonus, a holiday period, a time in which they can express without interference from other responsibilities their caring for each other. They may be surprised to find how rewarding this period can be.

Only after the spouse's death does grief truly begin. It is at this point that a new set of psychological and social phenomena, the phenomena of bereavement, become apparent. These are the phenomena we have described here.

One element of the process of grieving that seems of special importance is "distancing," that is, the avoidance of unmanageable distress by the device of keeping disturbing thoughts away from the focus of one's attention. Many of our widows, and somewhat fewer of our widowers, tried at

[5] Paula J. Clayton, James A. Halikas, William L. Maurice, and Eli Robbins, "Anticipatory grief and widowhood," *British Journal of Psychiatry*, Vol. 122, (1973), pp. 47–51.

first to fend off disturbing thoughts and memories. Some kept busy and some avoided people or situations that would remind them of their loss. Many got rid of the spouse's clothes or shut them away out of sight.

The widows also generally recognized that grief needed to be expressed, that too much inhibition of feeling was unnatural and itself could cause difficulties. Widows sometimes feared that if they permitted themselves to be overwhelmed by grief things would go badly; but so might they also if they failed to express their grief. They worried not only about too little distancing, but also about too much inhibition of feeling, in which case, they feared, the feelings become "bottled up," eventually to burst through in uncontrollable form.

There is some evidence that there is justification in the fears widows sometimes have that they are grieving either too much or too little. Parkes's study of bereaved psychiatric patients found that people who had been admitted for psychiatric treatment after a bereavement were likely to have reacted to their loss either by immediate overwhelming grief, lasting for some time, or by little or no emotional disturbance at the time of the loss followed by a severe reaction some weeks later.[6] It may well be that an ability to express grief while yet not permitting it to overwhelm one is an important method of coping.

Some of the widows in our study were concerned about the effect of their grief on their children. Most hid their tears; only a few extended to their children the recognition that expression of grief within limits was good. Just as a dying husband, in the hope of saving her from pain, sometimes ordered his wife not to mourn for him, so a bereaved mother sometimes tried to save her children from

---

[6] C. Murray Parkes, "Bereavement and mental illness," *British Journal of Medical Psychology*, Vol. 38, No. 1 (1965), pp. 1–26.

the pain of grief by controlling her own feelings and by avoiding mention of the father's death. What effect a protective attitude has upon the children is hard to assess. It may well sustain the notion that the expression of grief is harmful; in a few cases it may sow the seeds of later emotional difficulties. Data from child guidance clinics[7] and from psychoanalytic studies of adults and adolescents who were bereaved in childhood[8] suggest that the inhibition of grief in childhood is sometimes damaging.

If appropriate distancing is important for adults and children alike, how can it be fostered? A person who is overwhelmed with grief may need to escape for a while from the perpetual reminders of the loss—perhaps by taking a trip, if there are friends to visit who can see to it that isolation will be avoided. And a person whose grief is bottled up may find relief in being given permission to grieve more openly.

It seems that different grievers might be helped in different ways. Are there any general rules that seem to apply across the board? The ideal situation is one in which, during the early postbereavement period, the bereaved person can begin little by little to look at the reality of what has happened and to express the feelings that accompany the realization of loss. Among these feelings are likely to be anxiety and fear. Anything that promotes security and provides a sense of safety will make grieving easier, and anything that confronts the griever with danger or uncertainty will make it more difficult.

---

[7] B. Arthur and T. L. Kemme, "Bereavement in childhood," *Journal of Child Psychology and Psychiatry*, Vol. 5 (1964), pp. 37–49; A. C. Cain, I. Fast, and M. E. Erickson, "Children's disturbed reaction to the death of a sibling," *American Journal of Orthopsychiatry*. Vol. 34 (1964), pp. 741–752.

[8] H. Deutsch, "Absence of grief," *Psychoanalytic Quarterly*, Vol. 6 (1937), pp. 12–22; M. Wolfenstein, "How is mourning possible?" *The Psychoanalytic Study of the Child*, Vol. 21 (1966); pp. 93–123.

What are possible sources of security for the newly bereaved person? We might suggest safe places, safe people, and safe situations.

To most of us the safest place in the world is home. This is where most bereaved people prefer to withdraw to during the period of their grieving. Unfortunately home may also be the place most likely to remind them of their loss, and bereaved people sometimes react to this by giving up their home. Yet it is often the case that the bereaved person who has given up his or her home feels less safe than before. Although brief excursions to another familiar place may do no harm, permanent change made too soon is likely to be regretted. The newly bereaved should be dissuaded from giving up their homes in the early stage of their bereavement. Nor should they expect to escape their grief by taking a long holiday, though a brief change of scene may help them manage to introduce some distance.

Safe people are of two types. First, there are loved persons, usually family members, and not uncommonly friends, who can be relied on to protect and cherish the bereaved person. Then there are all those people whose roles or behavior lead them to be defined as safe: clergy whose professional role it is to support the bereaved, lawyers who are paid to defend the interests of their client, and friends or acquaintances who take the trouble to give practical help and emotional support. In this last category we do not include all those who express anxious concern and pity. Pity too often increases feelings of weakness and insecurity, and anxious concern may convey an expectation of further disaster to someone who is already overstretched. Emotional support, on the other hand, implies a willingness to get involved, to protect and stand by the bereaved person.

Safe situations are those that provide the bereaved person with worthwhile roles to perform without taxing his limited resources. If we bear in mind that the newly bereaved person is tense, anxious, restless, and unable to concentrate on any task for long, it will be clear that such roles need to be clearly defined and uncomplicated. In relation to more complex tasks and to tasks that impose emotional stress, the presence of another person who can lead the way can be invaluable. The important thing is to avoid a situation in which the bereaved person feels trapped and without the possibility of escaping a possible rise in level of anxiety.

It is always easier to approach a danger if an escape route is assured. One of the tasks of the early phase of grief seems to be to secure such escape routes. An escape route may be a next door neighbor who says, "Come round when things get bad," or a job that gets a widow away from her home for a few hours each day, or a corner bar to which a widower can go after work. It may be a comforting sense of the presence of the dead person or it may be a tranquilizer or a sedative. Our impression, based on the few relevant instances in our study, is that alcohol is a dangerous escape route. It is too easy for the griever to cease caring whether he or she becomes addicted, and this can permit addiction to occur.

By prescribing "mourning" as the expected behavior of the bereaved, society provides them with a set of roles that come close to being the roles they are best able to perform. The widow or widower, as "chief mourner," takes on a certain distinction that may help to balance the sense of weakness and vulnerability often felt at this time. The rituals of wake, funeral, and mourning may provide a setting in which public grief can be expressed and shared. Too often this is not the case; then the ritual, far from being an opportunity to express grief, may become still another occasion at which feelings must be strictly controlled.

Still, it is not the case that the early expression of grief makes a dramatic difference to its subsequent course. The widows and widowers in our sample who thought they could "get it out quick" were usually disappointed. Grief fades slowly and unevenly and even years after a loss there are likely to be times when sudden grief will flood back.

Loss seems to produce not only deep and lasting sorrow but also disorientation, a failure of trusted meanings. Widows and widowers sustain a loss of a major part of their lives and with it of assumptions about themselves and their futures, about their roles and responsibilities, about the fundamental meanings of their lives.

In *Loss and Change*,[9] Marris points out that any event that invalidates or destroys a large segment of the understandings an individual has maintained causes that individual grief. Loss of meaning is in Marris's view the explanation for the long period of bewilderment and anxiety that may follow such events as bereavement.

As long as a person can live in a life space where death does not enter (even though he may know in theoretical terms that it might), he can develop a structure of understanding that ignores the fact of death. When a loved person dies, this is no longer possible. Now death and personal vulnerability must be explained, made a part of cognitive structure. Death, being in most instances irregular, unpredictable (except within limits), and uncontrollable is hard to make meaningful. The provision of meanings for death has been the concern of all the major religions and is among the tasks of the rituals of burial and mourning.

The widows we interviewed often did not entirely accept the doctrines regarding death and life after death propounded by their religious leaders, nor did they typically have a well worked out system of belief of their own. However they seemed to obtain comfort from the reassuring tone of the funeral service and from the assumption that a structure of belief did exist.

The two essential messages of the rituals of death were that there had indeed been death, but that nevertheless there was continuity and persistence, the dead one's work or spirit

[9]P. Marris, *Loss and Change* (London: Routledge & Kegan Paul, 1974).

or memory lived on, and therefore all was well. Neither of these messages was entirely accepted. The first message, though literally true, could not be fully assimilated as yet; the second conflicted with the sense of disaster that surrounded the whole occasion and with the overwhelming reality of personal loss. Taken together, however, the two messages provided both a spur to reality testing and a means of mitigating the pain of that reality. They constituted social supports for appropriate distancing.

The rituals of death have some of the characteristics of a *rite de passage*. But they only mark the beginning of the process of reestablishment of a new life organization. Widowers seem not to begin this process by entrance into the social status of mourning, but widows still do, and thereupon encounter some uncertainty regarding how and when that status should end. There might for them be value in a further ritual or set of rituals to mark the end of mourning and the return to social participation. Many of our widows expressed considerable perplexity concerning the extent and duration of expectations that they would wear sombre colors and restrict their social activities. Some complained that they could get no adequate guidance from others. Friends and relatives were anxious to avoid imposing their ideas on the widow, and tended to emphasize her freedom to choose for herself. In some cases the husband's family more or less explicitly gave permission for social mourning to end. In some cases the widow developed her own ending ceremony—a shopping trip, for example.

As we have pointed out, guilt and anger were often, although not always, associated with grief. They seemed especially likely to be associated with grief among those who would later display problems of recovery, including grief that would not abate, inability to move toward a potentially gratifying reorganization of life, and continued emotional instability and disorganization. Marked guilt or anger early in bereavement would seem to be a danger signal.

We can at this point only speculate why the complicating of grief by guilt or anger should be associated with relatively poor outcome. Anger is often disruptive of on-going social relationships and sometimes establishes a vicious circle of anger leading to rejection leading to loss leading to further anger, the end state of which finds the individual quite isolated. Guilt can sponsor feelings of unworthiness and unacceptability that may also lead to isolation. Guilt may also promote a desire to atone, or to demonstrate contrition through self-punishment, and so become a reason for frustrating the attempts of others to help.

Recognition that these feelings may develop can be valuable in helping those who may soon be bereaved. The opportunity to nurse a dying husband or wife or to maintain a bedside vigil until the moment of death seems to enable many people to make restitution for prior deficiencies in their relationship with the dying person. Nurses who discourage a woman or man from staying at the bedside of a dying spouse or who fail to notify relatives of impending death may be depriving them of an opportunity to give to the dying person a last gift that might partially clear old debts and repair old injuries. In just this way the rituals of the wake, funeral, and interment can also be a last gift to the dead as well as a statement of continuing love and loyalty.

At a later point the opportunity to talk about feelings of anger and guilt, and so to clarify their nature and origin, may help a widow or widower to come to terms with them. Insofar as these feelings express only the insecurity and perplexity of the new status they will lessen as time passes. The discovery that others understand and are not driven away by irritable behavior can provide useful support. Insofar as the bereaved individual's guilt is justified, as perhaps with a man who was in some way responsible for an accident in which his wife died, it may be helpful to emphasize that punishment, even self-punishment, must have its limits, and that endless self-recrimination is futile. Religious leaders are sometimes in a position to grant absolution but they should not be the only ones capable of acknowledging and permitting the reality of guilt and at the same time offering understanding.

Sometimes a man or woman who is at odds with the marriage partner carries in his or her mind an image of the world as it might be if only the other would change. Refusing to accept the other as that person really is protects a dream of how good life could be if the other were different. When the spouse in such a marriage dies the individual may feel a double loss: not only has the spouse been lost but also the possibility of a more nearly ideal world. The interruption by death of these clearly unhappy relationships can give rise to intense bitterness toward the spouse and the self. Family, friends, and professional advisors may need to be prepared for apparently interminable complaints and criticisms of the dead spouse and of the self before the bereaved person begins giving primary attention and energy to the world in which he or she actually lives.

This brings us to the final task of the mourner, the discovery of new objectives and of a new set of roles in life. The bereaved man or woman wants to make a fresh start, to discover purpose in the life that remains, but he or she also wants to put the clock back, to hang on to the old way of life, to seek the earlier supports and gratifications, which it is so difficult to see as irretrievably lost.

At the same time that the process of distancing allows the bereaved person, little by little, to approach the painful discrepancies between the-world-as-it-should-be and the-world-as-it-is, a new, modified model of the world is being constructed that is or should be closer to reality than the model it supersedes. Of importance in this process are *linking phenomena* that tie the person to the past and *bridging phenomena* that lead him or her to the future.

Linking phenomena are those objects, people, environments, and occasions that are associated with the dead person and that tend to maintain the old view of the world. They include mementos, photographs, people who resemble the deceased (such as a dead husband's brother), furniture, and music associated with the deceased. They also include certain times especially associated with the deceased—birthdays and anniversaries. All of these have the power to evoke the presence of the lost person and to maintain the feelings and perceptions of the time when that person was alive. Early in bereavement this is the most comfortable state, and the widow or widower may seek out linking phenomena in an attempt to reduce anxiety. Thus a widow may visit her husband's grave, and even carry her husband's tobacco pipe in her handbag. A man may keep his wife's photograph on his desk, or tell his children not to forget.

It is doubtful how much use should be made of linking phenomena as a routine means of helping bereaved people who seem to be recovering satisfactorily. Where there are early difficulties—unmanageable grief, for example—their use may perhaps be encouraged. In any event, in the early period recognition of the comfort to be derived from such phenomena is useful and the understanding helper will not oppose the whim of the widow who wants to wear her husband's dressing gown or of the widower who wants to visit at his wife's grave before going to work. But just as mourning can become ritualized and habitual, so the use of linking phenomena and linking behavior can be taken too far. The widow who closets herself month after month with her husband's things is stuck in a limbo between life and death and her linking objects have become fetishes.

With the passage of time the intensity of pining diminishes to a level that allows the bereaved individual to give attention to the class of phenomena we have termed bridging phemomena. These too may be objects, people, environments, and occasions, but they differ from linking phenomena in providing a bridge to a new world rather than sustaining a tie to the old. A bridging phenomenon may be the new car in which a widow learns to drive, a school in which she takes evening classes, or it may be the relationships a widower establishes with neighbors who look after his preadolescent children until he returns from work. These phenomena are important for what they symbolize as well as for what they are. They represent commitment to going on, to fashioning a new life. Unlike linking phenomena they lead on to other new things and then they may themselves be left behind.

In most cases grief seems to resolve itself in time. Among the widows and widowers with whom we talked three to four years after their bereavement, some were happily engaged by a life that seemed to them to be as rich and full as anything they might have hoped for had their earlier marriages continued. Most were far less depressed than they had been earlier. With very few exceptions the widows and widowers had not forgotten their earlier marriages, nor did they wish to. Nor had they forgotten the dark days after their loss. But most had moved toward recovery, all of them different for having suffered the loss, but many of them stronger for having succeeded in going on.

INDEX

307